ARTIFICIAL LIGHTING
FOR PHOTOGRAPHY

ARTIFICIAL LIGHTING FOR PHOTOGRAPHY

FIRST EDITION

JOY McKENZIE AND
DANIEL OVERTURF

DELMAR
CENGAGE Learning

Australia • Brazil • Japan • Korea • Mexico • Singapore • Spain • United Kingdom • United States

Artificial Lighting for Photography, First Edition
Joy McKenzie and Daniel Overturf

Vice President, Career and Professional Editorial: Dave Garza

Director of Learning Solutions: Sandy Clark

Senior Acquisitions Editor: James Gish

Managing Editor: Larry Main

Product Manager: Nicole Calisi

Associate Product Manager: Meaghan O'Brien

Editorial Assistant: Sarah Timm

Vice President, Career and Professional Marketing: Jennifer McAvey

Marketing Director: Deborah S. Yarnell

Marketing Manager: Erin Brennan

Marketing Coordinator: Jonathan Sheehan

Production Director: Wendy Troeger

Content Project Manager: Angela Iula

Art Director: Joy Kocsis

For product information and technology assistance, contact us at
Professional & Career Group Customer Support, 1-800-648-7450

For permission to use material from this text or product, submit all requests online at **cengage.com/permissions.** Further permissions questions can be e-mailed to **permissionrequest@cengage.com.**

Library of Congress Control Number: 2008937098

ISBN-13: 978-1-4283-1804-5
ISBN-10: 1-4283-1804-6

Delmar
5 Maxwell Drive
Clifton Park, NY 12065-2919
USA

Cengage Learning products are represented in Canada by Nelson Education, Ltd.

For your lifelong learning solutions, visit **delmar.cengage.com**
Visit our corporate website at **cengage.com.**

Notice to the Reader
Publisher does not warrant or guarantee any of the products described herein or perform any independent analysis in connection with any of the product information contained herein. Publisher does not assume, and expressly disclaims, any obligation to obtain and include information other than that provided to it by the manufacturer. The reader is expressly warned to consider and adopt all safety precautions that might be indicated by the activities described herein and to avoid all potential hazards. By following the instructions contained herein, the reader willingly assumes all risks in connection with such instructions. The publisher makes no representations or warranties of any kind, including but not limited to, the warranties of fitness for particular purpose or merchantability, nor are any such representations implied with respect to the material set forth herein, and the publisher takes no responsibility with respect to such material. The publisher shall not be liable for any special, consequential, or exemplary damages resulting, in whole or part, from the readers' use of, or reliance upon, this material.

Printed in Canada
1 2 3 4 5 XX 11 10 09

CONTENTS

PREFACE

Background of This Text

What is artificial lighting? Some photographers refer to this type of lighting as studio or commercial. Such a definition is vastly limiting. All light sources, except the sun and moon, are considered by many as artificial and can be used for any project that requires controlled lighting. There are photographers who will simply resist the term *artificial* light. They would ask, "What is artificial about any light? Light is light, regardless of the source." There is certainly merit in that open-ended definition that suggests that we should embrace any form of illumination as simply *light*, without unnecessary categories.

This open-ended question naturally prompts the question of why, or even how, one authors a book about artificial lighting. There are many lighting books on the market, and many address specific lighting techniques. The authors were grounded in the goal of presenting a comprehensive text complete with artificial lighting techniques that would offer instructional material in easy-to-understand language, diagrams, and images. The outline of the text is intended to bridge the gap between classroom instruction and practical application. The authors are educators who understand the importance of artificial lighting skills and the value of a text that addresses these issues.

The contemporary classroom environment also informs this book. Students are using lighting to craft images with a wide array of image-making tools. Approaches range from the still to the moving image, from analog to digital, from the ephemeral or time-based to the yet-unseen avenues of art making. The current interdisciplinary teaching environment owes much to earlier collapses of categories and disciplines. Traditional lighting techniques, such as the continuous source, have returned in modern forms, and current lighting technique instruction is typically all-inclusive. The student who is experimenting with lighting technique is met with many options and alternatives. Students have many role models in contemporary practice. Many artists use artificial lighting to create gallery works wherein the set is the means to an end—a photograph intended for exhibition in galleries instead of commercial applications. Through it all, light and lighting remain a constant consideration in all of the imagery created. This book's comprehensive outline reflects that criterion.

Many photographs are created using both artificial and natural light for visually aesthetic effects. The strength of these images relies on the photographer's understanding of how to visually balance the different sources of light. Photographs are a language, and light is the raw material from which this language is conceived. A successful photograph relies on the photographer's ability to use the tools at his/her disposal effectively, whether it is artificial or natural light, in a studio or on location. Using artificial lighting does not require a studio; it requires knowledge about lighting and the ability to effectively use light sources for a desired effect anywhere.

Chapter Contents

This book is divided into three sections: Section I, *Lighting Techniques: Basic Concepts and Theories*; Section II, *Lighting Application: Light, Equipment, and Portraiture*; and Section III, *Grip Glossary*.

Section I: *Lighting Techniques: Basic Concepts and Theories* has four chapters, and each chapter discusses specific lighting issues. Chapter 1, *Light*, introduces the principles of light, the basic equipment, and the terms used in subsequent chapters. Chapter 2, *Shadows, Shapes, and Multiple Sources*, presents information on the relationship between light sources and the shadows they create. How light shapes objects and how to use more than one light in a setup is also explained. The authors have included the basic lighting techniques for portraits in this section because so much of portraiture is about shaping the face and working with light and shadows. However, more advanced portrait techniques are found in Section II. Building on Chapters 1 and 2, Chapter 3, *Reflective Surfaces*, discusses the principles of lighting reflective surfaces, specifically metal and highly polished surfaces. Chapter 4, *Transparent Objects*, addresses various techniques for lighting glass.

Section II, *Lighting Applications: Light, Equipment, and Portraiture*, offers advanced information, including practical application and historical contexts for light measurement, light sources, and lighting equipment. Chapter 5,

Light Measurement and Color Temperature, begins with basic information on these topics. Building on these principles, the text continues to describe how to analyze light intensity and color under more complex circumstances. Chapter 6, *Light Source*, introduces much of the lighting equipment available to photographers and shows them how to use the equipment safely. Also included in the lighting equipment discussion is information on the historical background: the first application, who invented it, and how it got its name. Chapter 7, *Modifiers and Accessories*, presents the various attachments for lighting equipment, how to use them, what function they perform, and the light pattern created by these light modifiers and accessories. Chapter 8, Portrait, contains advanced techniques for photographing the portrait. A continuation of the portrait introduction in Section I, this chapter reviews the specialized options for additional light sources and modifiers which have been introduced in Chapters 6 and 7.

Section III, *Grip Glossary Handbook*, contains only one chapter: Chapter 9, *Bannister's Guide*, so named for the individual who gathered the information and created this list of equipment. It serves as a reference guide that describes the proper name, *also known as* (a.k.a.), and *incorrectly known as* (i.k.a.) information on numerous pieces of equipment that photographers may use in the course of their careers. The authors believe this will serve as a valuable resource for beginning and advanced photographers.

Photographers at Work

Profiles on working photographers are located at the end of each of the chapters (except chapters 1

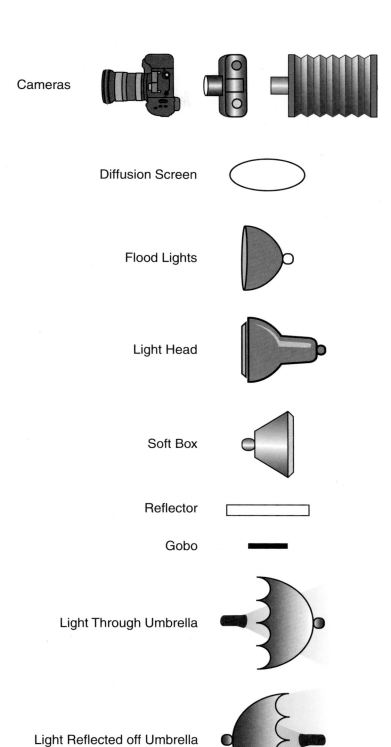

Cameras

Diffusion Screen

Flood Lights

Light Head

Soft Box

Reflector

Gobo

Light Through Umbrella

Light Reflected off Umbrella

Lighting diagrams accompany many of the lighting examples throughout this text. The icons above will assist in deciphering the symbols used for lighting equipment in each diagram.

and 9). These profiles include a short biography, one or more images of the photographer's work, and their lighting diagrams. This diverse group of talented artists is included to augment the text by explaining the skill and creativity required to make their featured photographs. Included are photographers whose varied styles extend from beautifully simplistic images to extremely complex images.

How to Use This Book

This book was written as a textbook to be used by educators in assisting students learning lighting techniques. An E-Resource is available to educators for this purpose. The best way to learn the material is to start at the beginning of the book, learn the principles of light, and then move on to the basic lighting techniques. Students can move between Sections I and II, combining basic skills in Section I with the advanced information found in Section II. Section II also provides a wealth of information on lighting equipment and modifiers to further control lighting arrangements both on location and in the studio. Section III is an invaluable reference resource for anyone working as a photographer's assistant or for a photographer looking for specific equipment for an assignment.

Instructor Resources

The accompanying CD was developed as a guide to assist instructors in planning and implementing their instructional programs. It includes sample syllabi for using this book in either an 11- or 16-week semester. Also included are sample projects to assign students, PowerPoint slides highlighting the main topics of each chapter, and additional instructor resources.

ISBN: 1-4283-1805-4

About the Authors

Joy McKenzie

Born in Columbus, Ohio, McKenzie has been a photographer since receiving training in the U.S. Army in 1969. McKenzie received her Bachelor of Fine Arts in Photography from the Kansas City Art Institute, did graduate work at the Memphis College of Art, and received her Master of Fine Arts in Photography from Southern Illinois University at Carbondale. McKenzie is a Professor at Watkins College of Art&Design, and, previously serving as department chair, she built the Bachelor of Fine Arts photography program there. McKenzie's previous book, entitled *Exploring Basic Black & White Photography*, was published in 2004.

Joy McKenzie.

Daniel V. Overturf

Born in Peoria, Illinois, Overturf has been a photographer since his teens. Educated at Southern Illinois University, he received his Bachelor of Arts in Photography in 1980 and Master of Fine Arts in Printmaking in 1983. He lived, taught, and worked in Nevada, New Mexico, Alberta, and Kansas before returning to his alma mater to teach photography in 1990. He is presently an Associate Professor in Cinema and Photography at Southern Illinois University. His previously published book, entitled *A River Through Illinois*, was published in 2008.

Daniel V. Overturf.

Acknowledgments

This textbook would not have been possible without help from many friends, colleagues, students, and, of course, the Delmar Cengage Learning production team. The authors wish to extend sincere gratitude to all who assisted with this publication, those we have listed and those we apologize to for unintentionally omitting from specific notice. Thank you to Richard Newman and Calumet Photographic for their generous equipment loans and technical advice. Also, thank you to the Paducah, Kentucky Chamber of Commerce for graciously allowing the authors to use their meeting rooms and Robert Shapiro for making the arrangements. Thank you to Lowel Manufacturing for technical assistance on front lighting technique for glass and to the Yard Shop for product loans. We thank all the folks at Cengage: Jim Gish, Senior Acquisitions Editor; Nicole Calisi, Product Manager;

Meaghan O'Brien, Associate Product Manager; Angela Iula, Content Project Manager; and Sarah Timm, Editorial Assistant. A special thanks to Vincent Pepe for his legal advice and support. Thanks to Maggie Tucker for creating the skull drawing for this book. Lisa Deal, thank you for your photograph and studio assistance with the book's illustrations. Also, thank you to Samantha Angel, Robin Paris, and Mandy Springer for their studio assistance on illustrations in the book. Thank you to Amanda Nagy for her assistance with the glossary and to Beth Hartman-Peters for her general support and operation of the photography lab at Watkins College of Art & Design. We offer a special thanks to President Jim Brooks and Vice President John Sullivan from Watkins College of Art & Design for providing student assistance on illustrations and their support during this project. A special thanks also to Brian Matsumoto (Canon USA) for all of his specialized knowledge, equipment loans, and technical advice. Jeff Goshert and the good folks at Bogen gave their assistance in providing equipment for the illustrations, so we would like to thank all of them. Also, thank you to Eileen Healey and the good folks at Chimera for providing specialized Chimera instruments and an illustration from their own collection. A big thank you to Ann Dodge for her tireless work on the book's images and overall organization. Greg Landrum, thank you for your technical advice and insight provided from teaching a studio course and years of professional experience. Thank you to Lyle Fuchs for his general support in the making of the book's photographic illustrations and overall computer support. A special thanks to Jennifer Haselhorst, Alex Wasilewski, Eric Robinson, Bridget Ryan, Sarah Hyde, Ernie Ashby, Carl Hileman, Josh Denmark, Chrystal Nause, Josh Gates, and Roderick Brown for the their work on the cover and other illustrations in the text. A very special thank you to all of the photographers who provided materials for the "Photographers at Work" sections. The book would not be complete without their additions. Thank you to Clay Bannister, who generously granted his permission to reprint his Grip Glossary. Also appreciated was the advice on stop action photography and the photograph of Doc Edgerton, both provided by friend and colleague Andy Davidhazy from RIT. Stan Lawrence, thank you for your caring support, helpful advice, and understanding during the entire project. Last, but certainly not least, thank you Heather Lose, for your skillful design advice and overall encouragement during the entire project.

There are a select few illustrations included in the text that were supplied by longtime and new colleagues. Thanks to those who helped with the included historical and technical images.

Delmar Cengage Learning and the authors would also like to thank the reviewers for their valuable suggestions and expertise:

Bob Carey
Photography Department Chair
Gardner-Webb University
Boiling Springs, North Carolina

Peter Glenndinning
Department of Photography
Michigan State University
East Lansing, Michigan

Mark E. Hamilton
Department of Photography
Winthrop University
Rock Hill, South Carolina

Jay Reiter
Department of Photography
McIntosh College
Dover, New Hampshire

Questions and Feedback

Delmar Cengage Learning and the authors welcome your questions and feedback. If you have any suggestions that you think others would benefit from, please let us know, and we will try to include them in the next edition.

To send us your questions and/or feedback, you can contact the publisher at:

Delmar Cengage Learning
Executive Woods
5 Maxwell Drive
Clifton Park, NY 12065
Attn: Media Arts & Design Team
800-998-7498

Or the authors at: Joy McKenzie: jmckenzie@watkins.edu
            Daniel Overturf: dvo0201@siu.edu

LIGHTING TECHNIQUES: BASIC CONCEPTS AND THEORIES

Introduction

This section introduces chapters on the basic concepts for all lighting techniques, beginning with the principles of light and the basic tools for artificial lighting techniques found in Chapter 1. These foundational principles are subsequently used throughout Section I. Chapter 2 discusses the basic techniques for lighting arrangements for front, side, back, and top lighting. Further examples will show the overall effects of different illuminations in relation to the aesthetics of highlights and shadows. Applying those basic concepts, Chapter 2 will also introduce basic portrait lighting. Chapter 3 discusses how to illuminate and control highlights and shadows on metal and reflective surfaces. Chapter 4 addresses lighting glass subjects from various directions.

Light forms the space and contour for photographs; it creates the environment for the *look* and *feel* of the photograph. Understanding the principles of lighting arrangements in controlling image aesthetics is the foundation for creating more complex, interesting photographs.

CHAPTER ONE

LIGHT

Figure 1-1   Controlled artificial lighting creates abstract form and shape from Fresnel lenses.

Photography is *all* about light. It is the physical source with which photographers communicate in images. It is how photographs are *read*. It describes, molds, and shapes objects to appear as expected, or it can obscure the object to become abstract. Learning to sculpt an object, to create an illusion, or to create a representation is to understand light as an art form and to use it as a tool to communicate in fine art, advertisement, or editorial images.

When shooting outside with ambient light, the photographer has little control over light intensity, light direction, or shadows. Conditions can be influenced by camera placement, using filters or fill cards, reflectors, and diffusion screens. The photographer cannot change the shadow placement but she can move the subject or the camera to include or eliminate the shadows. One cannot create overcast conditions from a bright, sunny day or vice versa. Sometimes the only solution is to reschedule the shoot and watch the weather for the desired lighting conditions. Another option is to use artificial lighting to create the desired lighting for the subject, which is the subject of this book.

Using artificial lighting opens up unlimited potential *if* one understands the characteristics of the light and knows how to take advantage of the possibilities. Lighting is also about becoming a problem solver—controlling light to give form, shape, and texture to an object. It is effectively using light to convey a three-dimensional object on a two-dimensional surface. Other art forms, such as drawing, demonstrate this visual shape by shading in some areas and leaving other areas alone, allowing the white paper to represent the highlights of the object. There is a long history of artists representing events and portraits in painting and drawing until J. L. M. Daguerre introduced the Daguerreotype in 1839.

Drawings and paintings are the artist's representation of the object, but they are always understood as *representations*. Photographs seem to take on the existence or the life of the object or person; people do not refer to photographs as "a photograph of my sister"; instead, they say "here is my sister." Artists *observe* light and create the environment on paper or canvas with pencil, charcoal, or paint; photographers *use* light to create the environment and record it on film or digital capture. Figure 1-2 illustrates a drawing and a photograph of a steer skull. Both images are representations of the object. What an artist does with

Figure 1-2b
The drawing has shape and form because the artist used colored pencil to create shadows, midtone, and highlights. The photograph has shape and form because the photographer positioned the artificial light to create the shadow, midtone, and highlights.

pencil, charcoal, or paint, a photographer does with light and the camera.

What Is Light?

We all know that light is a very complicated subject, and most photographers would agree that light is the foundation of the photographic medium, but consider that light is the foundation for *everything* we see. Although the authors do not intend to write extensively about the physics of light, it is important to understand the basic principles of light.

Light Waves

Light is composed of waves containing energy and magnetic fields called electromagnetic radiation. These waves travel at right angles to each other in varying sizes called **wavelengths** (fig. 1-3). Wavelengths are measured from the distance of one point of a wavelength to the point of the next

Figure 1-3

Wavelengths travel
vertically and horizontally
at right angles to each
other.

which occurs because the light wave traveling outside the water, in air, is moving faster than the light wave traveling in the water. This phenomenon also occurs when one glass object is placed in front of another, and the edge of the glass object in back appears to bend. In figure 1-6, the rosemary twig is refracted in the water. It appears as though the stem simply stops and another begins on the left side at the water's edge, continuing down to the bottom of the jar. Also, note how the horizon line travels from left to right and then drops down at the point it meets the left side of the jar. It resumes from the right side of the jar and continues out of the frame.

Figure 1-4

Wavelengths are measured
from one point to another.

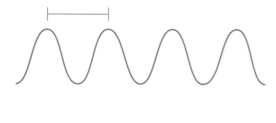

Polarized Light

Polarized light results when lightwaves travel in only one direction or on a single plane (fig. 1-7) instead of the combined vertical and horizontal planes of normal lightwaves. Polarized lightwaves are the primary cause of unwanted reflections or glare on objects. Generally, rough surface texture will not have polarized light reflecting from the surface because the surface reflects lightwaves in different directions. Smooth or shiny surfaces like glass, water, and polished wood will have some polarizing effects, and the amount of polarization will depend on the incidence and angle of light. Polarized light can be controlled with so-called polarizing filters. Placing a polarizing filter on the camera lens or the artificial light partially blocks these lightwaves, as illustrated in figure 1-8. The filter allows all other lightwaves to pass through unchanged. If two polarizing filters are at right angles to each other, no light will pass through because all light waves would be blocked.

Figure 1-5

Light waves slow down
when they move through
material, causing them to
refract or bend.

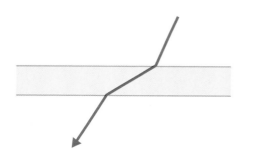

wavelength (fig. 1-4). Furthermore, these energy wavelengths fluctuate at different rates. The rate at which waves pass through space, measured in a one-second interval unit referred to as a Hertz, is called its frequency. The more energy a wavelength has, the faster it fluctuates.

Light waves also slow down as they pass through material such as water or glass. This causes the light to refract, which gives the illusion of bending or shifting (fig. 1-5). For example, if a spoon is placed in a glass of water, the spoon handle appears to shift,

Typically, polarizing filters for cameras are on a rotating ring so the photographer can adjust the ring to the direction of polarized light. These filters can reduce the light reaching the film or digital capture by as much as 2× or 4× (one or two f/stops). Exposure adjustments must be made if the

Figure 1-6

Light waves travel at different speeds as they pass through different materials. In this illustration, the water is causing the light waves to slow down, giving the appearance that the rosemary twig splits and shifts.

photographer is using a light meter for exposure information. Of course, if the camera has through-the-lens metering, the exposure adjustments are indicated in the readout. There are two types of polarizing filters, linear and circular. Each produces the same visual effect; however, a linear polarizing filter will interfere with autofocus and autoexposure camera functions. A circular polarizing filter does not interfere with these camera functions. The camera manufacturer's manual should provide compatibility recommendations. The visual effects of polarizing filters placed on lights are demonstrated in Chapter 7, figures 7-8 and 7-9, that show disappearing Plexiglas.

Color

All light is made up of photons moving through space in electromagnetic waves (figs. 1-9 and 1-10). Although photons move at the same speed, the more energy

the photon has, the faster it fluctuates. Photons have no mass; they are pure energy that can move even in a vacuum. No one sees a photon until it exerts force against an object. All objects absorb some photons and reflect others, which is what makes them visible. The fluctuation rate of the electromagnetic field of photons determines the **color** of visible light. All light waves traveling in the same direction are absorbed or reflected by the object surface. It is the reflected light that is visible as color.

Three Principles of Light

Light is controlled by three basic principles: (1) light travels in a straight line, (2) light is equal and opposite to the angle of reflection, and (3) light intensity changes proportionally to the inverse of the square of distance.

Light Travels in a Straight Line

Light travels in a straight line. It can scatter in different directions, but each light wave will travel in a straight line, as shown in figure 1-11. The direction of the light waves defines texture, shape, and volume. It also determines where a shadow falls or where the brightest area on an object appears. *Light travels in a straight line.*

Angle of Incidence

The **angle of incidence** is the direction light travels from the light source toward an object. The angle at which the light reflects off an object is exactly the opposite of the angle at which light strikes the object. This is called the **law of reflectance**. However, different light sources and different textures affect how the light is received and the angle at which it is reflected (fig. 1-12). For example, a flat surface will reflect light exactly the opposite of the angle of incidence in a predictable direction. Light will strike a textured surface in different places, sending reflected light in different directions, but always opposite and equal to the light rays creating them (fig. 1-13). The law of reflectance states that *the angle of incidence is equal to and opposite the reflection.*

Figure 1-7

Polarized lightwaves travel in one direction either horizontally or vertically along a single plane instead of both the vertical and horizontal planes of normal light rays (refer back to fig. 1-3).

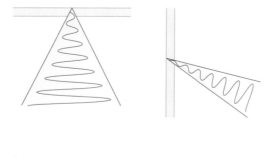

Figure 1-8

When a polarizing filter is introduced, it blocks polarized light, which significantly reduces reflection.

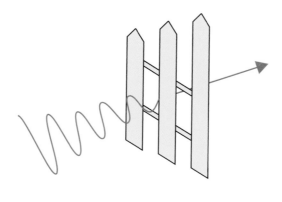

Figure 1-9

A wavelength travels through space around a photon at different frequencies with a positive field half of the time and a negative field half of the time.

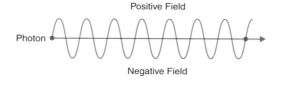

Positive Field

Photon

Negative Field

Figure 1-10

The frequency of a wavelength is measured in one-second intervals. The frequency of a red light wave is slower than the frequency of a blue light wave.

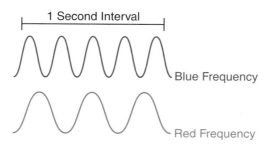

1 Second Interval

Blue Frequency

Red Frequency

Inverse of the Square of the Distance

Light will diminish and spread out as the light source moves farther away from the subject. The principle of this law states that if a square beam of light is placed one foot from a flat surface, the illumination on the surface will equal one square foot (fig. 1-14). However, if the light is moved to a distance of two feet from the flat surface, the beam of light will spread out to four square feet, and the intensity of the light would be reduced to 25 percent of the original illumination. This beam spread and intensity reduction is called **falloff**. The opposite will occur if one starts at a distance of two feet and moves closer; the area illuminated will become smaller, and the light intensity will become greater. *Light intensity changes proportionally to the inverse of the square of distance.* This is also called the **Inverse Square Law**; it is discussed in depth later in this chapter.

Language of Light

Photographers use many different terms to describe light: *intensity of light* or **brightness**, *quality of light* or **contrast**, and color. All of these terms refer to both natural light and artificial light. These terms are also used to refer to the subject. When discussing light, it is very important to be specific.

Brightness

Brightness describes the **intensity** of the light source. Typically, the brighter the light source, the better. A brighter light source means greater exposure control for the photographer in shutter speed and aperture settings, which allows more creative control in the image. Photographers learn early on in basic photography that low-light conditions may require compromises in image quality. There are some low-light instances where a shot may not be advisable. Every photographer knows that it is nearly impossible to take a portrait using very slow shutter speeds and an open aperture because of some subject movement and minimal depth

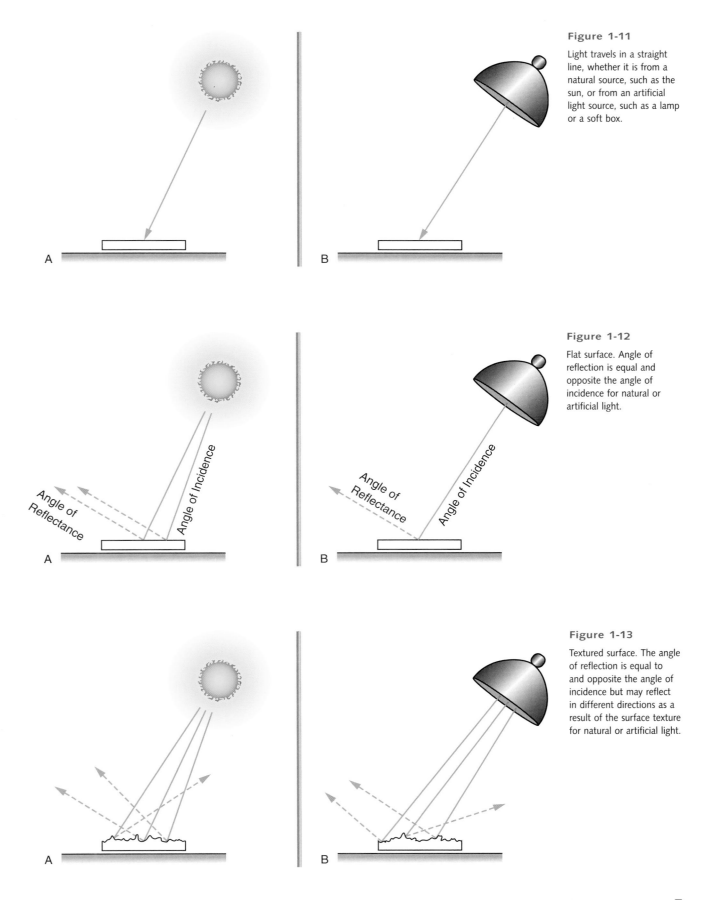

Figure 1-11

Light travels in a straight line, whether it is from a natural source, such as the sun, or from an artificial light source, such as a lamp or a soft box.

Figure 1-12

Flat surface. Angle of reflection is equal and opposite the angle of incidence for natural or artificial light.

Figure 1-13

Textured surface. The angle of reflection is equal to and opposite the angle of incidence but may reflect in different directions as a result of the surface texture for natural or artificial light.

Angle of Incidence

Angle of Reflectance

A

B

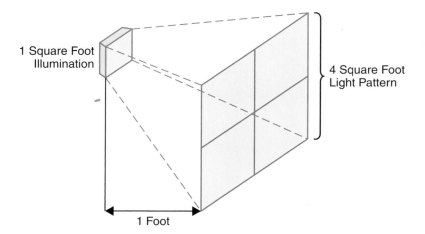

Figure 1-14

Principle of Inverse Square Law.

1 Square Foot Illumination

4 Square Foot Light Pattern

1 Foot

of field. If the intensity of the light is not bright enough, image aesthetics may suffer. Because most artificial lighting systems are designed to accommodate different power levels, the photographer can select the light source that produces enough intensity or brightness for the best possible photograph for any given subject. Section II discusses a variety of lighting equipment a photographer might select, depending upon lighting requirements, to produce a properly exposed photograph. Chapter 8 will focus specifically on advanced portrait lighting equipment and techniques.

Contrast

In basic black and white photography classes or workshops, image quality is generally discussed in terms of highlights, midtones, and shadows. Terms used are **high contrast** and **low contrast** when discussing the scene, negative, or print. High contrast indicates very bright highlights and dark shadows but few midtone areas. Low contrast describes even lighting but few bright highlights or dark shadows. Both terms are referring to the relationship between highlights and shadows (or lack thereof). The same terms apply in artificial lighting, except they are called **lighting ratios**, that is, the difference between the brightest area of the scene or subject (highlights) and the darkest area of the scene or subject (shadows). Measuring for lighting ratios is discussed in Chapter 2.

In high-contrast scenes, all light waves are hitting the subject at almost the same angle, which blocks light from other areas creating dark shadows. For example, when light waves strike a tree on a bright sunny day, it blocks light from striking the ground, causing deep, dark shadows with clearly defined edges (fig. 1-15). Any experienced photographer recognizes a high-contrast scene and the difficulty in producing a print that has detail in both areas.

When the scene is low contrast, everything is, for the most part, evenly illuminated. Light waves are striking the subject from many different angles and reflecting at many different angles. The reflecting light fills in the shadow area with additional illumination. As a result, there are no definitive shadows. The shadow edges are soft and diffused (fig. 1-16).

The same high- or low-contrast situation can be applied and controlled with artificial lighting by selecting the specific type of lighting or light source for the desired effect as illustrated in figures 1-15 and 1-16.

Color

Color is simply the visible light waves reflecting off of an object. However, color also creates an emotional response and plays an important part in the visual communication and aesthetics of a photograph. Consider how the photographer discusses color; reds and yellows are "warm," and blue and green are "cool." Color is assigned emotional

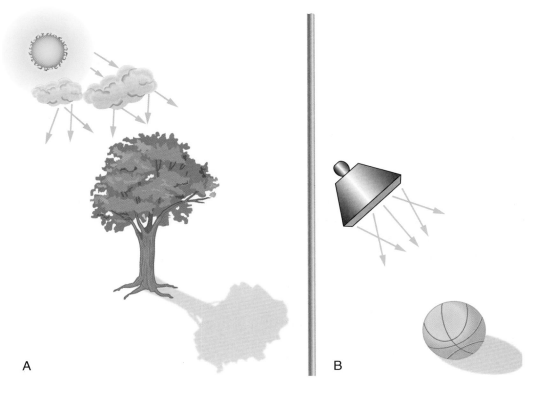

Figure 1-15

Light travels in a straight line from the sun on a bright day, creating dark shadows with hard edges. A small artificial light source also creates dark shadows with hard edges.

A

B

Figure 1-16

Light rays are scattered in a low-contrast day, creating diffused shadows with no clear edge definition. A soft box functions in a similar manner, diffusing and scattering the light on the subject.

A

B

responses, such as passion when referring to red or "seeing red" when speaking of anger. Different people respond to color saturation in positive or negative ways; one color may be too vivid, another too dull, or too pastel. Color and the response to color can also be the result of cultural influences; black represents darkness and depression on or elegance, and white is light and airy, pure. These are the cultural influences of most western countries, and their interpretation may be different in other parts of the world. Choice of object colors, background, and environment, or using gels in front of lights can produce visually exciting images wherein color is a powerful element in the photograph (fig. 1-17).

Basic Tools of the Trade

Before beginning discussions on light, there are some basic tools that must be addressed. First, lighting knowledge is independent of the camera or medium used to create images. Whether using digital capture or film, the lighting equipment and vocabulary describing light remain the same. Although both digital and film capture can be used with artificial light sources, the photographer must understand the camera operation

to achieve successful exposure, including selecting the correct film for film cameras or setting the white balance for digital cameras. Eventually, all decisions regarding exposure and lighting information will be included in a lighting plan or diagram. Why would one need to use a lighting diagram? Planning lighting requirements and materials for studio or location work ensures that: (1) all equipment and accessories are available when needed, and (2) time is not wasted on figuring out what to do on the set. This level of organization saves time and avoids frustration and unnecessary stress. Most figures in Section I will have a lighting diagram for lighting-setup illustrations. The key for the lighting symbols used in these diagrams is located in the Preface.

Photographic lighting can either be **continuous** or **flash**. The sources can be simple or complex. A common flashlight can be an artificial light source, producing visually aesthetic images (fig. 1-18). Continuous light source simply means that a light source is turned on, and it remains on until it is turned off. A basic continuous light source is **tungsten** or **fluorescent** light. Tungsten comes in the form of **hot lights** as shown in figure 1-19, so named because they get very hot during use. Photographic

Figure 1-17

The photographer has used a monochromatic color to convey a somber mood in this image. It is offset by the elusive figure behind the star at the far left. Courtesy of L. Deal.

fluorescent lighting uses tubes that are similar to common household lighting fixtures.

Flash generally refers to a **strobe** light that fires a single burst of light when the shutter button is pressed (fig. 1-20). This can be as simple as an electronic built-in flash on a point-and-shoot camera to a basic, low-budget system, or it can be very specialized strobe lighting equipment costing thousands of dollars. It is more difficult to see how the subject is lit when using strobe lighting equipment. To deal with this, manufacturers have built in **modeling lights**, which are low-wattage tungsten lighting. The modeling lights allow the photographer to see how the subject will be lit, but because of the low wattage of these modeling lights, it is still difficult to determine accurate lighting. Ways to determine accurate exposure for strobe lighting are discussed in Chapter 3. Digital capture enables the photographer to see the *potentially* finished product immediately either on the back of the camera or on a computer screen, and their ability to change the ISO allows photographers to use lower wattage light sources. In fact, some photographers use speedlights as a light source for photo shoots (fig. 1-20). These are usually attached to a light stand and used with an umbrella to shape and control the light.

All artificial lighting equipment should be secured to light stands, as shown in figure 1-21. When placing the light head on a stand, it is important to position the light head over an extended leg to counterbalance the weight of the light. Weights should also be placed on braces on the bottom of the light stand to secure the entire set (Chapter 7, fig. 7-40). Some photographers also use **gaffer tape** to tape the cord in place to prevent anyone from tripping over the cord.

Artificial lighting requires power. Batteries **(direct current, or DC)** are used in some cases, and **alternating current (AC)** is used in others. Regardless of the complexity of the system a photographer uses, safety must be followed, especially

Figure 1-18

A laundry line is illuminated using a flashlight.

Figure 1-19

An example of a hot light with barn doors attached. The barn doors are light modifiers that allow the photographer to modify the spread of light with the adjustable blades.

Figure 1-20

Speedlights can be used with various light modifiers for an efficient, low-budget source light in artificial lighting.

Figure 1-21

Monolight head with umbrella attached to light stand.

Figure 1-22

Detail shot of power pack.

when using units requiring AC power. There are numerous potentially dangerous circumstances that should be regarded when using artificial light. There are two basic power supplies for strobe lighting: **power pack** or **monolight**. Additional information on these light sources is located in Chapter 7.

A power pack is a single box that controls light output for multiple lighting units (fig. 1-22). Each cable is plugged into a separate **cell** or **channel**. Each channel of the power pack functions independently from the others, similar to household plugs or outlets operating on different breakers. The photographer can control how much power the unit produces by turning the power dial up or down to adjust the power level; furthermore, power output to each cell can be controlled using the dial designated to that particular section. The

modeling light can also be controlled in these units. The camera **PC** cord is plugged into the sync receptors. When the camera shutter button is pressed, all light heads plugged into the power pack fire simultaneously. Every power pack is different, and the photographer should follow the manufacturer's instructions when using a power pack. Safety precautions must be used with these units because of the large wattages produced by the power pack. It would be an important precaution to know the location of the electrical breaker to the studio in the event of power outage or emergencies.

The monolight is a self-contained power unit built into the light head. Each unit is plugged into an electrical outlet and functions independently from the others. Power adjustments for the modeling light and the amount of light output are controlled on the back or side of the unit (fig. 1-23). One light is **synced** to the camera. The other units have **slaves** built in so that when the shutter button is pushed and the light synced to the camera fires a flash, the other lighting units automatically flash. There are many different types and manufacturers of monolight equipment, and photographers should follow the manufacturer's instructions when using them.

Here are a few terms associated with strobe lighting that every photographer should know:

a) **Recycle times** refer to the amount of time that a flash requires to recharge for the next burst of light. If the photographer does not allow for adequate recycle time, the illumination will be inadequate for proper exposure.

b) A **watt second** is a basic unit of measurement that will help a photographer determine the size of a light unit. A watt is a unit of electrical energy. This measurement is a simple equation when regarding a continuous source bulb. A 250-W bulb is roughly 2.5× brighter than a 100-W bulb. Flash units are also rated in a similar manner. A 4800-W power pack contains twice the flash output as a 2400-W unit. In the case of the latter example, this means that the photographer will be gaining a full stop of additional light when using the 4800-W pack. Photographers should be aware that some manufacturers name light models with a number, and these do not necessarily represent the watt-power of the unit. Always check manufacturer information to ascertain the watt-power of the light unit.

c) **Sync speed**, abbreviated from synchronization, is the term that indicates a camera's minimum shutter speed that can be used with flash. Each camera will have its own setting for the sync speed; photographers should follow manufacturer's instructions.

d) A **modifier** is a device that is fitted to a light source to change the quality of the light. The most common modifier is a reflector, and they come in many shapes and sizes for both tungsten lights and strobe lights. The modifier can make the light source more focused or more diffused, can change the color of the light, or can change overall shape of the light beam and can effectively be adapted to whatever purpose the photographer may require. Examples of modifier terms are **snoots**, **umbrellas**, **grid**, **barn doors**, **soft boxes**, and **gels**. An extensive discussion on lighting equipment and modifiers can be found in Chapter 6.

A light meter is an essential piece of equipment in the toolbox of artificial lighting. Beginning photographers learn the difference between reflective and incident light meters. Another meter used by photographers is the flashmeter. The flashmeter measures the strobe flash produced by the light unit. Often, a more expensive light meter will have all three functions (reflective, incident, and flash) built into the meter. The strobe sync cord

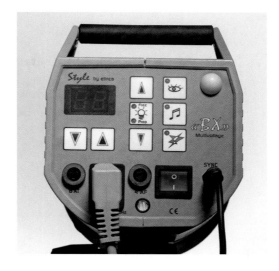

Figure 1-23

All monolight controls are located on the lighting unit. In this example, the controls are located on the back, but other monolight heads may have some controls located on the side of the unit as well.

is plugged into the PC receptacle of the light meter. The meter is placed in the area to be illuminated by the lighting units, and the white dome is directed at the camera. When the photographer pushes the button, the exposure reading is shown in the **LED** (light-emitting diode) display window. There are many different manufacturers of light meters, and photographers should always read the manufacturer's instructions.

Summary

Understanding the principles of light is the foundation for all artificial lighting techniques. Lighting equipment is referred to by many different acronyms and names. These can vary depending on the location and region from which a photographer may work or the terminology used to describe equipment by the supplier or manufacturer. Many of these terms are thoroughly discussed in Section II of this text, and there is a *Grip Glossary* in Section III to assist with learning the common names for a variety of other equipment. Learning the names of equipment is essential to avoid confusion when working as a photographer or a photographer's assistant. No professional likes to hear her expensive piece of equipment called a "thing-a-ma-jig" or a "whatcha-ma-call-it"!

SHADOWS, SHAPES, AND MULTIPLE SOURCES

Figure 2-1   Light and shadow create form and shape. A form with random cut-outs, called a cookie, in the upper right corner is producing the shadow pattern on the license plates in the image.

By now, it should be apparent that it is the combination of light *and* shadow that defines a shape. In this chapter, two antique cameras, one painted white and the other black, are used as the subject to illustrate lighting. Hereafter, these cameras will be referred to as the *object* or *subject* to reduce possible confusion between the photographer's camera and the subject camera. In figures 2-2 and 2-3, the object is used to demonstrate the effects of backlighting and flat lighting on a white object. If the object is photographed with light shining on the background but no illumination on any visible side of the box, it appears like a flat, black shape with no volume, as seen in figure 2-2. The resulting image becomes a silhouette. Most photographers have experienced a similar result when shooting backlit subjects; for example, someone sitting in front of a window where the sun is behind the subject. Compensating for backlit subjects requires opening up either the aperture or the shutter speed to correct the exposure on the subject. Another option is to use a fill flash to illuminate the subject while keeping the background correctly exposed. Chapter 5 will answer all questions regarding fill flash with ambient light, color temperatures, and metering.

If this same object is photographed so that all visible sides receive the same illumination against a dark background, it appears light and flat (fig. 2-3). Again, there is only a two-dimensional shape without volume. Figure 2-3 contains some clues to object form because the subject (in this case, a white object) is positioned at an angle, and slight texture is visible on the right side. In addition, the viewfinder, aperture, and seams on the front are indicators of object form. Ansel Adams demonstrated these examples in his very early photography book, *Artificial Light Photography, Basic Photo Five*, published by Little, Brown and Company, written in 1956. In his example, a tent was created to eliminate stray light to demonstrate the effects of backlighting, and diffused light was used for the flat lighting. A wonderful aspect of photography is that the principles of light and lighting *never* change. Photography styles and technology may change. The manner in which the image is captured and subsequently presented may change. The photographer may need to adjust the lighting intensity or arrangement or to compensate for different media, such as film versus digital, but the principles of light and its relationship to objects remain the same.

Figure 2-2

Backlit objects become silhouettes, offering no information about surface texture or form.

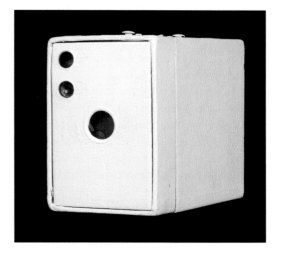

Figure 2-3

There are small indicators of form in the object because a small amount of light is reflecting onto the object. The lack of surface texture and form reduce the object to a two-dimensional form.

Creating Surface Texture

Light rays reflecting off objects define the surface texture. There are four basic actions that affect how object surfaces appear: *quality of light, reflectance of light, distance from light,* and *intensity of light*.

Quality of Light: What Kind of Light Is It?

To repeat, light is what defines photography; it is the key element to visually describing any object for all photographers.

Recognizing the quality of natural light is to understand how to use artificial light effectively. What do they have in common? How can this knowledge of natural light be used effectively and applied to artificial lighting for a studio or location set? The key to artificial lighting is that *it should not look artificial* unless, of course, that is the photographer's intention! The same definitions used to describe natural light also describe artificial light.

Lighting conditions outside may range from bright sunny days to overcast days. The light qualities of these two lighting conditions are vastly different, as are the shadows produced by them. Light produced from the sun on a bright day is a **hard light**, resulting in bright areas and distinct, dark shadows. The light source (the sun) is a *small* light source. Light produced from a cloudy day is a **soft light** that creates even illumination and less defined shadows. The light source for a cloudy day is a *large* light source. However, the light source also describes the shadow it creates. A small light source is a *hard* light producing *hard* shadows. A large light source is a *soft* light producing *soft* shadows. Shadows appear lighter or darker because of the contrast of the overall scene. *The smaller the light source, the harder the shadows will appear; the larger the light source, the softer the shadows will appear.*

Hard Light/Hard Shadows

Bright, sunny days produce **high-contrast** images. Contrast refers to the difference in brightness between shadows and highlights. All beginning photography students recognize that a high-contrast photograph has greater differences in tonal values between shadows and highlights, and has fewer midtones. The sun is a single light source from which light rays travel in a straight line. The lightwaves are striking the subject at the same angle, which means the shadow created from this light source is dark with clearly defined hard edges, or a **hard shadow**. The light source creating a hard shadow is called a hard light. Even though the sun is the largest object in our solar system, it is described as a small light source because it is a single-point light source in the same way that a bare bulb is a single-point light source. They are called single-point light sources because of the direct path of the light rays to the object and the type of shadows created from the hard light source.

Artificial lighting uses the same terms describing the qualities of light as those produced by the sun. The light source creating a hard shadow is a small, hard light source, like a **hot light**, as shown in figure 2-4a or a **strobe** light with a **reflector** (lighting diagram, fig. 2-4b). The light travels from the light unit toward the subject in a straight line, just as light travels in a direct path from the sun on a bright sunny day. Predictably, the shadow created from this type of artificial light source appears similar to the shadow produced from a bright, sunny day, that is, a dark shadow with hard edges. In figure 2-5, the small light source is coming from the left, so the hard shadow falls to the right of the white object. There is very little visible detail in the shadow area.

When a small light source is used, and very dark shadows are produced, it can reduce the objects to basic shapes. The shadow side of the white object in figure 2-5 becomes a black rectangle, as does the shadow. The aperture and viewfinders become circles. The dark shadows create a sense of depth, but not much volume or shape.

Soft Light/Soft Shadow

Overcast days produce shadows that have no clearly defined edges, and the light produced by an overcast day is **low contrast**. The cloud cover on an overcast day has the effect of a large soft-box, making the sun a large light source because it causes the light rays to scatter in different directions. Even though the light is traveling in a straight line, there is no direct path from the sun to the object. When the light rays are scattered, they hit the subject from different directions, creating a *soft shadow*. The shadow

Figure 2-4a

In this example, the single hot light is a hard light. The result is a bright object with hard shadows.

area receives some illumination from stray light. This type of light is called soft light. A low-contrast photograph will have more midtones than dark shadows and bright highlights.

A hard light source can be changed to soft light by placing a **diffusion panel** in front of it (fig. 2-6a). A translucent material such as thin white paper or cloth scatters the light rays in different directions, producing diffused lighting. Care should be taken when placing material too close to the front of a hot light because the lights are exactly what the name implies; they are very hot and can cause a fire. A strobe light source with a reflector is also a small light source. It can produce diffused light if it is placed behind a diffusion screen in the same way a hot light will when it is placed behind the diffusion screen. The diffusion screen acts as a filter, reducing the amount of light that goes through the material to illuminate the subject. The photographer must consider two issues when using a diffusion screen

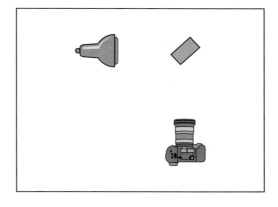

Figure 2-4b

This diagram indicates the light-subject-object relationship. In this example, the hot light (tungsten) is indicated (refer to symbol key in the *Introduction*).

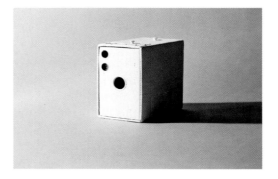

Figure 2-5

A subject illuminated by a hard light will produce dark shadows and a high-contrast image.

Figure 2-6a

Placing a diffusion screen in front of a hard light source (hot light) creates a large light source, turning a hard light into a soft light.

Figure 2-6b

Using a soft box (large light source) diffuses the light, softening the shadows and spreading the light.

with hard light: (1) A hot light must never be placed too close to a diffusion screen. The hot lights produce intense heat and can burn (or even set fire) to the material; and (2) The distance at which the light is placed from the diffusion screen will affect the size of the light source and the appearance of the shadow. The closer the light is to the diffusion screen, the brighter the light on the subject. It is also a smaller light source compared with placing the light farther from the screen, which creates a larger light source but reduces the intensity of light on the subject.

A soft box, which is a light modifier that has a diffusion panel on the front, can also be used to produce diffused light (fig. 2-6b). Soft boxes come in different sizes, which produce different sizes of diffused light, from small to very large. Both methods increase the size of the light source, producing the same type of light as the sun under overcast conditions. The soft box or diffusion screen scatter the light source in the same way the cloud cover scatters the sunlight, causing the light rays to travel in different directions. The examples in figures 2-6a and 2-6b demonstrate how to achieve soft shadows using the diffusion screen or the soft box. This type of lighting is called soft or **diffused light**.

The methods used in figures 2-6 produce a soft light that wraps around the object, producing the soft shadows shown in figure 2-8. The film advance key, shutter release, and viewfinder are clearly visible because the shadow on the left side is not a deep, dark shape as that produced when using a small light source. The contrast between the shadow and the highlight is reduced, and texture is visible. These features are also more visible because the object is white. White reflects more light than darker colors. If a black or dark-colored object were used in the example, these features would not be as visible because black reflects very little light.

Because soft light is a larger light source than hard light, it produces a sense of depth *and* volume because three sides are now visible. Shadows appear less dark, with transitioning between lighter and darker areas. This transition is called the **penumbra**. The center of this shadow at its darkest value is the same as the whole shadow cast by the small light source in figure 2-5.

Perspective

Perspective means different things to different people depending on occupation, education, and understanding of the word. In the language of photographers, perspective provides depth, shape, and spacial relationship to an object. A photograph is, after all, a two-dimensional image of three-dimensional space, and everyone is familiar with the image of railroad tracks in which perspective creates the illusion that the tracks are receding and converging in the distance, at the vanishing point. Consider how an object's planes appear to change when viewing it from the top, sides, front, below, or at an angle. The shape and form change as the camera angle of view is moved from one position to another.

Perspective is about perception, and the perception about an object's physical properties and spatial relationships can be

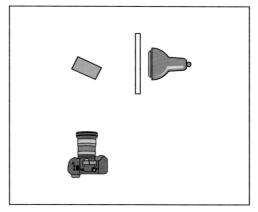

Figure 2-7

Lighting diagram for hot light with diffusion screen.

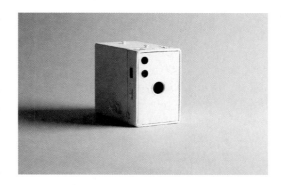

Figure 2-8

Shadow produced by soft box transitions from dark in the center to a lighter tone at the edges. The shadows are very soft at the edges.

manipulated. **Perspective distortion** happens when an object appears much larger than it is relative to the rest of the scene and when the spatial distance appears shorter between foreground and background objects. These distortions are produced by the lens focal length and subject-to-camera distance, as discussed in most beginning black and white textbooks.

Reflectance of Light

Objects are visible because some light rays reflect off the surface while other light rays are absorbed. **Reflectance** is how much light is reflected off the surface, and it varies with the object. Four properties determine reflectance: *surface texture, surface color, type of light striking the surface,* and *amount of light striking the surface.*

Types of Reflections

Earlier in this chapter, light was described as small or large. The type of lighting directly affects object reflections. Hard lights produce either **direct reflections** or **diffused reflections**, depending on the surface. Soft lights produce diffused reflections. *The type of light is determined by the light source, and the reflection is determined by the object surface.* Types of light and reflection will be discussed at length in Chapter 3.

Color and Surface Texture

Perceived object color is not only a function of the fluctuation of the light wave, as discussed earlier in this chapter. Light intensity and polarized light will also affect how color saturation appears. Furthermore, extremes in object color, e.g. black and white, against background color and other objects in the scene can also affect the overall appearance of color in the image. Choosing hard or soft light sources, backgrounds, gels, and other considerations affecting color and surface texture are determined for aesthetic reasons depending on what one wants to communicate.

Although surface texture itself can range from a highly polished to a rough, matte surface, lighting types, light direction, and light intensity play an important role in determining the appearance of surface texture. The photographer may select specific lights to increase or reduce surface texture.

Surface texture can be exaggerated or hidden, depending on how the subject is lit. Figures 2-9a and 2-10a demonstrate how surface texture is controlled using a single, small direct light source. In figure 2-9b, the lighting diagram indicates that the light source is placed at the camera angle and directed at the object. This lighting results in a flat two-dimensional surface with little indication of surface texture (fig. 2-9a). To show surface texture, there must be shadows to provide information about the object surface. Figure 2-10a reveals the rough texture of the tablet, which is visible in the pitting on the bottom of the image. In addition, the shadows give the flowers and bird form and shape as the relief becomes more visible. This is achieved by placing the light to the right or left of the object, causing the light to shine directly on the side of the object as the lighting diagram indicates in figure 2-10b. This technique is known as **raking** the light. This is beneficial when shooting a low-relief object requiring visible texture and shape.

Lighting Direction

The direction of light plays a major part in determining how one interprets object depth and shape. There are six basic directions to illuminate an object: front, back, side, top, three-quarter, and below. The directional descriptions are from the *subject position.* Discussions in this chapter will cover all directions except below, which will be discussed in Chapter 4.

The surface on which the object is setting also plays a part in defining the shape of objects. If the surface and background is white or a light tone, it will reflect light back onto the object. Light reflecting back onto an object helps fill in the shadows. However, surface color and texture will affect how much light, if any, will be reflected back onto the subject. For example, if the surface and background is black or a dark tone, little or no light will be reflected back onto the object. Fill-in reflections will change depending upon whether the surface is textured or highly polished. The type of light source also affects how shadows appear on the background and surrounding objects. As discussed earlier in this chapter, small light sources produce dark shadows, whereas large light sources fill in the shadow areas. When working with artificial lighting, it is very important to consider all aspects of the set, including the backdrop and background materials.

Front Lighting

Front lighting comes from the direction of the camera (fig. 2-11, a and b). It is very even and flat, giving few clues to the shape of the object photographed. The shadow falls behind the object, obscuring perceived depth. Because the object is turned slightly toward the right in figure 2-12, a and b, the front of the object receives most of the light and appears brighter than the left side and top of the object. However, there is very little information provided in the image about the environment. The lighting in figure 2-11a is higher and pointed slightly down, so the gray backdrop material transitions from light to a darker shade of gray. Although this does not offer much information to define the object, it does result in providing limited depth clues within the overall image. It prevents the white object in figure 2-12a from appearing to *float* on a sea of gray. Figures 12b demonstrates front lighting for a black object on a gray background. There appears to be less information supplied for the black object because of the nature of black material and its lack of reflective qualities. Even though the light is coming from the front, there is very little surface information. Adjustment of exposure is required to show more detail in the black object. This adjustment would result in a brighter background because more light would also strike the background material.

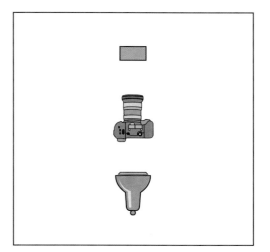

No exposure compensation was made in the example shown in figure 2-12b.

Backlighting

Lighting the object from the back creates a silhouette. Figure 2-13a demonstrates backlighting, and figure 2-13b illustrates the lighting diagram for backlighting an object. As discussed earlier in this chapter,

Figure 2-9a

Hard light shining directly on a surface creates a flat, undefined surface texture.

Figure 2-9b

Lighting diagram showing light-to-object relationship, resulting in little or no surface texture.

Figure 2-10a

Raking the light across the surface from an angle creates shadows and highlights, which define the surface texture.

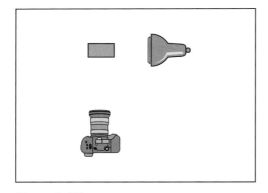

Figure 2-10b

Lighting diagram demonstrating light-to-subject position for raking the light.

a silhouette offers no information regarding object texture or shape. The object in figure 2-14 is not a silhouette because the object is not isolated from light reflecting from the backdrop onto the object. Even though light is reflecting onto the object, there is still not enough visual information for shape and form. The front appears flat and gray. The only thing preventing it from appearing completely two-dimensional is the physical features of the object, such as the film advance key and mechanical aperture on the front. The exposure was set to show some detail on the front, but it results in eliminating all detail on the top of the object, which is so bright that it blends into the background. This further emphasizes the two-dimensional aspects of the image. Backlighting is typically used for lighting glass (lighting transparent objects such as glass is discussed in Chapter 4).

Top Lighting

Placing the light directly over the subject will illuminate the top, but the front and sides will receive approximately the same illumination. A variation of this lighting is used for many **tabletop sets**. A tabletop typically refers to small setups that literally sit on a table. Although the example in figure 2-15, a and b, illustrates the illumination of direct overhead lighting, a typical tabletop lighting setup would have the lights positioned overhead but more to the rear and tilted to shine in the direction of the object so that the backdrop gradates from light to dark. The overhead light could also be positioned to the front and tilted so that more light falls on the front of the subject and illuminates the background. The subject in figure 2-16 demonstrates the result of overhead lighting. The light is directly overhead; therefore, the gray surface appears much brighter because of the directional lighting. Figure 2-15a also demonstrates how to use c-stands to create top lighting when a boom (Chapter 7, fig. 7-37) is not available. Note the counterweights on the end of the arm to balance the light head and soft box. Not shown in the figure are weights on the legs of the C stand to provide additional stability and balance (Chapter 7, figure 7-40 demonstrates weight placement on a C stand).

Figure 2-11a

Light setup for front lighting.

The top of the white object appears much brighter than the front or sides because the front and sides are receiving some illumination from light reflecting off the surface of the background material and bouncing back onto the subject. There is a slight shadow on both sides of the subject because the illumination from the soft box is lighting the white object evenly. In fact, if one could see all sides of the object at once, there would be shadow information all around because of even lighting.

Side Lighting

Placing the light to the side of an object creates a visible shadow. The shadow is dark and distracting in a typical still life setup, but can produce dramatic results if that is the desired effect. Moving the light source closer to the object or using a larger light source will make the shadow softer, which occurs because more light strikes the surface, surrounds the object, and reflects back into the shadows, thus filling them in. Moving the light source farther away or using a small light source will produce a darker shadow.

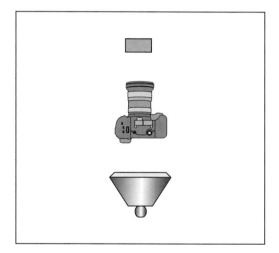

Figure 2-11b

Lighting diagram for front lighting. In this example, the symbol for soft box is used to represent soft lights. If hard lights were used, the symbol for hot lights or reflector would replace the soft box symbol.

Again, this is a function of how much light is reflected from the surrounding surface back into the shadow areas. However, if the light is moved farther away, the subject will receive less illumination, requiring an exposure adjustment. Figure 2-17, a and b, demonstrate the lighting diagram and lighting setup for left-side soft light. The effect of this setup is shown in figure 2-18.

Figure 2-12a

A white object on a gray background shows some detail because of the position of the white object, but there is little information about the environment or background. The shadow falls behind the white object with front lighting, providing minimal information about the subject's surface or shape.

Figure 2-12b

A black object on a gray background shot at the same exposure produces less detail than a white object on a gray background. Black material does not reflect as much light, thus reducing visible texture.

Side lighting is used in figures 2-19 and 2-20 to demonstrate the relationship among lighting, object reflection, and background surface/color. In these illustrations, the white and black objects are used with white, gray, and black backgrounds. The gray background is used for the basic exposure setting for each object and placed in the center of the figure as a reference. An incident light meter was used to make lighting exposure for the white object against the gray background and the black object against the gray background, and the same exposure was used for the other photographs in each example.

Starting first with figure 2-19b, the white object has shape, form, and depth; detail in the shadow areas on the right are dark but visible; and the bright areas of the top and front also have detail. There are three distinct tonal values to the white object, and the gradation of the background material and the shadow falling on the surface provide volume.

The white object on white (a) in figure 2-19 has lost some detail along the left edge and on the bottom edge. It is disappearing into the white background material. The white background material is reflecting back into the object, which is further illuminating the subject. However, the right side has shadow detail on the object and the surface of the background material. It is easily viewed and has form. White on white can be a difficult subject to control.

The white object on a black background material (c) has good detail to the front and top, but the shadow detail is lost on the right side. There is little information on texture or background. It appears as though the front and top are *floating*. It is apparent that the black background material has a slight sheen on the surface because a reflection is visible just below the front of the object. This is the only clue to the background material's surface texture.

Figure 2-20a shows the black object clearly on the white background, even in the darkest shadow area. Surface detail is visible on the front and top; the edge is clearly defined on the right side in the shadow. It has form, shape, and depth. The subject on the neutral gray background is also clearly visible, although the right, bottom edge in the shadow is not as clear. The subject in (c) suffers the same fate as the white object on white. Black does not reflect much light; therefore, the black object is disappearing into the background material. We see some illumination behind the object because of spillover from the soft box shining behind the object and illuminating the background material. The front of the black object has a subtle sheen to the leather and is reflecting the light, resulting in a slightly lighter tonal value. The top is receiving some light and is a darker tonal value than the front. The right side and the shadow area have lost all detail and appear as a black void in the image. Once again, because the background material has a slight sheen, it transitions from a dark gray to black as a result of the light reflecting off the surface.

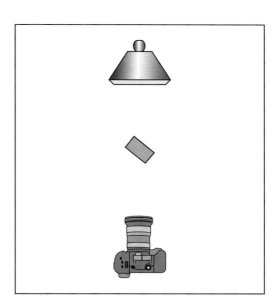

Figure 2-13a

Lighting setup for backlighting.

Figure 2-13b

Lighting diagram for backlighting.

Figure 2-14

Typically, backlighting creates a silhouette. In this figure, light is reflected from the backdrop onto the object, which gives some visual clue but not enough information for form and shape. The top of the object is lost in the background.

Three-Quarter Lighting

Three-quarter lighting requires the light to be placed at a 45° angle between the camera position and side-light position. Strict side lighting often creates shadows that are too deep, requiring a second light or fill card to illuminate the shadow side of the object. Three-quarter light allows light to wrap around the front and side of the object so that the shadow area receives some light (fig. 2-21, a and b). Figure 2-22 illustrates three tonal values created from the

Figure 2-15a

Figure 2-15a

Light setup for top lighting. A boom is preferable for this type of lighting, but a C stand can be used if a boom is not available. The long arm of the C stand should be over the longest leg, and weights must be used at the end of the arm to counterweight the light head and soft box. It is also good practice to place weights at the base of the C stand in the same manner as a standard light stand.

Figure 2-15b

Lighting diagram for top lighting. It would be difficult to draw a lighting diagram for top lighting from an aerial perspective, so the diagram is drawn from the side view. If more than one light is used, there may be two drawings: an aerial view and a side view to make the lighting setup clearly understood.

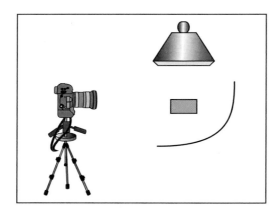

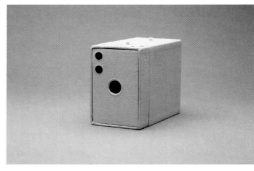

Figure 2-16

Placing the light directly overhead creates a bright highlight on the top of the object while the front and sides are in shadow, but the light is even. A light shadow is visible on the right side of the object from the overhead lighting. There is also a shadow on the side of the object, which is not visible.

three-quarter lighting. The brightest area of illumination is the front, followed by the top. The left side of the subject is in shadow because the three-quarter light position is on the right side from the camera shooting position. This lighting gives shape and volume to the object. The shadow from the white object falls back toward the backdrop at an angle, emphasizing visual depth in the image.

This section presented basic lighting techniques for directional lighting using two different light sources. In addition to the two basic light sources and directional light, light modifiers can be used to control intensity and to create different patterns of light. Light modifiers offer unlimited possibilities for controlled lighting and creative images. Illustrations of light modifiers can be found in Chapter 7.

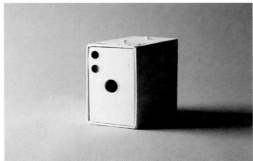

Figure 2-17a

Light setup for side lighting.

Figure 2-17b

Lighting diagram for side lighting.

Figure 2-18

Soft-light side lighting on gray background. The edge of the shadow transitions from the dark center to the diffused outer edges of the shadow.

Distance from Light

The distance of an artificial light source from the subject affects the level of illumination: the closer the light, the higher the intensity; the farther away, the lower the intensity. When placing the light farther away it spreads out, but decreases the illumination. This is called **falloff**. The amount of falloff can be calculated using the **Inverse Square Law**. The law states that light is inversely proportional to the square of the distance. For example, when a one-foot-square source light is one foot away from a surface, it will provide one square foot of illumination. Moving the

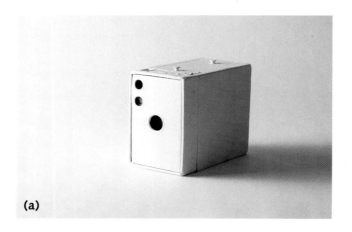

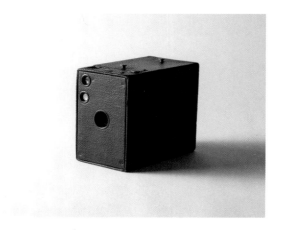

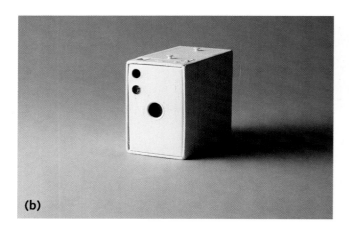

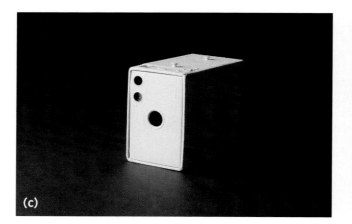

Figure 2-19a, b, c

Compare the exposure for the white object against a gray background with the white object on white and the white object on a black background.

Figure 2-20a, b, c

Compare the exposure for the black object against a gray background with the black object on white and the black object on a black background.

Figure 2-21a

Three-quarter lighting setup requires that the light be placed at approximately a 45° position between the camera and the side-light position.

light source two feet from the surface (or doubling the distance) will decrease the illumination not by half, but by 75%, resulting in 25% of the original intensity. If the light is moved farther away from the surface it is lighting, the illumination decreases proportionally to the square of the distance it is placed from the surface to the light source as discussed in Chapter 1. What does this mean when using artificial lighting on a subject? Simply stated, if one moves the light farther from the subject, the lights spreads out to cover a larger area, but there is less light on the subject; moving it closer increases the amount of light on the subject and reduces the area of coverage. If the source light is placed one foot from a surface, and the meter reading is f/22 at 125, it covers four feet of area. If the light is moved two feet away, the illumination on the subject changes from f/22 to f/11 for proper exposure, and the light spread is a four- × four-foot spread. At four feet, the f/stop must be set at f/5.6, and the spread is 16 × 16 feet. Each time the distance is doubled, the light illumination is reduced exponentially, and exposure compensation

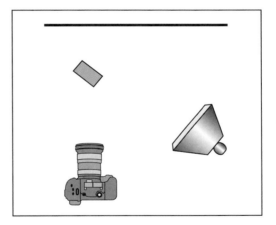

Figure 2-21b

Three-quarter lighting diagram.

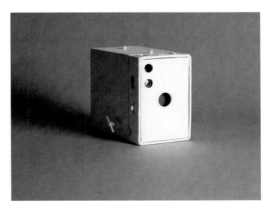

Figure 2-22

Three-quarter lighting allows the light to wrap around to the shadow side, reducing scene contrast.

must be made to achieve the same exposure on film or digital capture. The area of illumination increases by the square of the previous illumination. In practice, changes that photographers make in lighting distances are often done intuitively, but consider the fact that because of the Inverse Square Law, small changes in lighting will result in large changes in illumination.

As the light travels, it spreads out. The illumination in the center of the surface will be brighter than the outer edges of the surface. Figure 2-23 demonstrates the effects of the Inverse Square Law. The light was placed above and behind the camera position. Three white cards were used to demonstrate light falloff. Card 2 is two feet behind card 1, and card 3 is four feet from card 2. The distances are increasing proportionally to represent light reduction with the square of the distance. Although it is not possible to *exactly* reproduce the Inverse Square Law, this example demonstrates what happens with objects placed at different distances from the light source. Remember that the camera will record the exposure based on the *light-to-subject distance*, not the camera-to-subject distance. Because the illumination on the white cards decreases with distance, the farthest white card appears gray. What does this mean to

someone learning lighting? It means that even white can appear gray and gray can appear white, depending upon brightness and distance of lighting from the subject, thus giving the photographer substantial control over the subject.

Intensity of Light

Intensity is the level of light brightness. An incident light meter measures the intensity of the light falling on the subject, and a reflective meter measures the intensity of the light reflecting off the subject. For example, if the incident light meter is set at a shutter speed of 125, an f/stop reading of f/16 indicates four times the light intensity (or two stops) than an f/stop reading of f/8. The light is brighter, which causes the meter to indicate a smaller aperture for proper exposure. The photographer has little control over light intensity under natural lighting conditions. Camera accessories such as neutral density filters must be used to reduce the intensity of the light, but the only solution to increasing light intensity under natural light conditions is to use artificial light.

The photographer can completely control light intensity and exposure with artificial light units. This is accomplished

Figure 2-23

Inverse Square Law effects. The cards are all identical in size, material, and white color. The light is bright, with close objects allowing the first card to appear white. As the light falls off, the white cards appear to be light gray and then dark gray the farther they are from the light source.

by increasing or reducing the amount of light output produced by the lighting unit or changing the distance between the light source and the subject (fig. 2-24). The photographer's choices in adjusting exposure using the shutter speed or aperture depend on the light source. Tungsten lighting is similar to natural lighting in that it is a constant light source. The exposure can be adjusted by either the shutter speed or aperture or a combination of shutter speed-aperture adjustment. Strobe lighting illuminates the subject only when the shutter button is pressed. The illumination for strobe lighting is a quick burst of white-balanced light. It is so fast that the shutter speed has little effect on the exposure. Therefore, exposure is controlled through adjusting the power of light intensity on the light unit and/or aperture selection. Exposure cannot be adjusted using the shutter speed when using strobe lighting. However, if the modeling light remains on during long exposures or slow shutter speeds, both image color and exposure will be affected. The first of two examples of this scenario occurs when an image requires a very small aperture for depth of field, but the lights are not powerful enough to stop down to the desired

aperture. The photographer can then fire the flash multiple times, thus building exposure and allowing the photographer to use a smaller aperture than the power of the lights can provide with one flash. The second example occurs when the photographer desires subject blur or movement in the image, which would require a slow shutter speed. In this case, the photographer would balance the two light color temperatures (strobe and tungsten). This depends, of course, on how long the aperture is open after the strobe fires. Additional information on color temperature and light sources is found in Chapters 5 and 6.

If light intensity cannot be controlled by adjusting the power of the light unit. Moving the light closer to or farther away from the object, as shown in figures 2-25 and 2-26, will increase or decrease the light intensity. However moving the light away affects the overall illumination of the scene, objects, and the shadows. A light source that is repositioned for one object may cause too much or not enough illumination on another. Of course, the subject itself receives light in its own way, and multiple subjects may present the necessity for additional lights or light modifiers.

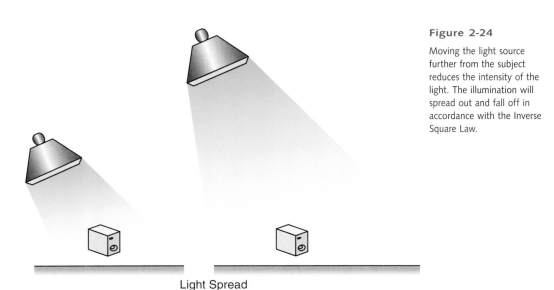

Figure 2-24

Moving the light source further from the subject reduces the intensity of the light. The illumination will spread out and fall off in accordance with the Inverse Square Law.

Light Spread

Figure 2-25

A light source close to an object will produce a brighter intensity and softer shadows.

Figure 2-26

Moving the light source further from the subject will reduce the intensity of the light but could also include unwanted illumination on other objects. The shadows will be darker, creating more contrast in the overall image.

Shaping the Object

To demonstrate how lighting affects form and shape, one light source (a hot light or a soft box) was used in figures 2-27, a–f, and 2-28, a–f, on mannequin figures and backdrops.

A word about the setup: The mannequins are positioned to show how the shadows and highlights affect different planes of the body figure and how the figures relate to each other as the lighting arrangement is changed. Sand was chosen for its textured surface, and

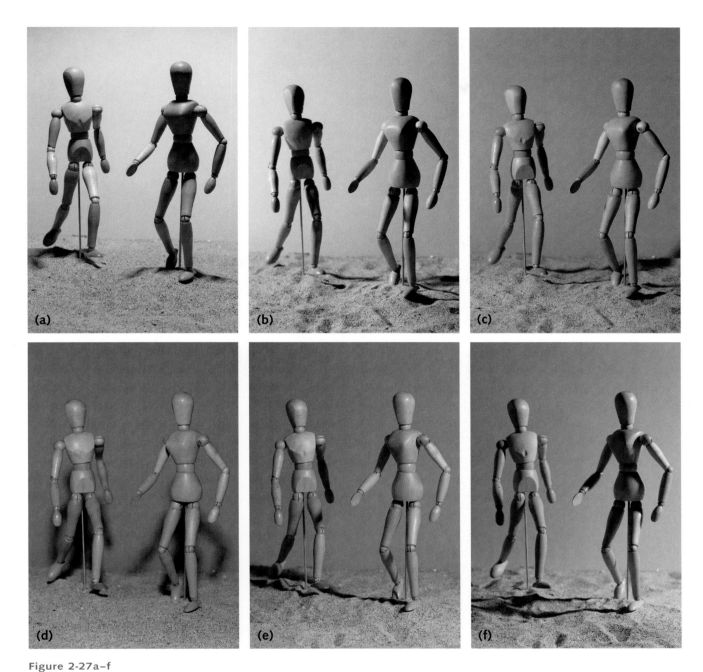

Figure 2-27a–f

A hard light source is used in this figure, causing dark harsh shadows. As the light moves from the top of the mannequins and then horizonally 180°, the mannequins take on different shapes and forms. Figure 2-43c has less shape because the lighting is from the front. Only the shadows on the backdrop give depth to the scene. Moving the light also affects the illumination on the backdrop. Top lighting illuminates the backdrop most because it is falling directly on it.

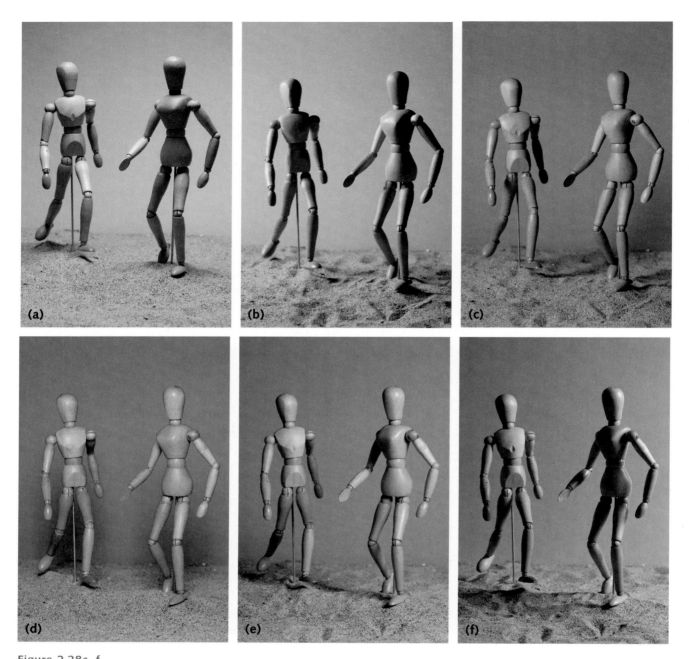

Figure 2-28a–f

A large soft light source was used for this figure. As with fig. 2-29, the form and shape change as the light moves 180° around the mannequins. Because the light source is large, the shadows appear less defined and soft.

a neutral gray background was used to best see the effects of the shadow as the lights are moved around the figures. A shallow depth of field was used to emphasize the light and shadow effects on the figures.

Particular attention should be paid to the following when comparing all illustrations:

1. Hot lights are small, bright, round highlights from overhead lighting. As the lighting moves around the figures, it may elongate form shape, but somewhere there will be a clue about the type of light used.
2. Soft boxes produce softer lighting. The type of lighting can be identified by the shape of the highlights.
3. Shadows from hot lights are dark and hard; soft boxes produce lighter, less defined shadows. The light wraps around the figures and fills in the shadow areas when a soft box is used.
4. The direction of the shadows and where the highlights appear are indicators of directional lighting.
5. The background material changes with the different lighting. Note how the material gradates when the lighting comes from the side or how even the lighting becomes when it is front lighting.

All of the above comments regarding the two figures and the different lighting should be considered when setting up any shot. Where are the shadows? Do they interfere with other areas of the shot? Where are the highlights? Are they too bright? How are the shadows/highlights working with the background? Is it the right background for the shot? Is this the best composition for the shot? Should the camera angle be changed? Successful lighting begins with the overall composition and ends with attention to detail.

Shaping the Object with Multiple Light Sources

Multiple lights, **gobos**, and fill cards can be used to shape objects for specific lighting requirements. Often, there may be areas requiring additional illumination to *fill in* shadow areas, to prevent shadows from becoming dark holes, devoid of detail. These dark holes create a distracting element in the photograph. Using multiple lights, fill cards, and gobos give the photographer nearly absolute control of how the photograph appears.

To understand how to use multiple sources for effectively lighting a setup or scene, the photographer must understand contrast and brightness as they apply to the lights, subject, and scene. They all work together to produce a successful image. Earlier in this chapter, contrast was discussed as it applied to lighting the object (the white object) and the shadows created from two different types of light sources. The difference between the brightest area (that area receiving the most light) and shadow area of any scene (that area receiving the least light) is called the **lighting ratio**. For example, a two-to-one lighting ratio (written as 2:1) means that the brightest area is two times (or one stop) as bright as the area receiving the least amount of illumination; 4:1 means there is four times more illumination in the brightest area in relation to the area of least illumination (or two stops). If all areas of the scene receive the same illumination, then the lighting ratio is 1:1. This relationship functions in the same manner as the *amount of light* calculated for *number of stops* learned in basic photography, i.e. $2\times$ = one stop, $4\times$ = two stops, $8\times$ = three stops, and so on. Therefore, the 8:1 lighting ratio means that the brightest area is $8\times$, or three stops, brighter than the shadow area.

The light meter will identify the f/stop differences. Figure 2-29 demonstrates the setup for using two soft boxes to illuminate the subject. Side lighting was selected for demonstration purposes only. A photographer should place the lights where appropriate to illuminate the subject for the desired effect. Any multiple-light placement combination will produce a lighting ratio for the scene setup. One light is the **main light**, and the other light is the **fill light**.

Figure 2-29a, b, c

a, meter reading to determine exposure for the main light; *b*, meter reading to determine exposure for the fill light; *c*, meter reading for overall exposure.

The main light provides the primary illumination, whereas the fill does exactly as the name implies; it fills in the shadow or adds additional illumination to a darker part of the setup. Increasing or decreasing the intensity of the fill light changes the lighting ratio, e.g., from 4:1 to 2:1 or vice versa. This change can also be accomplished by increasing the intensity of the main light. The photographer can also move the light source closer to or farther from the setup to achieve this change, remembering that the illumination will spread over a larger area as the light is moved back.

So, how does one determine the lighting ratio? It can be determined by taking an incident meter reading on both sides of the subject for the main light (the brightest area of importance) and the fill light (darkest area of importance) while both lights are illuminating the setup. Reading the main and fill lights for lighting ratio does not necessarily mean reading the darkest part of the scene; rather, it means reading the *important* shadow areas and the *important* highlight areas. This method may not be as accurate as others because light will spill over from the main light into the shadow area when taking a reading of the shadow side.

Another method is to turn off the fill light and take an incident meter reading of the main light (fig. 2-29a) and then turn on the fill light, turn off the main light, and take an incident meter reading of the fill (fig. 2-29b). This method will give the absolute lighting ratio between the two lights. The meter reading is taken by pointing the incident meter directly at the lights instead of the camera. However, this does not provide an accurate exposure reading for the overall scene. Therefore, a third reading must be taken to give an accurate reading of the overall scene for exposure (fig. 2-29c). The lighting ratio simply provides the photographer with information about how much light is illuminating different parts of the scene and the relationship between shadow

and highlight areas. Sometimes, a photographer will take many readings in different areas around the set to determine exposure readings for specific areas and to identify the lighting ratio between many areas of the setup, which provides previsualization for each area and how it may be recorded in relation to the other areas in the scene.

The examples used in figure 2-29, a–c, demonstrate how to determine lighting ratio. However, if a more complex image is used, the photographer must consider all aspects of the image. Figure 2-30, a–c, illustrate how the lighting ratio affects the background and the surrounding objects in the scene. In figure 2-30a, everything is illuminated evenly; depth of field is used to determine the spatial relationship. Shadows from other objects appear on the ground and the sails because of directional lighting. The overall scene is light and bright. Figure 2-30b has 2:1 lighting. It appears to have more texture and depth. The ship and the small wooden figure have shape. Figure 2-30c appears to be darker, projecting a more somber mood. More detail is lost on the right side because less light fills in the darker spaces at a 4:1 ratio. The sails on the ship in figure 2-30, b and c, have more form, shape, and depth created by the lighting ratio between the main and fill lights. However, the shadow from the small wooden figure on the left remains the same because the light coming from the left was not adjusted. The lighting ratio for the image was controlled by reducing the fill light to produce the desired results.

Although only two lights were used in the examples shown, photographers may need to use three, four, or many more lights to accomplish the desired effect for a complicated set, particularly with location shooting. There is no set number of lights required, and lighting arrangements will vary from set to set. Lighting ratios can also be created using one light and reflectors (gold or silver panels) or fill cards (large and small white cards) to reflect illumination

(a) (b) (c)

Figure 2-30a, b, c

a, lighting ratio of 1:1 relies on depth of field for spatial relationship; *b*, lighting ratio of 2:1 and *c*, lighting ratio of 4:1 display more form, shape, and environmental aesthetics created by the main and fill lighting ratios.

back into the scene onto specific objects. More information about different lighting equipment and uses is discussed in Chapters 6 and 7.

Subject Contrast

Subject contrast refers to the *difference between the most reflective surface and the least reflective surface within a subject.* **Scene contrast** is the *comparison of reflective surfaces of many objects within the scene.* A reflective light meter is necessary to determine the subject and scene contrasts. Taking a meter reading for various objects will determine the amount of light reflected from the surfaces; the photographer should take readings from many objects and compare them to determine scene contrast. A spot meter is often used because it reads small areas of the single-subject surface. The reflectance of the sand, the surface of the boat, and the polished surface of the mannequins in figure 2-30 together are an example of how scene contrast would be evaluated from subject to subject. Comparing the reflectance of the sails and the dark surface

of the boat demonstrates subject contrast evaluation.

Basic Portrait Lighting

The basic techniques thus far have addressed using light to form and shape objects, the shadows created by different types lighting, and the relationship between highlights and shadows on the subject and the scene. Now it is time to apply this information to one of the most common subjects for artificial lighting: the portrait. The authors have included basic portrait lighting in this section because it is the natural progression from foundational lighting techniques for creating shape and form. However, it should be noted here that portrait lighting generally requires more than two lights for advanced techniques, and the following sections will not address this. Advanced techniques are built around the basic lighting setup of one or two lights. Chapter 8 will address the different types of light sources used in portrait lighting and some advanced lighting techniques, such as catch lights, hair lights, kicker lights, and the like.

There are four basic lighting techniques for portrait lighting: **Rembrandt lighting**, **broad lighting**, **short lighting**, and **butterfly lighting**. These are the foundations for portrait lighting, and any photographer can create variations to enhance individual portraits from these techniques.

Rembrandt Lighting

This lighting technique is named after the seventeenth century Dutch painter Rembrandt Van Rijn, who used this dramatic effect for his portraits. An examination of his portraits reveals an inverted triangle of light over one eye, traveling down the cheek to a point even with the base of the nose. This technique is used by many photographers because it can be used as subtly or dramatically as desired for effective portraits. As in Rembrandt's paintings, the basic technique for photographic portraits is to create the inverted triangle of light on the subject's face (fig. 2-31). The size and shape of the triangle will vary depending on light placement and head position. This technique is achieved by placing the light high and at a 45° angle, as shown in figure 2-32. The height and the direction of the light determine the size, placement, and length of the triangle of illumination. Using a fill light affects the light ratio; the greater the lighting ratio, the more dramatic the effects. Therefore, an open, brighter portrait would require a reduced lighting ratio. Conversely, a greater lighting ratio is required for a more dramatic effect (fig. 2-33, a and b).

Broad and Short Lighting

These two lighting techniques are similar in that the description on how to achieve the lighting is relative to the subject's ear and the camera position as shown in figure 2-34, a and b. Figure 2-34a illustrates a broad lighting setup. Notice that the subject is sitting at an angle, and the light is positioned on the same side as the subject's ear (fig. 2-35). It is called broad lighting because the face is illuminated across the side of the face and it wraps around the head (fig. 2-36, a and b). This lighting may be used to widen the face for individuals with a thin face.

The lighting ratio can be reduced for each lighting techniques by adding a fill light or using a reflector card to illuminate the darker side of the face.

Short lighting requires that light placement is on the side of the subject's face where the ear would not be visible to the camera, as illustrated in figures 2-34b and 2-37. This illuminates a small portion of the face opposite the camera position (fig. 3-38). Sometimes, photographers use this lighting for a plump or full, round face to make it appear slimmer. This lighting can produce challenges for the photographer if the subject wears eyeglasses. Because the subject is positioned toward the light, a reflection from the light source may appear in the lens of the eyeglasses.

Butterfly Lighting

Butterfly lighting is achieved by placing the light in front of the subject and raising it high enough to create a small shadow under the nose and beneath the chin. The depth of the shadow is controlled by the height of the light relative to the subject position. This is often referred to as *glamour lighting* because it was used by Hollywood studio photographers, such as George Hurrell, for early movie star headshots in the 1930s.

Summary

Understanding the basic qualities of light is essential if a photographer is to understand artificial lighting. The ratio between light areas and shadows defines and shape all objects, giving each object volume and the entire scene depth. This chapter discussed the complex relationships among basic light characteristics and principles, the different lighting types and reflection, the language of light, controlling light intensity and light ratios to control object shape, and texture and scene aesthetics. Lighting portraits is no different from creating form and shape for anything that is photographed. These concepts only provide the beginning in understanding and using artificial light. Observation and practice will produce successful images.

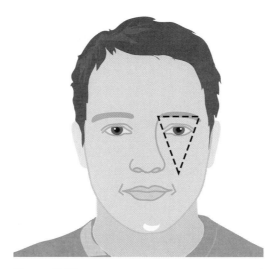

Figure 2-31

The inverted triangle on the drawing represents the area of illumination on the subject to achieve Rembrandt lighting.

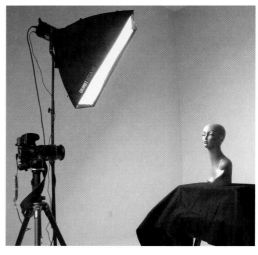

Figure 2-32

Basic light setup for Rembrandt lighting. The light is placed at the three-quarter position, high and positioned at an angle toward the subject's face.

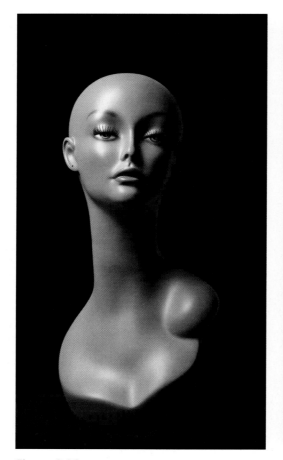

Figure 2-33a

Rembrandt lighting. Note the triangle on the mannequin's right eye created by the single three-quarter light; the right side is dark, creating a dramatic effect.

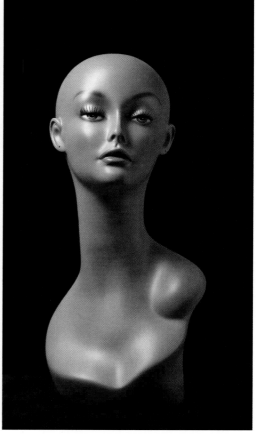

Figure 2-33b

A bright, white fill card was used close to the subject's face for additional illumination on the side of the face.

(a) (b)

Figure 2-34a, b

Lighting diagrams for the broad lighting technique (a) and short lighting (b).

Figure 2-35

Broad lighting illuminates the ear side of the face. A fill card was used to reflect additional light onto the left side of the face that was receiving little illumination from the soft box. Placing the fill card closer to the face would result in brighter illumination on the side of the face that is turned away from the light.

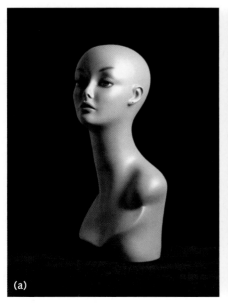 

(a) (b)

Figure 2-36a, b

a, broad lighting without fill card. *b,* broad lighting with fill card. The mannequin in this example is not facing the camera, but the subject's head position is at the discretion of the photographer for a successful photograph. The key element here is the light position is on the visible-ear side.

Figure 2-37

The light is positioned high, behind, or near the camera position and angled down toward the subject.

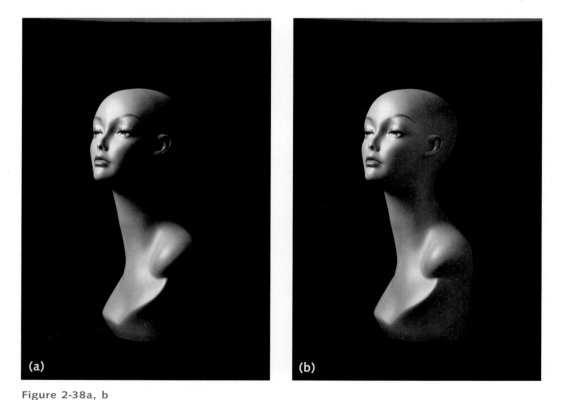

Figure 2-38a, b

a, short lighting without fill card. *b*, short lighting with fill card. Generally, the subject is facing toward the light but may not necessarily be looking into the light. The light position is on the opposite side of the visible ear.

Figure 2-39

Butterfly lighting requires a front lighting setup. The light is positioned high, behind, or near the camera position, and angled down toward the subject.

Figure 2-40

This lighting is identified by the shadow under the nose and the chin. The mannequin's features make it difficult to display the nose shadow because they are unnaturally small, but the shadow below the chin demonstrates the front lighting setup required for butterfly lighting.

Photographers at Work

Polly Chandler

Polly Chandler, from Austin, Texas, works for the Texas House of Representatives as a photographer. You won't see her government work here, though. Polly maintains an active alternative career as a photographer. She has exhibited her work nationally, and her photogr aphs have been published in magazines such as *Photo District News, American Photo*, and *Silvershotz Magazine* (www.pollychandler.com).

Title: *Sara, 2005*

This photograph is from an ongoing series of narrative images that I have been working on for a number of years. The content is derived from an exploration of my own identity and how that translates visually.

I chose to use a handheld Sunpak flash to counterbalance the intensity of the sun. It was about 2:00 p.m. on a spring day in Texas, and the sun was extremely bright. Although I wanted the

Figure 2-41

Sara, 2005. Courtesy of Polly Chandler.

Figure 2-42

Lighting diagram for *Sara*.

intense natural light, I also wanted to dial it down a bit to create a darker background. This was a great opportunity to use artificial light to provide separation. The small flash allowed me to use a fast shutter speed on my view camera lens. The combination of the darker tones of the background, and thanks to the strength of the flash, the viewer is able to focus attention on the subject in the foreground.

The film is Polaroid Type 55, and the negative was printed on silver gelatin paper.

Figure 2-43

Polly Chandler. Courtesy of Jonathon Edwards.

Greg Landrum

Greg Landrum, from St. Louis, Missouri, is a commercial photographer whose specialties of work extend from product to architectural photography. He also specializes in large-format camera negatives and platinum/palladium printing for his personal work (www.landrumphoto.com).

Title: *Dried Miniature Daisy*

I had envisioned this portfolio shot to be made in black and white. Because of a happy accident, it was fully realized in color. This image was planned as a new portfolio addition, but the image can also function as fine art, too.

The size of the flower is quite small, three inches from top to bottom. I photographed on a background that was distorted, for lack of a better word. The wall and base did not meet at a 90° angle, more like 120°. In other words, the wall leaned back, and the base leaned down. This is why I was

able to lean the flower against the wall and, with the correct lighting angle, have separation to create the shadow that is so integral to the photograph.

A spotlight was place to the left of the set and positioned in a manner to create a pleasing shadow. A small soft box with a diffusion screen was placed to the left of the set as well. Placed between the soft box and the set was a 20-inch-square foam core card with a round hole. The hole was about 8 inches in diameter. Because the flower was so small, the hole was cut to effectively reduce the size of the soft box illumination. The soft box added directional fill from the same side as the main light, and I adjusted it to soften the contrast of the spotlight without filling in the shadow too much.

Because a black and white image was my intention, I placed a number 8 filter (yellow) over the lens to add some tonal separation. At some point in the process of making the color image, I became curious to see what the image might look like in color. I exposed a color Polaroid and was

Figure 2-44

Dried Miniature Daisy.
Courtesy of Greg Landrum.

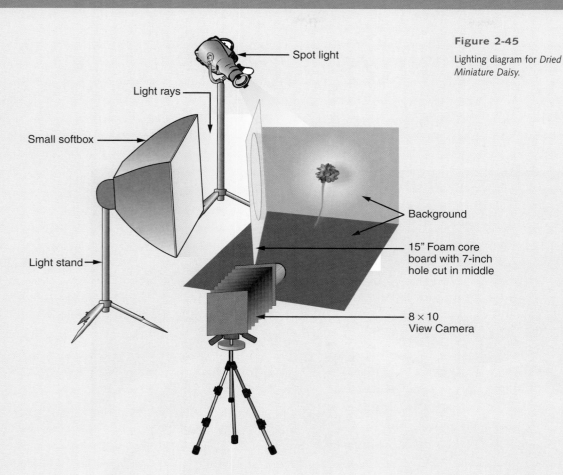

Figure 2-45

Lighting diagram for *Dried Miniature Daisy.*

Spot light

Light rays

Small softbox

Light stand

Background

15" Foam core board with 7-inch hole cut in middle

8 × 10 View Camera

stunned when it came out of the processor. I had forgotten to remove the number 8 filter before shooting the Polaroid Type 809. After comparing the black and white and color proofs, I felt that the yellow filter transformed and heightened the overall impact of the image.

I wanted to achieve shallow focus with this image, so an 8 × 10 view camera was chosen. Because the flower was so small, a bellows draw (space between the rear standard/film and front standard/lens) of about *five feet* was necessary to compose the image as seen. I used front tilt and swing to try to achieve focus on just the petals and a fairly wide aperture for such a large camera. In a darkened studio, each strobe was fired individually multiple times, with the shutter set to T to achieve proper exposure. Because I was shooting at around f/11, I didn't have to do all that many "pops" of the strobes. Unlike many instances in the studio with a large camera, a desired smaller

Figure 2-46

Greg Landrum. Courtesy of Matt Waltsgott.

aperture was not the reason for the multiple pops. In this case, the five feet of bellows length incurred a subsequent exposure factor, leading to the additional exposure.

CHAPTER THREE

REFLECTIVE SURFACES

Figure 3-1 Bright shiny metal reflects the light source. Evidence of the light source can be seen in the long reflections on the hammer head, which suggests a large light source was used to light the set.

All materials reflect light; light is what makes objects visible. However, reflections will often obscure surface information if light is not controlled. Controlling the reflection is not difficult, but knowledge of the light-object-camera relationship, light source, and reflection type is crucial. Chapter 2 discussed different light sources and their effects on objects and shadows. Some reflective surfaces, including those that are highly polished or shiny (polished wood, shiny metal, polished acrylic) can be particularly challenging. Observing the direction of light in relation to reflective objects is vital to controlling the reflection in the image. This chapter specifically addresses the relationships among light source, surface texture, and reflection and how the direction of light affects the reflection appearance.

Direction of Light

All surface reflections are a product of the light source that produces them, but they are also affected by the *direction* of the light. Chapter 2 discussed how shadows are affected by a light source and light direction; this chapter discusses how surface reflections are affected by the light source and the direction of light.

Chapter 1 discussed the principles of the Angle of Incidence and the **law of reflection**. Artificial light behaves the same way. Figure 3-2 illustrates a hot light illuminating a flat surface and the corresponding reflection. However, because artificial lighting is completely controllable, the photographer can control the Angle of Incidence and the resulting angle of reflection. In other words, reflections are predictable.

Reflection Types

There are three types of reflections: **direct reflections**, **diffused reflections**, and **glare**. Direct reflections are sometimes called **specular reflections**. Specular reflections should not be confused with *specular highlights*. **Specular highlights** are the bright, small highlights within a larger highlight or a small reflection from a small bright light. These types of reflections often add interest to the photograph and usually are not problematic.

Direct Reflection

A direct reflection is a mirror of the light source that produces it. In other words, the direct

reflection is a product of the relationship among the angles of the light source, the subject surface, and the camera's point of view. When using artificial lights, the photographer has to determine whether or not the camera will record the direct reflection based on the light-subject-camera relationship. To do this, the photographer must determine the angles where the camera will record a direct reflection. Following an imaginary line from the object surface angle away from the camera, but up into space, determines the angle at which the light source is recorded by the camera. This is the **family of angles**, as shown between points A and B in figure 3-3. If the light unit is placed anywhere within this family of angles, the camera will record the reflection. *Any light source within the family of angles is a direct reflection.* The camera will not record any light source outside the family of angles, as indicated

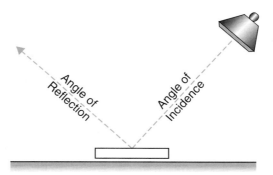

Figure 3-2

The angle of incidence is the direction of light traveling from the point source to the object. The law of reflection is the reflected light traveling from the object equal to, but opposite from, the angle of incidence.

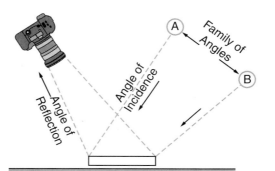

Figure 3-3

Family of Angles

Following an imaginary line from the surface edges away from the camera and up into space establishes points A and B to identify the family of angles: the distance between points A and B. The camera will record a direct reflection if the light is placed within this space.

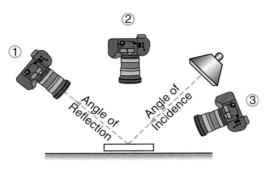

Figure 3-4

Camera 1 will show a reflection because it is within the family of angles. Cameras 2 and 3 will not show reflections because they are outside the family of angles.

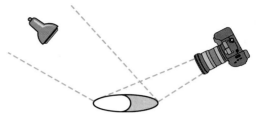

Figure 3-5

A small light source placed inside the family of angles will be reflected in the mirror and recorded in the image.

in figure 3-4. Cameras 2 and 3 are not within the family of angles and, therefore, will not record the reflection from the light source. However, camera 1 *will* record the direct reflection because it is within the family of angles. Do not confuse direct reflection with direct light. Direct light is a light source traveling straight from a point source to the object, usually a small, hard light source. Direct reflections are a mirror of the light source creating them, whether it is a small, hard light source or a large, soft light source.

What Does a Direct Reflection Look Like?

A direct reflection is *always* determined by the light source. For example, if the object has a highly polished surface, and a small, hard light source is used, the reflection will be a small, bright reflection. If a large light source is used on a highly polished surface, the reflection will be a large, bright reflection.

The best demonstration of this example is a mirror. Placing the light source for the mirror within the family of angles guarantees it will be recorded by the camera (fig. 3-5). The small, hard light source in figure 3-6 is clearly visible in the mirror, creating an undesirable reflection and a distraction to the overall image aesthetic. The mirror is also reflecting the strobe tube in the lower part of the dark mirror surface (the green tube circling the dark area). There is so

much brightness that lens flare is extending from the light reflected in the mirror, and lens aberrations travel down toward the strobe tube reflection. Although the light source is reflected in the mirror, it does not cover the entire surface of the mirror because it is smaller than the family of angles. As a result, part of the mirror surface area appears dark.

A small light source can produce dramatic effects *if* it is located outside the family of angles. Figure 3-8 demonstrates the light placement outside the family of angles, and figure 3-7 shows the effects of this small light source placement. The dramatic effects of the image are due to the hard shadows created by a small light source. The shadows define the mouth and eye of the moon face. The mirror surface is dark, and any dust or particles show up because they catch the light. The photographer must clean the mirror surface thoroughly and/or Photoshop the specks out of the image.

Figure 3-9 shows the actual setup used to produce the images shown in figures 3-6 and 3-7. Light A is inside the family of angles. Following an imaginary line, one can determine where the camera placement is located to create the results shown in figure 3-6. Light B is located outside the family of angles to produce the image shown in figure 3-7.

A bright surface is generally desirable when photographing a mirror, and the photographer will have a different set of issues, such as the type of light, how large the light

Figure 3-6

The small light source is visible in the mirror because it is positioned within the family of angles. The light source is recorded, leaving the remaining mirror surface dark.

Figure 3-7

The small light source is placed outside the family of angles, rendering the mirror surface dark. Small light sources emphasize dark shadows.

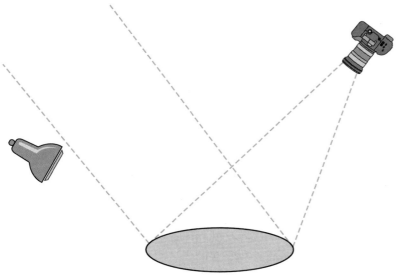

Figure 3-8

This illustration shows the lighting setup to place the light outside the family of angles.

Figure 3-9

A, small light source in the family of angles does not fill the entire surface of the mirror, rendering part of the mirror dark, while also showing the light source. B, a small light source placed outside the family of angles renders the entire surface of the mirror dark.

Figure 3-10

A large soft box ensures the light fills the entire family of angles.

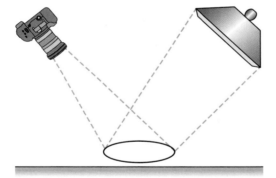

source should be, how bright the light source should be, and what happens to the surface of other objects in the image? A large light source should be used, such as a soft box. This is a diffused light source, but it creates a direct reflection when placed within the family of angles. If a soft box is unavailable, a small light source with a diffusion screen can be used to create a large light source. A large light source must be used for the entire surface area of the mirror to be bright; the *entire area* of the family of angles must be filled with the light source, as illustrated in figure 3-10. The soft box is a better choice

for this because it is a large, soft light source, which scatters the light in all directions. This light source and its intensity *will* affect the appearance of the other objects in the setup (this will be discussed later in this chapter). Figure 3-11 shows the lighting setup for a direct reflection with a large light source. The camera placement is directly in the path of the angle of reflectance in accordance with the law of reflection, which states that the angle of reflection is equal to and opposite the angle of incidence. It is better to have a light source that is larger than the family of angles to ensure that it completely fills the family of angles. The photographer can always block unwanted light with gobos, but if the light is not large enough to fill the family of angles, the entire surface will not be bright.

Figure 3-12 shows the effect of filling the surface area of the mirror with a bright reflection. Using a large soft light source produces softer shadows and even lighting over the surface of the mirror.

A comparison of figure 3-7 with figure 3-12 shows the different effects between these two light sources beyond the mirror

Figure 3-11

A large soft box is used to fill the entire family of angles. This renders the mirror surface bright in a photograph.

Figure 3-12

The large light source is reproduced in the mirror as a direct reflection filling the entire surface area, rendering the mirror surface bright.

surface. The shadows are softer and less pronounced in figure 3-12; the shadows in figure 3-7 are very dark, as illustrated in the eyes, nose, and stars of the mirror frame. In addition, the light refracting from the crystals is different because the light was scattered over the entire reflective surface (fig. 3-12) instead of creating one bright area (fig. 3-7). The crystals reflect the two different light sources in the same way the mirror surface reflects them. The metal surfaces on the small bells appear less harsh in figure 3-12, as is the cord connecting them. The colors are somewhat muted, and the texture of the paint on the mirror is less noticeable, appearing much smoother than the surface in figure 3-7. The differences between these two images are considerations for the photographer when initially setting up a shot: What light source should be used? How will it affect the entire scene? What effect is required for the final image?

The family of angles increases proportionately with the size of the reflective surface area. The larger the reflective surface, the larger the light source required to fill the family of angles. Distance also affects the family of angles. The farther away the light source is placed from the object surface, the larger it must be to fill the family of angles. This is because the family of angles will get larger as the imaginary lines are extended upward, as shown in figure 3-13. The family of angles will also increase as the size of the reflective surface increases. A larger light source would be required to adequately fill the family of angles if the photographer has a large reflective surface.

Diffused Reflection

Diffused reflections are a result of surface texture and color. It is a reflection that has been *changed* by the *object surface*. For example, light striking a rough surface sends the reflection in many different directions in the same way that a soft box changes the direction of light traveling from the light source to the object. Another factor in diffused reflection is the amount of light that is absorbed or reflected by the surface. A light color reflects more than a dark color, and the resulting reflections will be different for these two colors. Diffused reflections are recorded both inside and outside the family of angles. This occurs because the surface changes the angle of reflectance for all light rays striking the surface, regardless of the direction of the light source.

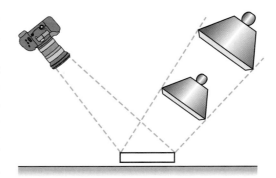

Figure 3-13

Moving the light source within the family of angles farther away from the object surface requires a larger light source to completely fill the family of angles.

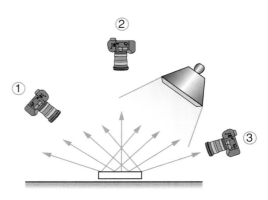

Figure 3-14

Diffused reflections will be recorded by the camera from all directions.

The camera records diffused reflections from all angles, as shown in figure 3-14. It will create a different aesthetic in the overall image than that created by a hard light source. This can be observed most effectively using a white object. White surfaces are almost all diffused reflection, and the reflection is the same whether using a small or large light source. Comparing figure 3-15, a and b, demonstrates how a white surface remains the same brightness whether using small or large light sources. However, there are visible differences in the two images created from using different light sources, such as the shadows and surface reflections.

Figure 3-15a was photographed with a small light source (hard), and figure 3-15b was photographed using a large light source (soft). The obvious differences in these images are the appearance of the shadows created from the egg and glasses. The small light source produces dark, hard-edge shadows; the large light source produces softer shadows.

It should be noted, however, that a fill card was used to throw light into the shadow produced by the bowl on figure 3-15b. This was done to prevent that part of the photograph from becoming a big, dark hole that occupied a significant part of the image.

(a)

(b)

Figure 3-15

The white object reflects the same brightness for both light sources. Differences between the two shots are in the shadow areas and reflections created by the different light sources on other objects in the scene.

If a fill card had not been used, there would be *no* detail from the lip of the bowl to the lower right corner.

Comparing figures 3-15a and 3-15b illustrates the differences in image aesthetics. The lens of the glasses in figure 3-15a is clear, allowing the earpiece to show through unimpaired. The lens of the glasses in figure 3-15b appears somewhat milky because of polarized reflection or glare. The light reflected in the egg yolk also appears different. The small light source in figure 3-15a produced a small circular reflection, and the yellow yolk looks brighter. The large light source used in figure 3-15b produced a larger, rectangular reflection, while also making the yellow yolk appear lighter and more subdued. The edge reflection on the bowl rim is different; figure 3-15a has small, bright reflections that mirror the small light source, and figure 3-15b has a long, soft reflection on the bowl rim from the large light source.

Glare

Glare is simply polarized direct reflections. The properties are similar in that the reflection is only visible when the light is within the family of angles. The difference between direct reflection and glare is that glare will be dimmer than the direct reflection. The simplest solution for controlling glare is using a polarizing filter on the camera or lights to reduce the amount of polarized direct reflection. Glare is visible in the liquid and the white saucer in both objects in figure 3-16a. Note, however, the small sliver of dark liquid visible at the top of the cup. It is dark because it is outside the family of angles and, therefore, is not reflecting direct polarized light. Placing a polarizing filter on the camera practically eliminated the glare on coffee and significantly reduced the glare coming from the reflective surface of the saucer in figure 3-16b. Once the polarizing filter was placed on the camera, it is evident that the backdrop paper was reflecting direct polarized reflection because of a slight sheen on the paper. The backdrop paper appears much darker in figure 3-16b than in figure 3-16a. A very faint reflection is still visible in the dark liquid because, as mentioned earlier, a polarizing filter may not remove *all* reflections but will significantly reduce them.

Light Reflecting from a Surface

Objects absorb some light and reflect the remaining light rays. However, they do not absorb or reflect in equal amounts. The more light reflected from the surface, the lighter the surface appears in a photograph (fig. 3-17a). The surface of the box appears light because part of the box is polished,

Figure 3-16

a, polarized glare is visible in the coffee and on the saucer, and the background appears lighter as a result of glare. b, placing a polarizing filter on the camera eliminated or significantly reduced the glare throughout the photograph.

and it is reflecting the light source within the family of angles. The reflection is obscuring the grain structure, making it difficult to see. To make the grain structure visible, the photographer has several options:

1. Move the camera so the family of angles changes; this, of course, also changes the composition.
2. Take the lid off the box, which changes the family of angles for the lid.
3. Move the light to change the family of angles. This will not change the composition, but it will change the aesthetics because the illumination is different.
4. Use a gobo to block the light striking the surface of the box. In some instances, a gradual transition from a reflection to the surface color or tone may be desirable; this will depend on the aesthetics of the photograph and the desired effects. The light was moved in figure 3-17b to change the family of angles, thus reducing the direct reflection. This change in light angle reduced the reflection, making the grain on the box visible. It also brought out more texture in the turquoise stone. Because the box in this example is not a flat, smooth surface, some reflection is still visible. However, these reflections offer visible clues to the polished surface and the uneven shape of the box lid.

A rough surface will create a diffuse reflection, scattering the light in all directions while the surface remains unchanged by the light source. A lighting setup that is perfect for one surface may not be adequate for the other. Different surfaces must be lit differently to achieve the desired effects; there is no *one size fits all* in lighting.

Terms describing reflections are **direct** and **diffused**. There may be some confusion about these terms because they are also used to describe light sources. Direct light is the light that travels from a point source (small light source) directly to the subject; diffused light is scattered light from a large light source. The light source determines the light type, but it does not necessarily produce the same kind of reflection. For example, a small light source produces direct reflections, but it can also produce diffused reflections. Reflections are *always* determined by the object surface. Glare is a polarized direct reflection.

Controlling Reflection

Every surface produces reflections. Controlling reflection depends on the angle of the light source in relation to the subject and camera placement. Learning to control reflections on shiny surfaces requires an understanding of the relationship between the light source and the surface texture of objects. It also requires recognizing when the light source will show a reflection in an object and when it will not. Following imaginary lines from the subject out and up can identify the family of angles, as shown earlier in figure 3-2. Any light source can be seen as a reflection through a camera lens (and recorded) if it is placed within the family of angles. The family of angles is particularly important when photographing metal. This will be discussed in detail later in this chapter.

There are four other considerations when working with reflections produced from small or large light sources. These are the reflection size, light-to-subject distance, camera-to-subject distance, and lens selection. Each will affect the overall aesthetics of the image.

Reflection Size

The distance of the light source to the reflecting surface controls the reflection size. The farther the light source is to the object, the smaller the reflection. The closer the light source is to the subject, the larger the reflection. Why is this important? If an object has a large reflective surface, moving the light farther away will produce reflections on only part of the surface area. Moving the light closer will spread the light to fill more of the surface area.

(a)

(b)

Figure 3-17

a, highly polished surfaces produce reflections that can obscure the surface texture. b, moving the light changes the family of angles, thus reducing or eliminating unwanted reflections.

Surface Reflection and Light Distance

When the photographer determines the aesthetic of an image, he will consider whether the image should be bright, dark, or have limited depth of field. This will require controlling the intensity of the light illuminating the subject along with camera exposure functions. If the intensity of the light is too bright, it must be reduced. The best solution for this is to power-down the light source. However, if this is not possible, the light source must be moved farther away. Moving the light farther away may cause the light to spread out, creating a smaller reflection on the object surface, but it may also create a situation where the light no longer fills the family of angles because the light source is too small. The result is a light source with

less intensity and one that may not produce the desired aesthetic effect for reflection control. If it is important to fill the family of angles, a larger light source is required.

The opposite consideration arises if the light is not bright enough for the setup. In this scenario, the light may be moved closer (creating a larger reflection and less light spread over the setup), the power may be increased, or the exposure maybe adjusted for proper exposure.

Reflection and Camera Distance

The photographer should have some idea of the overall effect desired for the photograph; creating a preliminary sketch and a lighting diagram can provide this. Typically, the photographer will build the composition from a specific camera angle and set initial light positions. Smaller adjustments are then made using gobos and fill cards, adjustments to the light position, or adjustments to subject composition. Elevating or lowering the camera may be a simple solution to an unwanted reflection. This will result in changing the family of angles enough to eliminate unwanted reflection, but it will also affect perspective.

Lighting setups are time consuming, and most photographers do not want to tear down the set and start over. However, if minor adjustments are not working, the photographer must reassess the entire lighting situation. Sometimes, moving the light source is necessary to change the relationships among the subject, camera position, and the family of angles. If the light source is moved closer or farther back from the subject but remains within the family of angles, the size of the reflection changes. Moving the light source closer increases the size of the reflection; similarly, moving the light source further away from the subject reduces the size of the reflection. This change in light source distance will also change the visual appearance of the scene. Evaluating the relationships among camera, lights, and composition is never wasted effort, even if the photographer must move lights and change the composition or tear down the set and start over.

Reflection and Lens Selection

The family of angles can also be controlled by the camera lens choice. A photographer might use a longer focal-length lens if the light is not large enough to fill the family of angles. Changing the lens can result in a narrower family of angles (fig. 3-18). Using a longer lens will also affect space compression, bringing the background closer to the subject. If physical space is an issue, the photographer may be required to use a wide-angle lens. This increases the size of the family of angles, as shown in figure 3-19. In this situation, a large light source would be required to ensure that the reflection covers the entire surface area of the object. It will also expand the appearance of space in the scene.

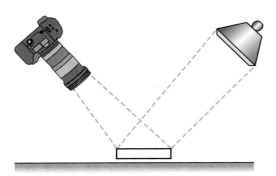

Figure 3-18

Shooting with a telephoto lens results in a narrow family of angles, allowing the photographer to use a smaller soft box.

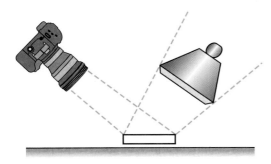

Figure 3-19

A wide-angle lens results in a larger family of angles, requiring a larger light source to fill the family of angles for reflection control.

Metal and Direct Reflections

This chapter is primarily concerned with shiny surfaces that may interfere with visual content or may simply be distracting in the overall aesthetic of the photograph. However, there are times when showing a direct reflection is necessary in a photograph to convey surface information. Some sets may require the metal to be rendered as a dark tone. Others may require a combination of dark and light metal. Controlling light placement in relation to subject and camera will determine whether the metal is light or dark. There is one principle used in determining whether or not the camera records the reflection. *If the light source is placed within the family of angles, the metal will be bright. If the light source is placed outside the family of angles, the metal will be dark.* Following this principle makes lighting metal predictable.

Bright Metal

Showing bright-metal reflections communicates metallic surface texture to the viewer. Highly polished metal, such as a mirror, reflects everything around it. Care must be taken to obscure the surrounding environment. Unlike the mirror example earlier in this chapter, the photographer may not want the entire surface to be bright. Often, a metallic object is best illustrated by allowing some of the metal to be bright, reflecting the light source that created the reflection and letting the remaining surface be dark or reflect the environment. In this scenario, the environment would be other objects within the scene or the backdrop/tabletop material on which the object rests. In figure 3-20, the photographer has selected a flat metal surface placed on a matte background to demonstrate the effects of metal placed within the family of angles. The knife blade is slightly serrated, placing part of the shape outside the family of angles. The gradated shapes on the knife show form to the blade edge.

Figure 3-20

Placing the knife blade within the family of angles renders the blade a bright tone. The serrated edge of the knife is a gradated tone because part of the shape is outside the family of angles.

Figure 3-21

Moving the light further away from the object results in less illumination on the background, but the metal remains the same brightness.

Figure 3-22

Moving the light source outside the family of angles renders the knife blade a dark tone. It also changes the scene illumination.

Metal remains the same brightness regardless of the light-to-subject distance. However, changing the distance of the light *will* affect the exposure for other objects in the scene. The knife blade remains the same brightness in figure 3-21 because the light source is still within the family of angles, even though it was moved further away from the subject.

However, comparing figure 3-20 with figure 3-21 illustrates how much the background has changed. This is because moving the light farther away resulted in less illumination, resulting in a poorly lit surface. Because the metal remains the same

intensity, the relationship between metal and background material can be controlled through exposure. The photo-grapher could also open up the aperture, but this would change the depth of field and could affect the aesthetics of the image. The photographer can increase or decrease the illumination on the scene by moving the light source closer or farther away without affecting the metal object in the scene. Moving the light will affect the light spread over the subject(s). A better option is to adjust the power output of the light head if the photographer wants more or less light intensity. This maintains the composition, depth of field, and general aesthetics of the setup.

Dark Metal

If the photographer wants the metal object to be dark, the light must be placed outside the family of angles, or a gobo can be used to block angle of incidence on the metal. Moving the light source will affect the aesthetics of the scene. How much the scene illumination is changed depends on where the light source is placed in relation to the subject scene. The light source in figure 3-22 was moved just enough to change the family of angles. The change in scene illumination is visible in the shadow placement of the lemon. Part of the knife remains within the family of angles: the rivets on the knife handle, the silver band above the blade, and the blade edge.

Controlling Exposure

The photographer must pay close attention to ensure that the remaining objects in the scene or set receive adequate exposure to communicate the visual aesthetic desired. Changing the distance of the light will also affect the size of the reflection, as discussed earlier in this chapter. Although the reflection on the object will increase or decrease in size, so will the illumination or light spread on other objects. Moving the light further away may cause unwanted stray light onto other objects. The photographer can use gobos to control light spilling onto other areas as a result of increasing the light-to-subject distance. In this way, the reflection is smaller but does not interfere with the desired effect on other objects in the scene. In other areas, a fill card might be necessary to illuminate areas of increased shadow as a result of moving the light. Adjusting the output power of the light head is an option for increasing or decreasing light intensity without moving the light source.

Figure 3-23 shows both reflective metal and matte objects in a scene. The light is placed within the family of angles, which renders the metal trivet bright, along with the scissors and pins. The distance of the light to subject is relatively close. Should the photographer want to render the metal dark, the light must be placed outside the family of angles. This can be accomplished by repositioning the light by moving it to a different position or possibly by raising the light head. Figure 3-24 is an example of dark metal achieved by keeping the light source at the same angle but raising it so it was no longer in the family of angles. In this scenario, the metal is now dark, but exposure must be increased to adequately light the other objects in the scene. To adjust the exposure, the photographer must increase the power output of the light source or open the aperture. The best solution between these two options is increasing power output because opening the aperture will affect depth of field. Changing the shutter speed should not be considered for two reasons: (1) the duration of the flash is so short, that using a slower shutter speed would have little or no effect on exposure; and (2) a change in shutter speed could produce an undesired color temperature shift in the image.

Keeping Yourself Out of the Image

Bright, highly polished reflective surfaces reflect everything, including other objects in the room *and the camera and photographer*! This only happens when the camera angle is perpendicular to the metal objects,

and should be avoided if possible. How can this be achieved? Short of shooting and digitally removing all reflections through Photoshop, there are two possibilities: use a view camera with adjustable standards or hide the camera.

Camera Adjustments

Any camera that can shift the front of the camera can remove the camera from an image. There are some manufacturers that have limited adjustable bellows for digital cameras, but the traditional way is to use a view camera to avoid camera reflections in highly reflective objects. Place the camera outside the family of angles and adjust the front and rear standards for proper perspective. Figure 3-25 illustrates proper adjustments to the lens-to-film plane relationship so the camera image is not recorded in the reflective surface. In this example, the camera is placed directly in front of a reflective object.

Hide the Camera

Another method is to aim the camera through a hole. If the reflective surface is lit so it is bright, a hole would be positioned in *white* material, such as boards, cloth, or some type of diffusion screen. Cutting a hole may not be an option, but positioning material, such as two strips of white cloth on either side of the camera so the camera lens can protrude, is a viable solution. The white cloth will produce a white reflection. If the photographer prefers a darker surface with bright highlights, the photographer would use a dark cloth on either side of the camera and allow the lens to protrude for the desired reflection. In this case, a large light source or a strip light (a long narrow soft box) is preferable because it produces long strips of light instead of the small round lights produced by a small light source.

Because all material near the camera lens is reflected in the reflective surface, there are two issues the photographer should consider: (1) protect the lens from stray light that can cause flare; and (2) be aware

Figure 3-23

The light source is close to the subject and within the family of angles, rendering the metal objects bright.

Figure 3-24

Moving the light further away from the object placed it outside the family of angles, rendering the metal dark. The exposure is adjusted to compensate for the reduced illumination on other objects in the scene.

that hiding the camera will not remove all reflections because the camera lens is still visible. However, it will not be as obvious as the camera, tripod, photographer, silver light stands, and the surrounding environment of the studio. The camera lens reflection can be corrected using digital software. Download the file from the digital camera, or scan the film, and replace the reflection with similar pixels surrounding the reflection using Photoshop or a similar software program.

Round Reflective Surfaces

This actually falls under the category of *hiding the camera* but requires more inventive measures. A round reflective surface may be one of the most difficult subjects to shoot. Because the object is round, there is no area that is not within the angle of incidence as shown in figure 3-26. So, how can the camera be hidden?

Build a Tent

There is no position where the camera, lights, or other objects are not visible when photographing a round metal or reflective object, as shown in figure 3-27. In this image, the camera, photographer, and studio lights are reflected in the image. A **tent** is an enclosure of material that reflects evenly and completely surrounds the round object, except for the small opening from which the camera lens will protrude. It can be made from white fabric, reflector cards, or diffusion screens. Removing all environment reflections can be accomplished by using a digital software program such as Photoshop.

Traditionally, photographers have constructed an enclosure from foam core or translucent material. It does not have to be pretty; it just has to work (fig. 3-28). The purpose of the enclosure is that the lighting evenly illuminates the round reflective object. Enclosing it with a portable room also ensures that no other objects will be visible as reflections in the object. There is a catch, though; there is no way to hide the camera lens. So, the round reflective object will always have a small dark spot in the center, which of course is the camera lens. As mentioned earlier, all unwanted reflections can be digitally removed.

There are also manufactured tents like the one shown in figure 3-29, which makes lighting round objects easier. The resulting image shows how the tent environment is reflected in the metal ball, but the camera lens cannot be hidden (fig. 3-30). This lighting setup requires two light sources placed on either side of the enclosure

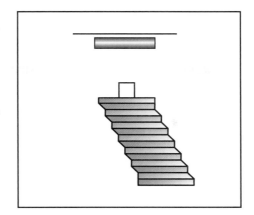

Figure 3-25

Adjusting the view camera front and rear standards can prevent the camera from appearing in the reflection of a metal object or a mirror.

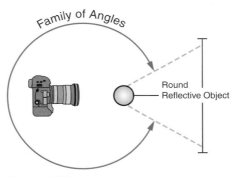

Figure 3-26

The family of angles for round objects includes everything around it.

Figure 3-27

A round reflective object reflects everything around it.

Figure 3-28

A tent built from translucent material hides the surrounding environment, keeping it from reflecting on the surface of the object. It may not be pretty, but it is functional. Many early photographers built enclosures like this for reflective objects; some still do.

Figure 3-29

A cocoon provides the perfect environment for round reflective objects. It is convenient and easy to use.

and high enough to evenly illuminate the interior of the tent or cocoon, as shown in figures 3-29 and 3-30. Because the tent is made of translucent material, small light sources are turned into large light sources.

Create an Environment

Photographing a round object in a tent controls the reflections, but it also makes a very dull, uninteresting image. Most of the time, these lighting arrangements are used either for catalog or other sales purposes

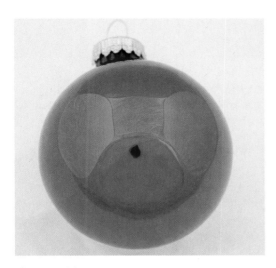

Figure 3-30

The tent is reflected in the metal ball. The camera lens is seen as the small dark circle in the center of the ball.

Figure 3-31

Using objects in the scene is a good way to hide reflections and provide a visually interesting photograph.

where an environment is not necessary; the purpose is to create a sterile environment to show the object clearly. Another approach to photographing round objects is to create an environment and allow some environmental reflections to appear on the surface. An environment can be created inside a tent; the photographer can carefully position objects so the reflected object obscures unwanted reflections, as shown in figure 3-31. The photographer can create an environment outside the tent or enclosure, but it is more difficult to hide the studio environment.

Summary

The key to controlling reflections on highly polished or metal objects is light source placement. The camera will record any light source placed within the family of angles. The reflections produced by light sources vary, of course, and the treatment of the reflections will depend on the desired results for the photograph. Reflections from the lights on highly polished or reflective objects appear as light areas, often obscuring the object texture, whereas metal objects are often enhanced by the brighter surface because this surface communicates the metallic surface to the viewer. Placing the light source outside the family of angles eliminates reflection from all reflective surfaces, eliminating the lighter surface area; metal objects will appear as a dark surface. Understanding the basic principles of the light-subject-camera relationship makes working with polished or metal surfaces predictable.

Deborah Fletcher

Title: *Untitled* (Self-Promotional Sample)

This image was made as a self-promotion piece. I wanted to create an image that emphasized a product but that also incorporated some kind of environment. Those close to me know that I am a tea drinker, and I had just received this teapot as a gift. To bring in a sense of environment, I used the glass block window from my studio. I also went through my prop room for the appropriate placemat and background props. The white rectangular shape in the upper right corner is the back of a chair. Another teapot is in the right foreground.

To light this image, I used a large Chimera soft box overhead. The glass block window was the main light source, also creating a very distinct reflection in the highlight of the main subject. There were two heads on the right side, and both had 20-inch reflectors and Lightsox diffusion material. One of the lights was for the foreground

Figure 3-32

"Untitled." Courtesy of Deborah Fletcher.

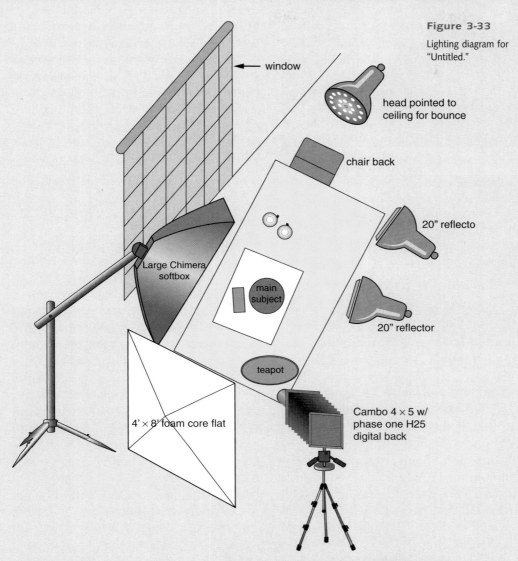

Figure 3-33

Lighting diagram for "Untitled."

window

head pointed to ceiling for bounce

chair back

20" reflecto

Large Chimera softbox

main subject

20" reflector

teapot

4' × 8' foam core flat

Cambo 4 × 5 w/ phase one H25 digital back

area creating the highlight on the right side of the main subject and lighting up the teabags in the canisters in the background. The other light was for the background and things beyond the table surface of the shot. There was another head in the deep background bouncing into the white ceiling. There was a large fill card, four by eight feet, in the foreground to the left of camera, which provided reflected fill. A small mirror was kicking reflected light into foreground, opening up the detail in the shadows.

Figure 3-34

Deborah Fletcher. Courtesy of Deborah Fletcher.

Dimitris Skliris

Dimitris Skliris, originally from Athens, Greece and now living in Dallas, Texas is a commercial photographer with many specializations. However, Skliris has spent the majority of his career photographing works of art, starting in Wichita, Kansas in 1993. To date, Skliris has photographed nearly a quarter-billion pieces and has been published in hundreds of catalogs and museum books. The museum expertise of Skliris extends beyond photography; he has been serving as the Director of Exhibition for the Trammel and Margaret Crow Collection of Asian Art in Dallas since 2004.

Devi, South India, Chola Period, 12th to 14th Century Bronze

In 2007, I was hired to photograph 100+ works of art for an upcoming art catalog to accompany the exhibition, *Texas Collects Asia*. The exhibition was planned as the main event to celebrate the Crow Collection of Asian Art's tenth anniversary in the Dallas art district. The art for the exhibition was assembled from private collections throughout Texas, and, in most cases, I had to travel to the homes of the collectors to photograph the art.

For this image, I had to travel to the home of Nanik and Suneeta Vaswani in Houston, Texas. Their collection consists primarily of objects from India, and the piece I was photographing is a

Figure 3-35

Devi, South India, Chola Period, 12th to 14th Century Bronze. Courtesy of Dimitris Skliris.

Equipment:

Camera:	Canon EOS 1Ds Mark II
Exposure:	f/16 @ 1/250 s
Lens:	Canon 100 mm f/2.8 USM Macro
Computer:	Apple MacBook Pro
Software:	Capture One Pro, by Phase One
Tripod:	Gitzo G-1504 with Geared Column and Bogen Deluxe Geared Head
Flash:	Visatec Solo 3200B, 1200ws moonlights, and Bowens wireless trigger
Boom:	Red Wing Compact Boom

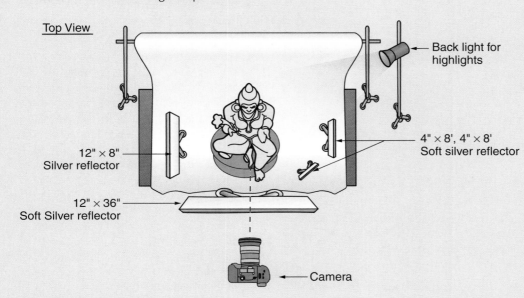

Top View

Back light for highlights

12" × 8"
Silver reflector

4" × 8', 4" × 8'
Soft silver reflector

12" × 36"
Soft Silver reflector

Camera

Figure 3-36

Lighting diagram for Devi, South India, Chola Period, 12th to 14th Century Bronze.

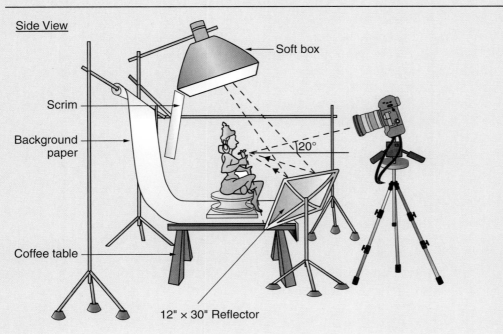

Side View

Soft box

Scrim

Background paper

20°

Coffee table

12" × 30" Reflector

bronze figure with very dark patina and a waxed surface.

As with most of the work for the book, I had to construct an impromptu studio setup in the collector's living room. After removing most of the furniture from the room and covering all of the windows with blackout fabric, I used their table as a shooting surface. I set up a portable backdrop stand with dark-gray four-foot paper over the table to create a seamless background. The main light was a Visatec 1200ws that was fitted with a Chimera Super Pro medium soft box with silver interior. The Visatec monolight and Chimera were

Figure 3-37
Dimitris Skliris.
Courtesy of Dimitris Skliris.

affixed to a Red Wing boom. The boom allows precise overhead placement of the light and also ensures the safety of the art. The soft box was placed inches above the bronze and parallel to the paper and the camera. The soft box's back edge was just over the artwork, so that I could control the light falloff to the seamless backdrop. To further minimize the light on the background, I installed a large customized open-end cutter, with triple black fabric. This was placed just inched over the art and thus feathered the light and produced a background with a very smooth light-to-dark gradient.

Next, I placed a second light, equipped with a 20° grid, at the right and far back side of the artwork. This head was set to a reduced intensity to serve as a secondary light to create highlights on the backside of the art. In addition to the lights, I placed four reflectors around the piece. The largest one, a two-foot by three-foot soft silver reflector, was positioned beneath and in front of the piece. The other three reflectors were placed at the right and left of the piece to increase the highlights at the edges to separate the dark tones of the bronze from the background. The camera was placed higher than the art to capture the three dimensions of the base. The camera was equipped with a 100-mm macrolens and was tethered to an Apple MacBook Pro.

TRANSPARENT OBJECTS

Figure 4-1 Taping the soft box with gaffers tape to simulate windowpane sections creates the illusion of a reflected window in the glass of the lantern.

Like metal, glass reflects primarily direct reflection, but glass reflections are usually polarized. Why is this relevant? When shooting most objects, the emphasis is on the surface; texture and lighting are set up to view the surface to the best advantage. Surface reflections on glass become a distraction if not controlled properly. One does not expect to see the surface of glass, although many glass objects have a surface design. Instead, one expects to see what is *inside* the glass.

Figure 4-2

Two lights set at 45°
angles were used to
light this set. Glass is
transparent and reflective,
and lighting it from the
front causes it to disappear
into the background.

Therefore, to light glass, it must be invisible,
which seems to be a contradiction because
the purpose of the photograph is to *see* the
object.

How does one photograph glass if it is
supposed to be invisible? Lighting glass
requires emphasis be placed on edge definition. Edge definition is what gives the glass
contour and form. One can light from most
directions effectively as long as reflections
are controlled with light modifiers, such
as a gobo. Standard front lighting using a
neutral backdrop produces flat lighting and
unwanted reflections, causing the glass to
disappear into the background, as demonstrated in figure 4-2. The glass in this example
has no form, shape, depth, or contrast; the

specular reflections created by front lighting
are distracting, appearing as a series of small
bright lines or dots. What appears through
the glass is the background material; in this
case, the gray backdrop, resulting in a dull
image. If a larger light source is used, a light
head with an umbrella, for example, the size
of the reflections would increase with the
size of the light source. So, the first issue with
lighting is the background; what should be
used? The answer is that the background
should be either bright or dark; there is an
exception to this when using color gels, and
this exception will be discussed later in this
chapter.

The next consideration is edge definition, which is determined by the angle of
incidence. The angle of incidence for a glass
subject is the same as that of a round reflective object; it surrounds the object from
one extreme side, around the front, and
to the other extreme side of the angle of
incidence, as shown in figure 4-3. And like
reflective, round objects, glass also reflects
everything in the area. Very specific lighting arrangements are required to effectively
photograph glass, and any light placed
within the family of angles, which is basically the entire circumference of the glass
object, is reflected in the glass.

There are many photographers who specialize in glass or, more specifically, liquids
in glass. There are photographs of liquid
being poured into glass, splashing out of
glass, bubbling or fizzing, or simply filled
with liquid. Many of these images rely on
creative techniques and controlled lighting
to achieve special effects, including multiple exposures and complicated lighting
setups. Others are simpler, using colored
backgrounds or gels to further separate the
glass from the background. Some photographers put colored water in the glass for
visual interest. There are many such variations that may create a visually interesting
photograph, and there are numerous books
on the market that specifically address
shooting glass products and specialized
lighting setups. The following discussions
are intended to provide basic lighting sets

Figure 4-3

Drawing of glass subject
and family of angles.

Angle of incidence of glass
extends from one extreme
edge around to the other
extreme edge of the family
of angles.

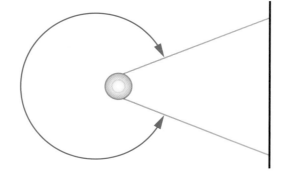

for glass that will provide a foundation for further experimentation in shooting glass objects and using specialized sets for shooting glass.

The most common methods of shooting glass are from behind. The goal for these lighting techniques is to produce either a bright edge or a dark edge. The edge definition is vital because without defining the edge, the glass is practically indistinguishable from the background. Other methods of photographing glass include shooting from below (often used in conjunction with colored gels or other special techniques), or shooting glass from the front using light modifiers and gobos.

Lighting Glass for Dark-Edge Definition on a Bright Field

Dark-edge definition means that one sees through the glass to a bright background called **bright-field lighting**, while dark material or cards are placed at either side of the glass to create a dark edge (fig. 4-4). The background must be a bright or light surface. There are three ways to create a dark edge on the glass with a bright field.

The first method requires placing a soft box directly behind the glass and a black card on either side of the glass, positioned against the soft box as shown in figure 4-5. The black cards are positioned at the extreme edges of the family of angles. The soft box provides back illumination, which creates a bright field, while the black card is reflected back into the glass, producing the dark edge. Sometimes, the soft box is much larger than the glass arrangement. In this case, all extraneous light should be blocked with flags, black foam core, or some other dark material so the only visible light is exactly what is required for the background of the photograph (fig. 4-6). The key to successfully lighting glass for a dark edge is to illuminate an area no larger than the camera's field of view.

Edge definition is controlled by the glass-to-light relationship. The closer the glass object is to the light, the more light shines into the angle of incidence, wrapping

Figure 4-4

Bright-field lighting is created by placing a light background behind the glass with dark material on both sides of the glass. Light placement will depend on one of three methods used to create the dark edge with bright-field lighting.

around the glass. The result is a less defined edge definition, as shown in figure 4-7. As the object is moved farther from the back light source (closer to the camera), the edges become darker, as shown in figure 4-8. This is because the intensity of the bright-field lighting is no longer wrapping around and dominating the glass object.

Moving the glass position also affects the size of the background-to-glass object relationship. The glass becomes larger as it is moved toward the camera, reducing the size of the background. As the glass is moved back toward the light, the size of the glass is reduced, while increasing the background field. The perspective of the object will also change as the glass object-to-camera position or camera angle changes.

The second method of creating a *dark edge* on a *bright field* is using flood lights (these can be strobe or tungsten) directed at a white wall or a white card (fig. 4-9), several feet behind the glass setup. The wall/card becomes the background for the lighting arrangement. The dark cards are placed directly behind and on either side of the glass at the extreme edge of the angle of incidence. The light source reflects off the wall or white surface and illuminates the back of the glass, making it bright, and the dark cards block the light and reflect back into the glass, creating the dark edge.

The last method requires the photographer to light from the front using a hot light. The authors recreated this lighting setup based on a technique created by Lowel Manufacturing to demonstrate the versatile qualities of this arrangement. Bright-field lighting is achieved by placing a long white board behind the glass object, and a dark curtain or dark boards is positioned on either side of the glass against the white board. Hot lights are positioned at the front, near the camera

Figure 4-5

Lighting diagram for glass with dark edge using rear soft box lighting arrangment.

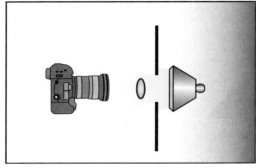

Figure 4-6

Lighting setup for dark-edge glass. Place the soft box directly behind the light, allowing the light to shine through the glass. All light is blocked except what is required for the camera's field of view. Black cards on either side of the soft box block extraneous light and create the dark edge on the glass.

Figure 4-8

The edge definition increases as the glass object is moved closer to the camera and away from the back light source.

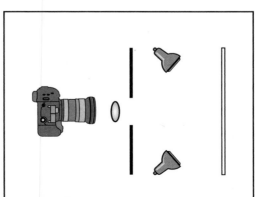

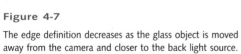

Figure 4-7

The edge definition decreases as the glass object is moved away from the camera and closer to the back light source.

Figure 4-9

Drawing showing alternative dark-edge glass setup.
Flood lights directed at a white wall will reflect back into the glass, creating the bright center required. The black cards on either side of the setup will reflect into the glass, creating the dark edge.

position, and a flag or gobo is placed between the light and the glass object (fig. 4-10), making sure it does not entirely obscure the light. The key element here is the flag or gobo because it blocks the light, thereby eliminating all reflections on the glass, but it allows the light to reflect off the background into the back of glass, as shown in figure 4-11.

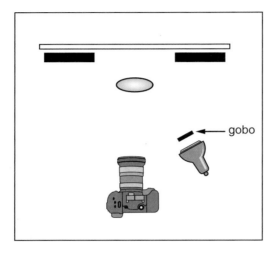

Figure 4-10

Lighting diagram for lighting glass using hot lights from the front. Note the position of a gobo between the light and the glass subject.

Metering for Dark Edge on a Bright Field

How should one meter for this setup? An incident meter will not work for bright-field lighting because the light falling on the subject has no relevance to this setup. The information required is how much light is shining *through* the object. Therefore, metering requires a reflective light meter reading, preferably a spot meter reading, of the source light illumination. In other words, point the reflective meter at the background. Once the basic reading has been established, the exposure must be adjusted for *more* exposure. Why? Because the basic reflective reading is for 18% gray (zone V), and the background should be a brighter tone than this. How much brighter is determined by the photographer. Opening up one stop makes the background a lighter gray, opening two stops makes the background a very light gray, and opening up three stops makes the background very bright (fig. 4-12, a–c). Where possible, power adjustments on the strobe light source should be used to control exposure because changing the aperture will affect the overall depth of field of the setup, and adjusting the shutter

Figure 4-11

Light setup for lighting glass from the front using hot lights.

Figure 4-12a

Opening up one stop
renders the background a
lighter gray than zone V,
but still darker than may be
desired for the image.

Figure 4-12b

Opening up two stops
renders the background
bright, while still controlling
edge definition.

Figure 4-12c

Opening up three stops
renders the background
very bright.

speed will have no affect at all. However, if the photographer is using a tungsten light source, then the shutter speed adjustments should be used so that the depth of field remains the same.

Lighting Glass for Bright-Edge Definition on a Dark Field

Creating a bright edge on a dark field might seem to be the opposite of lighting for a dark edge, and it is . . . *almost*. To create a bright edge, there must be no light striking the glass anywhere *except* at the extreme angle of incidence. The angle of incidence remains the same whether shooting for dark edges or light edges. It has already been established that defining the edge is what makes the glass visible.

A bright-edge definition requires a contrasting background. Because the glass is invisible, and it is the edge that the photographer is creating, the background must be an opaque, dark material. This is called **dark-field lighting**. Therefore, the object is to create a dark field behind the glass with a bright, light edge, as shown in figure 4-13. The next consideration is where the light should be placed. One might think that the light would be on either side of the glass for a light edge, especially because the background is opaque, but that would create reflections on both sides of the glass objects. The light position for the first two methods is behind the glass. Method three is the same setup as the bright field, wherein the light is placed in the front and near the camera with a gobo blocking the light to prevent reflections.

Method one requires a backlight with opaque material placed behind the glass object against the soft box. The soft box should be large enough to allow the light to extend beyond the opaque material on either side (fig. 4-14). The dark material only covers an area necessary to fill the camera's field of view. The bright-edge definition is created from the light reflecting into the family of angles on both sides of the glass, as shown in the lighting setup in figure 4-15.

The second method for producing a bright edge on a dark field is to position flood lights to reflect off a light wall or card behind the glass in the same manner used for bright-field lighting. However, the dark card or material is placed directly behind the glass. Light reflecting from the wall or card will spill beyond the opaque panel to the edges of the angle of incidence, creating a light-edge reflection, and resulting in a dark field with bright edges.

Once again, it is important that the dark panel is limited to the camera's field of view. If the panel is too large, light cannot reach the angle of incidence, and the glass disappears into the background because of weak edge definition (fig. 4-16).

An alternative to lighting from behind the glass for dark-field lighting with a bright edge is lighting from the front with a light modifier. This third method requires a long white card placed behind the glass setup, and a dark curtain placed directly behind the glass and against the white card, as shown in figure 4-17a. The lighting diagram (fig. 17b) illustrates the flag or gobo blocking the light from the light source. As long as

Figure 4-13

The light spilling around the background creates the bright-edge definition.

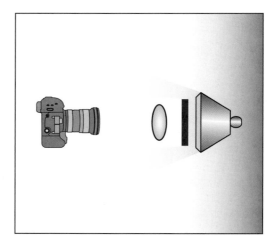

Figure 4-14

A dark background requires a dark, opaque material behind the glass with translucent panels from the soft box on either side, allowing light to spill around the dark material or card and into the extreme angle of incidence.

the flag or gobo blocks the light from creating unwanted reflections, the result is a dark field with a bright edge. The advantage of using a dark curtain as the dark field is that adjusting the width of the curtain will result in a more narrow or wider bright edge, as shown in figure 4-18. The curtain may also be visible through the glass, which may or may not be a desirable effect for an image.

Metering Glass for Bright Edge on a Dark Field

Metering for this setup is similar to the bright-field arrangement. Using the smallest diameter on the spot meter, aim it at the bright edge of the glass. It is important that the dark field is not included in the metering because the meter will average the two values. Again, the bright-edge reflective reading from the spot meter will give a medium gray, and opening up two to three stops will increase the exposure to achieve the desired edge brightness.

In the examples above, the photographer must deal with the horizon line (the edge of the table). There are many creative solutions for this problem, some of which

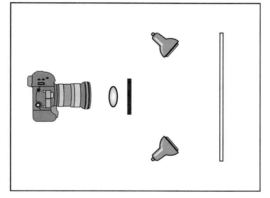

involve only showing part of the glass, thereby eliminating the horizon line. Other solutions involve creating an environment where the horizon line becomes part of the aesthetics of the image. Still others use the horizon line to emphasize the glass objects. Depending on the desired effects, the photographer must decide how to treat the horizon line in the image.

In addition to the horizon line, another challenge when using the method wherein the glass object is illuminated from behind is that there may not be enough illumination on any foreground objects or surface

Figure 4-17a

Front lighting setup for dark-field lighting and a bright edge. The flag is placed between the light source and the glass to prevent unwanted reflections.

Figure 4-17b

Front lighting diagram for dark-field lighting.

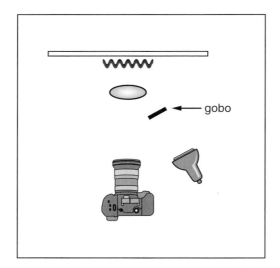

area. Therefore, it may be necessary to throw additional fill light into the scene to brighten specific areas. This can be accomplished by placing a second light illuminating the foreground or using a reflector card. However, any option that adds additional

illumination must be controlled because the glass will show the reflections from these possible lighting solutions. In this instance, a **snoot** could be used to illuminate small areas without creating specular highlights that could interfere with the aesthetics of the glass object. Using gobos to block the light from the glass or simply controlling where the light is placed in relation to the glass will help control unwanted reflections.

Lighting from Below

Because glass is transparent, it can pipe light through its structure to illuminate various parts of the glass. **Piping** consists of lighting the glass from the bottom and blocking all light, except the area in which the light must travel (fig. 4-19). The photographer must use a transparent table covered by opaque material. A hole is cut in the

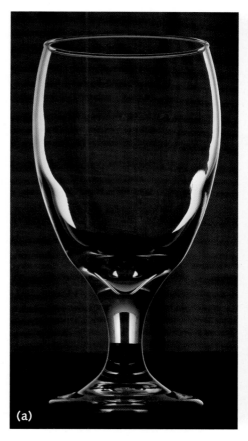

(a)

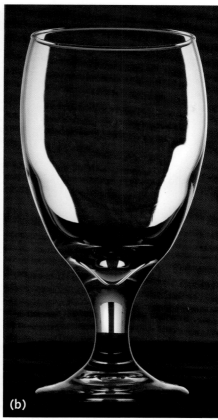

(b)

Figure 4-18a and b

Adjusting the material used for the dark field affects the size of the bright-edge reflection. In this example, the dark field was made smaller, allowing more of the white board to show on either side of the glass. This created a wider bright-edge definition.

material just large enough for the base of the glass object. A small light source is placed directly beneath the glass object. In figure 4-20, the glass object has a colored ball at the base. The ball is illuminated, and the color radiates from the light below. Light travels up the stem and into the glass edges. It gives the glass a brilliant-energy appearance. This technique can be used in conjunction with other glass-lighting techniques for creative visual effects. For example, this method could be used in conjunction with a dark- or bright-field glass setup.

Piping light produces very limited effects. Most glass objects are lit below with a larger illuminated area. This can be used in conjunction with gels for effect, as shown in figure 4-21. Illuminating from below with a background light and colored gel creates a colorful contrast and adds a glow to the image. To produce this effect, the table surface must be translucent. If a translucent tabletop is not available, this can be accomplished by putting translucent material, such as tracing paper, on a clear glass or acrylic surface and lighting from below using a reflector on a light head. Another light with a colored gel shines up onto the white background to create a glowing effect behind the glass objects. Light modifiers described in Chapter 7 can be used to create different light patterns on the background.

A word of caution here: tungsten light sources can be used to light from below, but they get very hot. If glass is used as a tabletop, it could get so hot it would break from the heat; if acrylic or Plexiglas is used, the lights could melt the plastic. Therefore, hot lights are not recommended for this setup; strobe lighting is preferred for piping or any lighting arrangement beneath the glass object. Although the modeling light does not produce the heat intensity of hot lights, the heat can build up; adequate air movement or ventilation is prudent when using the piping technique or any setup that requires lighting glass from beneath the transparent tabletop surface.

Figure 4-19

Lighting diagram of piping. The light is placed beneath a transparent surface; a small opening is cut from an opaque surface to allow light to shine into the glass object.

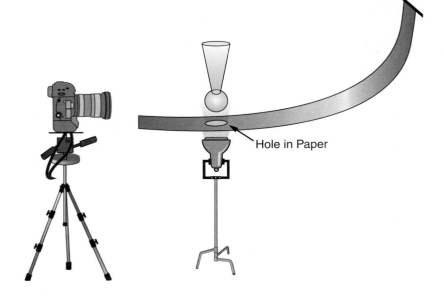

Hole in Paper

Figure 4-20

Piping the light up though the glass fills the edge structure of the glass with a brilliant-energy glow.

Top and Side Lighting

Glass can be lit from the top to create surface reflection for any liquid contained in the glass. Usually, the setup involves a soft box over the subject but angled at a light wall. This creates overhead illumination, but it also allows some of the light to reflect off the wall and into the back of the glass. Again, dark cards on either side of the glass will create a dark edge. Care must be taken to control unwanted reflections on the glass surface.

Side lighting is generally not employed as a means of lighting clear glass because edge definition is difficult. Many photographers use this technique when shooting dark glass, such as a wine bottle or glass vase. This would be handled in the same manner one would deal with metal or reflective objects, as discussed in Chapter 3. The reflection will mirror the light source used. Typically, a strip light is used to create an elongated, bright reflection by placing the light strategically for the desired reflection.

Adding side lighting can add visual interest by intentionally placing a reflection on a specific area of the glass to simulate the effects of a window (fig. 4-1). Using gaffer tape, the photographer simply tapes strips to the soft box or diffusion screen to simulate the windowpane effect.

Figure 4-21

The glass is illuminated from below using a reflector on a light head, creating a bright white surface on the table. The backdrop is illuminated with a 20° grid on a reflector head with a violet gel, which created a bright center with falloff around the edges.

Glass as a Lens

When glass has liquid in it, it functions in the same manner as a lens. The image is reversed. Figure 4-22 employs back lighting aimed at an extreme angle against the wall, raking the light (as discussed in Chapter 2). The light falls off as it travels down the length of the wall, becoming darker. The result of raking the light from right to left creates a transition of bright to darker tonal values left to right in the glass.

Summary

Lighting glass has two primary methods for edge definition: bright-field or dark-field lighting. Understanding the principles of creating edge definition is the beginning of creating more interesting images. Three ways to create edge definition are lighting from the back, lighting from the front with a gobo, or lighting from beneath the object. Other techniques can be added to these basic setups for experimentation. Important key aspects are object placement in relation to the light source, and limiting the background to fill the image frame.

Figure 4-22

Water placed in the glass acts as a lens, reversing the image. The light is raking the wall from right to left, but the water-as-lens effect is the tonal values transitions left to right, dark to light.

Todd Davis

Todd Davis, from St. Louis, Missouri, is a commercial photographer whose clients include Anheuser Busch, AT&T, and Coca-Cola. Davis also shows his personal work, mainly portraits, in various galleries. His professional work encompasses many areas, including tabletop and beverage photography, but his skills at lighting a complex interior are included for this example (www.tdavisphoto.com).

Title: "Six-Pack" Conference Room, Zipatoni Agency, St. Louis, 2001

I received the assignment to photograph the interiors of a long-time client's new agency. A separate client who is an industrial designer and sculptor was responsible for the design of a majority of the interior space. Thus, the assignment was to show the physical space and also feature the detail work done by the designer. We were given a week to photograph as much as possible, with only minimal guidelines. We were provided with a list of areas that were to be photographed but how to accomplish the images was up to us.

This considerable freedom came with a down side. The space wouldn't be completely finished until well past our deadline, and the agency employees were already moved in and working, so we wouldn't have the place to ourselves. This particular shot had two welders working just outside of the frame, one directly behind the "six-pack" conference room and a second just off camera to the right. They were kind enough to stop welding for a time once we started actually shooting.

Figure 4-23

"Six-Pack" Conference Room, Zipatoni Agency. Courtesy of Todd Davis.

The shot was lit with a mix of daylight and fluorescent sources. I augmented the existing light with my additional strobe and tungsten lights. To the left and behind the camera was a bank of windows providing a large amount of daylight. The decision was made to balance all the other light sources to the predominant daylight color temperature. Raised, black computer flooring with the reflective aluminum skin on the walls of the exterior of the conference room created an interesting lighting/contrast problem. We decided to keep some of the inherent color from the available light to help define the different areas and to bring some color interest to an otherwise rather sterile area.

The fluorescent lights in the conference room and the room on the left were wrapped with magenta gel to bring them halfway to daylight balance, while leaving a slight green cast. The tungsten lights were untouched to add some warmth to the wood ceiling and to the highlights on the

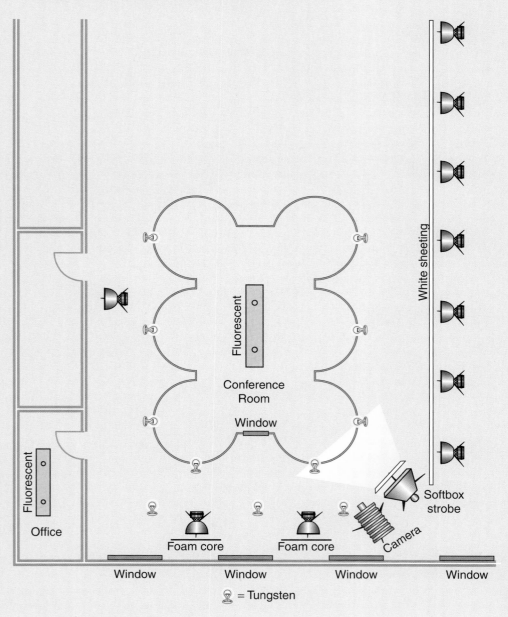

Figure 4-24

Lighting diagram for *"Six-Pack" Conference Room, Zipatoni Agency.*

aluminum surfaces. A series of strobe heads were placed along the right-hand side of the room and were bounced into a wall of white sheets. The sheets were constructed to act as a 40-foot long reflector. Polaroid proofs were taken to determine the correct exposure times for the daylight, strobes, tungsten, and fluorescent sources. With those times determined, an assistant was placed at each light source switch in each room to turn the lights off after the correct exposure time. Because we needed as much depth of field as possible, all bracketing was done with exposure times.

Film: 4x5 Kodak Ektachrome
Camera: Sinar camera with 58-mm Super Angulon lens

Figure 4-25
Todd Davis. Courtesy of Todd Davis.

Brian Wetzstein

Brian Wetzstein lives and works in the Pilsen artist district of Chicago, Illinois. Brian's clients include McDonald's, Quaker, and BP. Outside of commercial photography, he has continued creating work in photographing abstracts and everyday textures and in extensive projects with the nude figure (www.brianwetzstein.com).

Title: *Splash Shot: Blue Bottle*

Shot as a portfolio sample, this type of splash image is familiar in commercial and technical photography. However, the difference between recognizing this image and being able to create one provides for a steep learning curve. Multiple considerations regarding flash duration, lighting glass, timing, and repeated action are required to achieve a successful version of any splash photograph.

I used a vintage Ascor Speedlight with a Sunlight or "Sun Gun" head to arrest the action of the bottle entering the water. Decades ago, Ascor (American Speedlight Corporation) created a wide array of large, specialized electronic flash equipment. When using an Ascor, adding or subtracting an 800-W capacitor to a central power bank can regulate power levels. A Sunlight head could handle as many as 48 capacitors, which would bring the power level from that single source to 38,400 W. Connected by a very thick (two inches), short (18 inches) cable, the head-to-capacitor unit distance was kept to a minimum so that little energy would be lost. The Ascor units are rather legendary among photographers who have worked with the huge power banks, heard the loud flash bang, and experienced the Ascor "scent" that was produced at each flash pop. Equally storied are the polychlorinated biphenyls to be found in each unit, but that's another topic.

Flash duration is the most critical element to be considered in this photograph. The shorter the duration, the less blurred movement will be evidenced in the image. This frame is one of 130 images that were taken to get just the right moment. In other words, this is the best example from the 130 attempts in respect to the image framing and quality of the splash. I personally dropped the bottle for each exposure and simultaneously pressed the camera's cable release as soon as the bottle hit the water. The camera's controls were set to 1/125th at f/11.

The flash duration for this sample, created with a single Ascor 800-W capacitor, is hard to determine.

Figure 4-26

Splash Shot: Blue Bottle. Courtesy of Brian Wetzstein.

Figure 4-27

Lighting diagram for *Splash
Shot: Blue Bottle.*

Strobe

Splash Box

Camera

Diffusion

Figure 4-28

Brian Wetzstein.
Courtesy of Brian
Wetzstein.

After performing a moderate amount of research, I have found no real consensus on precise Ascor flash duration figures. Newer flash units, made by other manufacturers of flash equipment engineered to stop action, have duration rates of approximately 1/6000th. The Ascor can easily match those units for action-stopping capability.

The Ascor unit that used in this example had one condenser connected. However, an 800-W Ascor produces an extremely bright source because of the short cable and the efficiently designed Sunlight head.

Equipment:

Camera:	Hasselblad EL/M, 80-mm T* lens, Imacon 4040 Digital Back
Exposure:	f/11 @ 1/125
Computer:	Apple Powermac G5
Software:	Flexcolor from Imacon
Flash:	ASCOR 800-W condenser with one Sunlight head

II

LIGHTING APPLICATION: MEASUREMENT, EQUIPMENT, AND PORTRAITURE

Introduction

The following section contains chapters that describe the equipment used in creating light for film and digital capture. The breadth of lighting equipment stretches from the sophisticated to the crudely simple, from a delicate device to the nearly indestructible. Understanding the many methods of lighting instrument application requires experience and a healthy curiosity. Some photographers have been known to shy away from artificial light because of the great number of potential applications. However, once acquainted with the control afforded by artificial light, the photographer will find there are logical connections within the many layers of equipment.

Light measurement and color temperature will be discussed first. The basis for measuring light and the attendant factors regarding the temperature of light are interconnected. An overview of the specific types of sources and their varied qualities is next. The modifiers that permit the photographer to modulate the output are subsequently related to the appropriate sources. Lighting for diverse types of portraits completes the section.

CHAPTER FIVE

LIGHT MEASUREMENT AND COLOR TEMPERATURE

Figure 5-1 *Buck Barry, Hardin* by Daniel Overturf. Mr. Barry was placed in the shade during a sunny afternoon. A single Balcar Prismalite modifier provided the subject's lighting. In the initial tests, the flash illumination on the subject was measured and then balanced to the sunlit background. Because the color temperature of the flash and midday sunlight are similar, the color temperature of the subject and the surroundings are consistent. This bracket underexposed the background one stop by increasing the speed of the shutter, a technique described in this chapter. The original image was made with a Hasselblad Arcbody, 35-mm lens and Portra 160VC film.

The continuing advances in photographic technology have not altered the photographer's basic need to understand the role of light measurement in the creation of an image. Artificial light can be produced from a variety of sources, can come from a number of directions, and may possess an infinite range of qualities, colors, and intensities. Given the multiple and elaborate light metering devices available to photographers, how to measure light's intensity and gauge **color temperature** can be a matter of opinion. Like so many other components of photography, metering preferences will typically come from experience.

Light measurement can be divided into many subgroups, but in photography, there are two general elements of consideration: intensity and color temperature.

The technical foundation of any photograph begins by gauging the light intensity and setting the camera's exposure controls. The following pages will thoroughly describe the complete range of practices regarding light measurement.

Understanding color temperature and the ability to determine the color of the light on a numerical scale is absolutely critical for photographers who want to precisely control their chosen capture media's color response. Once the foundation of light measurement has been established, color temperature will be addressed later in this chapter.

Meters: Past through Present

The era of light measurement for photographers was initiated by reflective light readings from ingenious devices called **extinction meters**. The photographer looked into the extinction meter to see a series of letters/colors and then matched the least visible letter to a chart to determine exposure in aperture and shutter speed settings. Simple and dependable for many photographers, extinction meters relied extensively on the eyesight and judgment of the user. There are photographers who still claim to use, even prefer the simplicity of, extinction meters, such as the Leudi Exposure Meter (fig. 5-2).

Robert Hunt was known for an important refinement in reading light called the **actinograph**, based on a device called a **sunshine recorder**, or **heliograph**, invented by T. B. Jordan in 1839. The actinograph's light scale was exposed to photographic paper that in turn recorded a period of light. **Actinic** refers to how much actinism is found in the measured light. Actinism is known as the property of light that causes chemicals to combine and decompose.

Ferdinand Hurter and Vero Driffield patented a device to be used in conjunction with cameras and film that was also called an actinograph, although it bore little resemblance to Hunt's original. The inventors of the **H&D curve** invented this

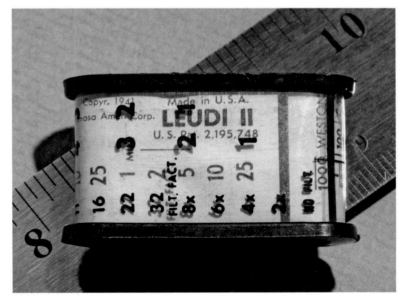

Figure 5-2

A Leudi Extinction meter, *ca.* 1930.

Figure 5-3

Actinograph, used for
estimating photographic
plate exposure, *ca.* 1900.
Courtesy of Richard F. Lyon,
©2005.

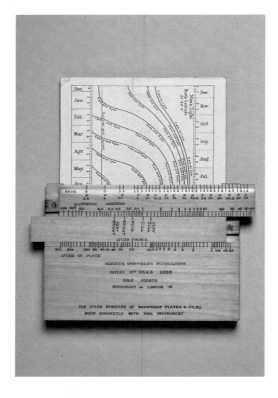

slide rule device that charted the time of day, the calendar, and other factors. The two pioneers of photography science invented their actinograph so that they could further develop a system for light measurement and exposure control.

Exposure meters would later become less dependent on an individual photographer's eye for reading light intensity. In 1932, light reading meters equipped with **photoelectric cells** arrived. The meters that used photosensors made from selenium, **cadmium sulfide (CdS)**, and silicon became the standards. **Selenium-type meters**, such as the popular Weston Master series, produced readings directly related to the sun's energy and required no batteries (fig. 5-5). Certain **silicon** and CdS sensor-type meters required batteries to provide their exposure readings. The classic Sekonic L-398, changed to Studio Deluxe III in 2007, is one example of a battery-less and amorphous silicon photocell meter.

For much of the early to mid twentieth century, light meters were located off-camera or handheld. The first 35-mm camera to be equipped with a built-in meter was the Zeiss Contax III in 1936. Other camera makers attached meters to the top of cameras to measure the scene from near the axis of the lens, such as the Leica MR-4 meter (fig. 5-6). Certain attached meters required a power source apart from the camera. Except for their meters, many cameras were entirely manual and did not require batteries. For a long time, the attachable or even the built-in meter was considered an accessory. Steadily, most 35-mm cameras were designed with exposure meters of varying types and patterns. The meters were integral to the essential design of the camera. Thirty-five mm and, if so equipped, medium format camera meters became increasingly more sophisticated. Still, handheld meters remained popular as separate light reading instruments for all formats. To date, many students and advanced amateur and professional photographers employ a handheld meter for film, digital, flash, continuous light, small- and large-format, studio, and location photography.

Recent developments in light meters point to the continued evolution of the photographer's need for accurate light readings when using modern image capturing systems. The **flashmeter**, the **spot meter** (down to 1° angle), and the reflective, incident, and darkroom meters can now all be found in one single, multiuse combination light meter. Other than the expensive and specialized color meter functions, most every light measurement can be found in a single unit. Recent, all-inclusive meters are available with wireless remote flash firing capabilities.

As shown in figure 5-7, advanced level meters, equipped with universal serial bus (USB) cord ports, can be connected to computer. These meters are engineered to accept digital camera sensor and/or film exposure profiles, created from targets that are downloaded from the photographer's computer. In reference to their 758DR,

Figure 5-4a

Vero Charles Driffield (1848–1915) helped establish the basis of testing the sensitivity of photographic emulsions. Courtesy of Science and Society Picture Library.

Figure 5-4b

Ferdinand Hurter (1844–1898), with Vero Charles Driffield, established the basis of testing the sensitivity of photographic emulsions. Courtesy of Science and Society Picture Library.

Sekonic states that their meter will be able to use programmed exposure profiles in flash/incident, flash/reflected, ambient/incident, and ambient/reflected modes. This advance is said to match the specific, profiled camera's digital sensor or film to the dynamic range programmed into the light meter. Once a profile is set, the meter could denote exposure extremes or **clipping points** to indicate that the capture is beyond the overexposure or underexposure limitations for the material/sensor.

Measuring Light Intensity

Understanding in-camera and handheld light meters is often the starting point for most photographers as they learn to make photographs. The basic, most essential knowledge when starting to photograph is how to determine a proper exposure based on a reading of the intensity of the light.

Figure 5-5

Weston Master Meter 715, with the baffle open halfway to reveal the meter's cell, *ca.* 1939.

Many photographers will start with natural or ambient lighting conditions. As their first foray into artificial light, there might be a flash built into one's first camera or a small unit that attaches to the top of the camera. The attachable units can be designed to work in conjunction with the

Figure 5-6

Leica M4 with a Leica MR-4 meter attached to the top of the camera, with interlock for the shutter speed dial, *ca.* 1968. The red dot indicates the 1/50th flash sync setting for the M4.

Figure 5-7

The Sekonic 758DR can be connected with a standard USB cable to any computer to set up profiles for films or digital capture. The meter is bundled with profiling software.

the photographer's preference of modes. The selected mode of exposure, based on the intended photograph, remains tied to the pattern and overall sophistication of the camera's meter.

For many decades, studio and location photographers proofed their images with Polaroid materials after their initial meter readings. The proof image could confirm correct settings or alert the maker to the need for further adjustments of lighting and exposure controls. The advent of digital capture has led to a smaller electronic capture preview, usually found on the rear of the camera. In many studios and sometimes on location, with camera and computers **tethered**, photographers preview their images by looking at computer monitor-sized versions of their exposures. The studio monitors may also be replicated or linked to other locations for feedback from off the set.

Contemporary exposure decisions, in many digital applications, are largely a visual determination that is tied to reading the **dynamic range data** that are supplied with each exposure. A term that is often heard in digital capture studios is *hitting the numbers*, which refers to maintaining a certain dynamic range in the capture that is suitable for an intended method of reproduction. Consumer-grade cameras are often equipped with a display option that includes exposure information and other settings such as **white balance**, lens focal length, and autofocus point. The main feature of the shooting information display will be the **histogram**. The histogram is a graphic representation of the image that indicates the range of darkness to light. Certain cameras are also equipped with a **highlight alert**, which will automatically signal any overexposed areas in the image. Learning how to read the simple histogram will assist the photographer in making accurate adjustments to avoid exposure errors such as extreme overexposure. Most digital cameras have similar histogram displays, but the photographer should review and thoroughly understand an individual camera's information panel readout.

camera's exposure system, which can make determining flash exposure setting considerably more assured.

So-called automatic exposure options flourished in the later stages of film camera design and have continued into recent digital units. Cameras typically offer some variants of the familiar shutter-preferred, aperture-preferred, or all-encompassing program settings for exposure automation modes. The camera's light meter is at the core of all automatic modes. The meter's information is processed through

Moreover, additional information called **metadata** or **EXIF** metadata, the most common form of metadata, is also typically stored with a digital image. Metadata is often defined as data about data, and EXIF stands for exchangeable image information file format. Depending on workflow or application, this information can be very useful for organizing and controlling one's images. The metadata can be extracted with a number of possible imaging programs.

The meter remains a key instrument in the creation of a photograph, regardless of capture media. Photographers initiate their photograph by reading the light with a meter, although they may rely mostly on visual feedback rather than meter data as the process continues. Understanding how to effectively manage that preliminary exposure data will enable a photographer to concentrate on the multitude of other visual and analytical decisions that will be required in the course of making the photograph.

The Gray Matter

The accepted target tonality for meters has long been understood as middle or **18% gray**. Eighteen percent refers to the popular standard that holds that a gray card reflects 18% of the light that is falling on it. Meters can dispense a wide range of information as the photographer examines the intended photograph, displayed in either an aperture/shutter speed combination or **exposure value (EV) scales**.

The photographer then interprets the provided information and determines the exposure. The middle gray reading is not necessarily the exposure setting. The photographer will apply those readings to the values of the scene and finally to the photograph that is to be created. Understanding that the light meter is seeking to render all light values to gray is at the heart of understanding how to apply the meter information to the exposure calculations. Figures 5-8 and 5-9 illustrate the difference between making a meter reading on a white surface versus the 18% gray card.

Curiously, Sekonic states in their specifications that their meters are calibrated to a 12.5% reflectance rating, and 14% is also mentioned as the middle reference level of reflectance in other applications. However, most major camera manufacturers claim to be holding to the accepted 18% standard.

In addition to the traditional 18% gray card, the so-called *digital* gray cards are also available. Digital gray cards, according to certain makers, are intended for creating a neutral color response, per the white balancing function for the camera's digital sensor. The digital version of the gray card, according to the manufacturer information, is not to be used to determine exposure because the reflectance is closer to 35% rather than the accepted norm of 18%.

Knowing the **latitude** of a film or digital capture will help to determine what extremes can be achieved in the lighting while maintaining detail. The latitude of film is easily related to the dynamic range of a digital sensor. Both terms describe the amount of acceptable under- or overexposure tolerated by the material or sensor.

Meter Types

Meters can be grouped into five basic areas for the purpose of understanding the how light and color measurement can be accomplished, as described in Table 5-1.

Meter Descriptions

There is a wide array of handheld and in-camera light meters available to photographers. Some have individual purposes; others are combination meters that feature many of the established metering options in a single unit.

Reflected Light Meter

Many photographers first determine and set the exposure controls by using a reflected light meter. The camera with a built-in meter or a handheld meter is aimed at the subject, and the meter responds by measuring the brightness of

Figure 5-8

Flash exposure set at f/22, based a reflected light reading from the 18% gray card. For the sake of comparison, a reflected light reading was taken off the white wall to determine the shutter speed to match f/22. The meter, reading the white wall, provided an exposure for this dusk photograph at 1 s.

Figure 5-9

The same exposure was determined for the flash, f/22. Compared with figure 5-8, the gray card was read to determine the shutter speed. Because the gray card is the accurate source of exposure data, the exposure is longer at 4 s.

Table 5-1

Meter Types

I. Reflected: reading light intensity as reflected from the subject
   A. In-camera
      1. Various subdivided patterns
      2. Spot
      3. Average
   B. Handheld
      1. Spot, 1° angle
      2. Averaging, 30° angle

II. Incident: reads light that is falling onto the subject
   A. Handheld
      1. Dome
      2. Flat panel

III. Flash: reads light that is emitted from an electronic flash; can be either or both incident or reflective; certain models also read ambient (continuous) light
   A. Incident dome or flat panel
   B. Reflected spot or averaging
   C. Modes
      1. Cord
      2. Cordless
      3. Multiple

IV. Combination: reads light in different modes; flash or ambient, spot or averaging; reflective or incident; incident dome or flat (recessed dome)

V. Color: reads the color temperature of light
   A. Ambient/continuous light, only reads blue-red balance
   B. Ambient plus flash reading models available
   C. Models that read blue-green-red light values for non-blackbody sources, such as florescent light

the light reflecting from the subject. The meter, guided by the 18% middle gray tonality baseline, presents the photographer aperture and shutter speed pairings for setting the exposure. As shown in Figures 5-10 and 5-12, the photographer points the meter directly at the subject for a reflective reading. In most instances, the meters that determine exposure settings in many of the latest digital cameras are identical to the light meter systems found in their film counterparts.

Reading specific areas within a photograph to understand the difference in intensities throughout the image remains valuable information. Many photographers use spot meters for reading areas of 1° (fig. 5-11). Spot meters can be handheld and pointed at the subject by looking through a viewfinder. Other reflected light meters may have a range of 30°, which does not allow for precise readings unless the meter is very close to the subject. Another specialized spot metering device can be inserted into the rear of a view camera and positioned to the desired area for a meter reading, near the film plane. This type of positioned sensor meter is often called a **metering probe**.

The difference between the shadow/dark areas and the highlight/light areas in an image requires individual readings of those values. Based on those readings, the lighting can be adjusted to create less or more contrast by changing the range of difference between the shadows and the highlights. Reflected readings, which are made from the combination of the subject's reflected tonality and the light intensity on the subject, can only be read with a reflected light meter.

Incident Light Meter

Incident meters read the light that falls on the subject, as shown in Figure 5-13. An incident meter is still based on the 18% gray goal, but the meter's design does not differentiate between variances in the reflected tones in the subject. The subject does not influence the incident meter readings, which may be preferable depending on the photographer's goals. A frosted half dome or a flat panel (fig. 5-14) measures the light intensity by placing the meter *at* the subject and directing the receptor *toward* the camera. The meter is only concerned with the intensity of the light that is landing on the frosted receptor and, in turn, the subject. Many photographers use the flat panel attachment or recessed dome when measuring the light on flat art or in the darkroom.

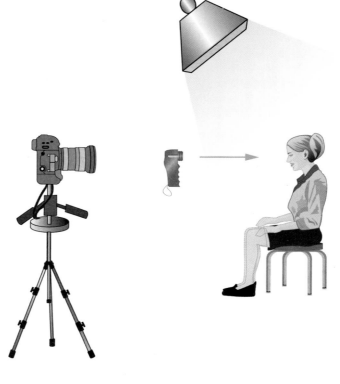

Figure 5-10

A reflective light meter reading is made when one points the meter at the subject to measure the light values reflecting off the subject.

Incident readings are, in effect, the most democratic. The meter is never pointed at the subject. Preparing to photograph a dark or black subject, the photographer will read the light that falls on that subject and receive the exposure options. In the case of the opposite value extreme, something bright and white in identical lighting circumstances, the incident meter will render an identical light measurement.

Flashmeter

Light meters that measure flash output are common for studio use, although flashmeters are equally important on location. A flashmeter differs from an ambient light meter in the same way that a burst of a strobe unit differs from continuous lighting. Meters that are capable of reading daylight can also read all forms of continuous artificial light. Only a flashmeter will also read electronic flash output.

When using a flashmeter in a closed studio setting, with a flash system as the

Figure 5-11

The dials on a Pentax Digital Spot meter are similar to most spot meters. The top row is the film speed designation. The middle numbers are the shutter speed and aperture combinations that are derived from setting the lowest row to the numerical indication shown in the meter's readout. In this example, at ISO/ASA 100, the reading was EV13. That EV reading translates to an exposure of f/16 at 1/30th or an equivalent combination. Many modern spot meters have the readout directly shown in the finder.

Figure 5-12

The photographer makes a flash exposure reading with a spot meter. Depending on the specific area she will read in this example, the reflected light readings will vary greatly as the meter seeks to turn all of the values to 18% gray.

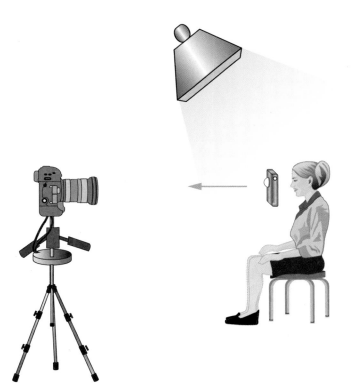

Figure 5-13

While pointing the meter at the lens, an incident light meter reads the light intensity that falls on the subject.

exclusive light source, the measurement procedure is relatively straightforward. Most flashmeters are designed to make incident readings (fig 5-21), although there are spot meters for flash readings that measure specific reflected targets. Either reflected or incident, the electronic flash is set off, and a measurement by the flashmeter delivers the appropriate aperture.

The shutter speed setting is not a functional, elementary factor in light measurement under these circumstances. The flash exposure determines the aperture, but in the studio, the shutter speed setting can vary considerably. The shutter remains an element to consider when measuring flash if there is any ambient or continuous light that will require consideration. However, under flash-only circumstances, the shutter setting may be largely inconsequential as long as the shutter speed is not too short or less than a prescribed sync speed. For additional information about synchronization and the role of the shutter, see the flash duration discussion in this chapter and in Chapter 6.

Metering: Combination Meter

A more recent trend in meter design is to combine spot, flash, incident, and other features into one single meter. Some models will perform these multiple functions through the use of attachments (fig. 5-15); others will have all the modes built into the meter (fig. 5-16). Certain models have also incorporated a zoom feature into the spot mode. Many photographers feel that one **combination meter** will often simplify their equipment needs, especially while on location. Functionally, the benefit to the photographer is the ability to measure in different meter modes for comparison purposes. This ability can be most useful in a complex scene with different sources and intensities. Before the advent of the combination meter, two separate units, or at least additional attachments, would be required for this comparison. The following section describes the metering advantages, in a given situation, when a foreground flash source is measured with an incident flashmeter mode, and the distant background ambient light is measured with a reflected spot meter mode.

Color Meter

Long considered a specialty tool for the location and studio photographer, the color temperature meter (figs. 5-17 and 5-18) is a unique type of incident meter. The **color meter** measures the color temperature of a scene, measured in what is called **Kelvin degrees.** The **Kelvin Scale** is the most common method to numerically express the color of light.

Depending on the capture media, the meter then compares that reading with the color sensitivity of the film or directs the photographer to adjust the white balance setting on a digital camera. The meter will denote the filtration that would be required for a neutral rendition with film. A digital camera can be set to the exact Kelvin temperature setting determined by the color meter or can be adjusted to be cooler or warmer by specific degrees. A more elaborate description of how a color meter functions and a complete description of the Kelvin temperature scale are included in the color temperature segment of this chapter.

Figure 5-14

An incident meter will function with either a flat panel or a rounded dome over the sensor. The flat panel (left) is typically used for flat subjects such as artwork. The rounded dome is for general light readings.

Flashmeter Applications

A flash and flashmeter can be utilized in a variety of applications, depending on the available metering modes and connections. The following descriptions cite a few general considerations and procedures for using flash and flashmeter readings.

Meter Connections and Modes

Reading flash output requires one of two methods or **metering modes** for connecting the flash burst to the meter. The corded method uses a PC cord to connect the flash system to the meter (fig. 5-19) and is usually called the **cord mode** on meters. The PC cord is usually the same cord, when switched back from the meter to the camera that connects the camera to the flash. (Some PC cords are **Y cords**, as shown in fig. 5-20, which connects all three elements—meter, camera, and flash—simultaneously.) Cordless radio remote units that are built into certain meters represent another method to directly connect the meter to the flash. With either of these methods, the meter fires the flash, and the reading is made instantaneously. A complete overview of meter triggering devices and techniques can be found in Chapter 6.

A second method of making a flash measurement is the **cordless mode**. The meter is made ready to receive the flash burst but will not make a reading until the flash is set off manually. Depending on the circumstances, the photographer will prefer one method of triggering and measuring the flash output to obtain the meter's suggested aperture setting.

A third possible flash reading can be made in the **multiple mode**, found on advanced flashmeters. Traditionally, many photographers have utilized a common method of building exposure intensity through multiple firings of a single flash unit or multiple units. The concept is quite simple. The lens remains open, in a darkened and perfectly still set, while the flash (once fully recycled) is repeatedly and manually set off. The procedure usually takes

Figure 5-15

Many models of meters accept attachments or are capable of different metering functions. Shown beside the meter's bare sensor are the 10° spot attachment the incident dome, the reflected light cover. The 10° attachment has a viewing eyepiece for aiming the intended spot. Although attachments are still used, many photographers prefer using a combination meter instead.

Figure 5-16

The Gossen Starlight meter is a combination meter with onboard functions that can read incident, spot, flash, and ambient light.

Figure 5-17

Minolta Color meter II, *ca.* 1982, an older model that will only read the color temperature of ambient light without the flash attachment.

Figure 5-18

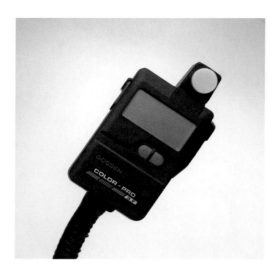

Lens Diffraction

For many photographers, digital capture has reduced the demand for extremely small working apertures. In digital systems with certain lenses, photographers have witnessed a sharpness decrease at apertures smaller than f/22. Lens **diffraction** at smaller apertures and the effects on sharpness has been a well-known optical artifact since well before the inception of digital photography. The absolute minimum (smallest) aperture on a camera and/or an enlarger lens was typically avoided because of diffraction, and the resulting decreased sharpness would be the most pronounced at that extreme. Digital capture sensors suffer from the same faults because their relationship to a lens is identical to film. There are also other optical layers that make up the digital sensor plane that add to the potential for increased diffraction and a further lack of sharpness.

The upshot of a photographer who has switched from using large format film to capturing the image digitally could mean that they are using an exposure that is two to three f/stops less intense. For instance, say the photographer had been regularly exposing film at f/45 but now finds that the digital capture's minimum aperture should be f/22. In terms of flash power and the need for multiple flash bursts, this change in aperture can routinely decrease the need for extra flash exposure beyond a single burst. In the example stated above, if the desired digital capture aperture is f/22, in an ideal arrangement, the flash system is metered as having f/22 as the output. A single exposure could be used, and there would not be any need for a darkened studio and other factors involved with making an exposure with multiple pops. Making film exposures with the same setup would have required a completely dark studio, the need to wait for the flash unit to recycle, and a completely static set. Based on a desired aperture of f/45, approximately four flash bursts of that single flash (f/22) intensity would need to be compounded.

place in a darkened room to ensure that the only lighting used is the selected flash, but the meter will also read coincidental light in the multiple mode. Most models of flashmeters are armed for one minute so the photographer can accumulate as many flash bursts as is practical. The example shown in Table 5-2 describes the effective cumulative intensity of multiple flashes, from 1 burst through 32.

Each flash burst compounds the exposure of the previous. The cumulative effect is that the photographer can use a less powerful flash setup that, with repeated flash bursts, can effectively immolate a more powerful unit. As the light intensity is built up with each burst, the smaller the functional aperture and the greater the depth of field created.

Filtration, bellows factor, and other light-diminishing factors can whittle away the effective power level of a flash source. To counter the reduced intensity, photographers often choose to employ the multiple flash method to achieve a target aperture. Once the shutter speed is set to either *B* or *T*, varying the number of flash pops can also create simple exposure brackets. One of the assignments traditionally given to studio assistants is to set off the flash units in a darkened studio while counting the number of bursts.

Another basic approach to examining the difference lies in a comparison of the basic

Figure 5-19

The end of a PC cord connects to the cord receptor on a flashmeter. The same end of the PC cord goes to the camera. The other end of the cord goes to the flash unit.

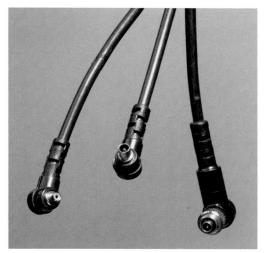

Figure 5-20

The three ends of a Y cord (from left): flash, camera, and meter. The dual end of the Y cord is for connecting both the meter and the camera, whereas the single end goes to the flash unit. The advantage is that the meter can remain connected at all times during a session. Otherwise, in a typical two-connector PC cord, the non-flash unit end of the PC cord must be switched between camera and meter. Note that the meter end has a locking collar for a more secure connection.

power requirements in the two examples. Without calculating for multiple pops, one must merely acknowledge that if a photographer achieves f/45 with a 4800-W power pack, then a 1200-W power pack will only reach f/22 under identical circumstances. Depending on the equipment intended for use and resources available, knowing the maximum power requirements for lighting a given photograph can lead to greater efficiency.

Shutter Speed's Visual Potential

The shutter is often fixed at a specific speed for flash exposures and is thus considered a minor exposure control with strobes. However, the shutter speed can play a visual role, with possibly critical adjustments when using flash under certain circumstances. The following three examples review situations when the photographer will need to carefully plan and/or take advantage of shutter speed effects after measuring for flash exposure.

Ambient Light Sources are a Factor When Calculating the Shutter Speed

If the light for the photograph contains flash and ambient sources, the shutter speed setting will either emphasize or minimize the role of the ambient light. To diminish or intensify the role of the ambient light, the shutter will be adjusted to add or deduct exposure to the areas not lit by the flash. A faster shutter speed will darken the ambient elements. A slower shutter speed

Table 5-2

Number of flashes	1	2	4	8	16	32
Example aperture	f/4	f/5.6	f/8	f/11	f/16	f/22

Figure 5-21

An incident flashmeter, similar to all incident meters, reads the flash's intensity as it falls on the subject. The flashmeter will read at one surface the combined output of one or more flash heads. Typically, the photographer will determine which light will be the key source and base the exposure on that output. The other heads may then serve to support that exposure with varying degrees of fill light. Or, as in this example, the photographer can use two heads with different spot lighting attachments to highlight two distinct surfaces. The light intensity is adjusted to be identical, although the light quality of each spot source is different.

will allow for a stronger presence of available light.

Arresting the Motion of a Moving Subject

Flash duration refers to the amount of time that the flash fires and is usually described in fractions that can sometimes be confused with shutter speeds. The flash duration figures will be different with each flash unit and make. When researching the characteristics of a flash unit, the duration time may be as critical as the power level if the application calls for arrested motion.

In terms of power, the logical relationship between power and duration exists; less power will normally equal shorter duration. The inverse applies as well. A 2400-W studio power pack's flash duration may be 1/1100th at 400 W while slowing to 1/300th at 2400 W or full power.

The camera shutter will enter into consideration if the chosen sync speed is faster

than the duration of the flash. A top-end limit to a camera's flash sync speed and the specific duration of its flash output can impact one's ability to freeze action, but one should also be careful to not exceed the duration of the flash. This relationship rarely exists, but certain cameras can achieve high-syncing shutter speeds that will cause the image to be only partially exposed once used with flash duration that exceeds that speed.

The Camera is Handheld with Ambient Light Sources Present

Handholding a camera when photographing in an environment with other light sources requires the shutter to be fast enough to freeze the intended subject and not drag the shutter to blur the background information. Sometimes a blurred background is an intended effect that employs the longer shutter speed as a visual device (fig. 5-22). The longer the shutter is open after or before a flash will allow for greater blur. The metering of the surrounding light is then factored into the exposure settings. The aperture determined by the flash is the basis for setting the complimentary shutter speed, long or short.

Mixed Light Sources: Flash and Ambient

Although the flashmeter takes into account existing or ambient light, the photographer will be looking primarily to judge how the flash source compares with the available light. Metering for flash exposure is chiefly used to determine the aperture component of the exposure setting. However, most flashmeters will read both flash output and ambient light intensities. Depending on the amount of ambient light and the shutter speed that has been set on the meter when taking the flash measurement, the readings for both flash and ambient may need to be analyzed to determine their relationship. The potential exposure variations within a complicated, mixed-light scene make meter reading critical to determining starting aperture and shutter speed settings.

For four different versions of a portrait, see the examples in figures 5-23–26. The photograph required meter readings for mixed flash/ambient sources. Using a flash to illuminate a dimly lit foreground in a scene with a brightly lit, ambient background source requires an analysis of the intensity of the two light sources. The photographer can vary the emphasis of different planes within a photograph by employing a thorough understanding of how to meld flash and natural light. The examples indicate four options for this photograph, although not all of them are acceptable as a portrait. The first two images, figures 5-23 and 5-24, are made without flash to convey the differences between ambient light intensities in the scene. Figures 5-25 and 5-26 show the difference in background details when adding a flash of an identical output and only adjusting the shutter speed in each example.

Flashmeters and Proofing

The use of strobe lighting requires a flashmeter to read the exposure in most applications. At one time, an instant print proof was required to verify the exposure and effect of the flash, at least in many professional applications (fig. 5-27). That was before digital capture and the nearly immediate capture became, effectively, a proofing system (fig. 28). Moreover, the digital capture "proof" might even be a finished or close-to-finished product, depending on the photographer's interpretation of the flashmeter readings and the quality of the initial capture.

Incidentally, Polaroid Corporation put the entire matter to rest with the February, 2008 announcement that the company would cease making instant film/print materials. At present, Fuji continues to produce a limited number of instant print products. Still, digital capture has effectively pushed instant materials out of the mainstream.

Despite the sophistication of camera meters, one question remained before the onset of digital technology. Why were there no in-camera flashmeters available? The technology certainly had been established, says one camera manufacturer, but the cost versus price quotient did not exist. Professionals who used studio flash units already relied on their handheld flashmeters or simply depended on their personal studio experience to arrive at an approximate beginning exposure.

Digital capture made the discussion of on-board flashmeters moot and the visual feedback that a photographer requires is now available long before an instant print would be. Additionally, many photographers presently use small, dedicated flash units in place of studio strobe units. As described later in this chapter, the dedicated units are completely linked with the camera's exposure system and make using a flashmeter somewhat redundant in certain applications.

The use of previews on a computer monitor or the digital camera's LCD

Figure 5-22

Toby, Starved Rock Lock and Dam by Daniel Overturf. The flash was set off at the beginning of an 8-s exposure made while on a slow moving barge. The warning lights inside the lock were blurred as the handheld exposure was finished after the initial flash burst. The image was made with an Xpan, 45-mm lens, Fuji Superia 200 film and a Metz flash unit on a bracket.

monitor replaced those instant prints as the standard proofing method. As before, the photographer will inspect the proofed image for exposure accuracy and the overall lighting ratio in a scene. Depending on that image and whether any radical changes are to be made, most photographers' adjustments will be made without the further use of a meter.

Dedicated Flash Units

A flash that is dedicated to the camera will have something of a flashmeter function relative to creating the ideal exposure on account of the through-the-lens exposure coordination of flash and camera. Often referred to as a speedlight, the small flash is a complex electronic device that can create a broad range of lighting applications while linked to the camera's central exposure control. The flash can be mounted on the camera's dedicated hot shoe fixture or placed anywhere via a light stand or other support. The dedication of the flash to the camera allows the exposure system of the camera to work in conjunction with single or multiple flash unit outputs. Multiple units can be linked together by cords or, in some cases, without. The wireless units may be placed anywhere within range and triggered by a camera-mounted transmitter or another flash unit on the camera. Depending on the sophistication level of the systems, the adjustments can be infinitely variable to create the desired lighting. The portrait session shown in Figures 5-29

and 5-30 illustrates the use of a dedicated flash and wireless connections.

Color Temperature

A potentially valuable element that can be measured, color, may seem secondary to the photographer because intensity has such a primary status to the creation of an image. However, for the purpose of understanding and accurately predicting color response, the color of the image should also be acknowledged as a critical characteristic. Color temperature readings apply especially to color images, but being aware of the color relationships within a scene can also factor into the creation of black and white images. The collective color temperature reading is created by three sensors, blue, green and red, as shown in Figure 5-31.

A beginning color photographer may learn the unavoidable lesson of what occurs when using daylight film or the daylight setting on a digital camera's white balance setting when photographing in tungsten or fluorescent lighting conditions. Typically, the tungsten-lit images will contain strong amber cast (fig. 5-32). The florescent-lit images, because of the increasing number of different bulbs available, can have a range of colorcasts. Traditionally, florescent bulbs required varying degrees of magenta filtration to counter an overwhelming green cast in daylight-balanced capture media (fig. 5-33). Newer bulbs require different filters as the phosphor color varies widely.

Figure 5-23

The following four images show exposure options when working outdoors, with and without flash exposure, and how to either separate or blend planes of exposure within a photograph. The natural light was bright overcast. The two flash exposures were made with a 1600-W monolight with a small softbox.

Exposure setting for foreground subjects, with no flash. The light intensity in the shade was quite dim. The camera was set at ISO 50. This would be the greatest amount of exposure of the set at ¼ at f/3.5.

Figure 5-24

Exposure setting for the background with no flash, 1/15th at f/11.

Figure 5-25

Exposure set to balance flash on the subject and the background. The flash reads f/11. The background exposure or shutter speed setting, based on the information derived from figure 23, is 1/15 when matched to the f/11 flash exposure. Note that this exposure is identical to the setting for the background, as shown in figure 24.

Figure 5-26

Exposure set to maintain the same flash exposure on subject, with the same aperture, as was used in figure 25. The shutter exposure, though, was decreased by 50%; thus, the background was rendered darker: 1/30th at f/11.

Figure 5-27

The instant, hard copy proof was at one time the standard for inspecting exposure, color, and light balance before making film exposures. The film photographer often sorted through Polaroid proofs and scribbled exposure/filtration notes and the resulting transparency film sheets on a light table.

Figure 5-28

Editing programs allow the photographer to simultaneously review digital capture thumbnail images, much like a proof sheet. One significant difference with the digital version is that one can click on an image and see an enlarged version almost immediately.

Importantly, the fact that florescent lights can never be fully neutralized by filtration is a byproduct of the bulb's **discontinuous spectrum**, a design attribute that will be explained in a following description.

The Kelvin Scale

Color meters measure and scale the color temperature of light. The color of light is expressed in a temperature scale that dates back to the 1848 proposal authored by Professor William Thomson, who taught at the University of Glasgow. Thomson would later be titled and made Baron Kelvin, named after the River Kelvin that flows near the university. His work at that time has been altered very little for modern usage and forms the basis for the system that remains today. The term color temperature indicates how physicists have arrived at the Kelvin temperature designation, which is commonly followed by °Kelvin or simply K. (Although not universal in practice, many sources typically omit the degree symbol when referring to color temperature on the Kelvin scale.) The measurement system compares the temperature required to transform a standardized blackbody,

often called a radiator, to a certain color. Intervals in the Kelvin temperature scale are identical to degrees Celsius, but the Kelvin scale begins at different point. Absolute zero, 0 K, equals –273.15 Celsius. To convert a Celsius temperature to a Kelvin, one must add 273° (fig 5-34).

Common photographic parlance opposes the essential basis of the Kelvin scale. Terms to describe a photograph, such as "warm" or "cool," run counter to the Kelvin numerical designations found in measuring color temperature. At the upper extremes of the Kelvin scale, as the blackbody is made warmer, the color pushes closer to blue. Hence, the radiator glows a deep amber color at 1527°C. This is the nominal rating that approximates the color of candlelight and known in color temperature as 1800 K. Warmed further to 2927°C, the amber color emitted is cooler in appearance than candlelight. This color has been assigned to tungsten B films that hold the familiar 3200 K rating and is the basis of many contemporary digital camera tungsten settings. The color temperature rating for the bygone tungsten A films, which were created for use with amateur movie lights and specific

Figure 5-29

The photographer is using an on-camera Canon Speedlight to fire the other three, stand-mounted flash units. The wireless operation allows the photographer to be untethered and move freely in a studio or on location.

photofloods, was 3400 K. White or neutral is produced at approximately 5500 K, or direct sunlight, in photographic terms. At the same time of day, the shadows might read much cooler in appearance at approximately 7500 K. Deep blues set in at the upper end of the scale, near 10,000 K, whereas the bluest skies in the natural world can be matched near 28,000 K. A typical sunrise is usually rated a bit cooler than sunset, 2500 versus 2300 K, respectively.

Interestingly, daylight films are matched to a mixture of direct sunlight and the cooler skylight. Specified at 5500 K, this temperature is generally designated as photographic daylight.

The Color of Electronic Flash
Electronic flash is nominally considered as balanced to photographic daylight, although the color temperature is typically cooler at approximately 6000 K. This is a well-known characteristic and is a basic consideration when photographing people with a flash.

The cooler light emitted by a flash has led many photographers, when photographing people, to automatically "warm up" their flash unit by applying a slight warming

Figure 5-30

The portrait created with the lighting arrangement shown in figure 5-29. Note the catchlights from the flash units. As described in Chapter 8, the photographer or subject may choose removal after the initial capture and/or alteration of catchlights, depending on taste.

gel filter. Depending on the surrounding ambient light conditions, such warming filtration can provide a greater separation between the subject (often called the figure) and any environment used as a location (supporting the figure, this is called ground). The subject is cast in a slightly warm, complementary light, while the surroundings are cooler, thus allowing for a desirable figure-ground separation. Many subjects, especially with a light tone, as shown in figures 5-35 and 5-36, can benefit from the warming of a strobe's cooler color rendition.

Using a warming gel on a flash is common practice, but as with all techniques, there are photographers who regularly invert the

Figure 5-31

The Gossen Color-Pro 3F with standard diffuser and +5 stop range extending diffuser. The bare blue, green, and red sensors can be seen without a diffuser in place.

3. Full CTO: converts 5500K to 3200 K or tungsten B
4. Quarter CTB: converts 3200 K to 3600 K
5. Half CTB: converts 3200 K to 4200 K
6. Full CTB: converts 3200 K to 5500 K or daylight

Florescent Light

Most systems have exceptions, and the Kelvin rating scale is no different. The system works well when matching a black radiator at different temperatures to certain colors of continuous light sources, such as tungsten or incandescent filaments. Florescent light sources are another matter because they cannot be wholly described or measured with the Kelvin scale. Florescent lighting is termed discontinuous because the lighting is pulsing or spiking at certain wavelengths, although not visible to the human eye. The term **color temperature (CT)** must be amended to **apparent color temperature** (ACT) or **correlated color temperature** (CCT) when regarding the color of florescent bulbs. Digital cameras are often designed with a florescent setting on the white balance that approximates 4000 K (figs. 5-38 and 5-39). ACT and CCT indicates how scientists and members of the photographic community have arrived at the correlated or closest approximate degrees Kelvin temperature for discontinuous sources.

Color Control: Film and Digital

When film is used, photographers base their color decisions around matching the predominant light source to a selected film. Daylight-rated film is used for daylight or electronic flash exposures, the latter's Kelvin rating being roughly the same as daylight. Tungsten film would be selected for tungsten light sources. After those two direct film/light matches, photographers must rely upon filters to adjust the color of the light before the image reaches the film.

Traditionally, specific filter recommendations by film manufacturers for each film and each lighting situation have been

warm subject/cool surroundings formula. Photographers have successfully tried to make the subject cooler than the surrounding environment two ways. One may be the most obvious, which is to apply a blue filter to the strobe. A color print or digital capture of a flash-lit main subject would then be balanced to near neutral while all around would be much warmer.

Equally effective is the common practice of using a daylight-balanced flash unit with daylight film or daylight capture setting under predominantly tungsten light or ambient light that consists of a warmer Kelvin rating. The results create the figure-ground separation by placing a neutral or slightly cool subject against a backdrop of warmth.

Two filter groups, warm (orange) and cool (blue), are commonly used as gel filters for the purposes described previously or when full conversion is required. The warm group is called **Color Temperature Orange (CTO)** and the cool is **Color Temperature Blue (CTB)**. Each group is available in 1/8, 1/4, 1/2, 3/4, full, and double density versions. The quarter and the half versions of each group are often used to warm or cool light sources when a full conversion is unnecessary, as in figures 5-36 and 5-37. The following list shows the most popular CT filters and their Kelvin conversions:

1. Quarter CTO: converts 5500 K to 4500 K
2. Half CTO: converts 5500 K to 3800 K

Figure 5-32

A daylight-balanced digital capture under tungsten lighting.

Figure 5-33

The same scene with the digital sensor adjusted to provide a neutral rendition under tungsten lighting.

published. In many cases, photographers purchased a range of filters to maintain neutrality or to create the look they desired. Those decisions were based on the film's recommendations, color temperature readings, lighting applications, past experience, and potential experimentation.

Digital imaging has essentially altered prior thinking on color temperature and balancing the color of the light to the capture media. An echo of every photographer's first experience with video capture quickly became a commonplace term in still photography. Digital cameras are equipped with white balance controls of varying sophistication. Put simply, a photographer can now alter the sensor's color temperature rating instead of filtering the light before that light reaches the media. Cameras are typically equipped with daylight, tungsten, shade, cloudy, tungsten, florescent, and flash presets in the white balance settings.

The white balance feature on digital cameras has effectively eliminated the need for the drawers and cases of filtration that were so common to the professional photographer in the past. A digital camera sensor can be adjusted to match the color temperature of a given situation. The ability

to dial in a specific color response on a camera is one of the most significant developments realized in digital capture. Given the ability to input an exact Kelvin setting to the sensor, the color meter can be even more useful and efficient. Readings from a color meter can be set directly into a digital camera. The numerical white balance response for the specific image to be made can be created by simply altering the balance on the camera. The photographer can switch throughout a range of changing color temperature circumstances. Regardless of how different the light may be, the source can be measured and adjusted to accommodate the variation. Contemporary color meters have been designed for the input of profiles for different camera sensors and/or films, so that the meters can be specifically related to the capture device/media.

Without the once necessary filtration located in front of or behind the lens, the photographer will also realize another benefit. The speed of the capture will not be affected by decreasing light intensity. When one or more filters are installed for color correction/light balance with film, the effective film speed is diminished. The amount can be as much as three to four stops or even more. An ISO 100 daylight

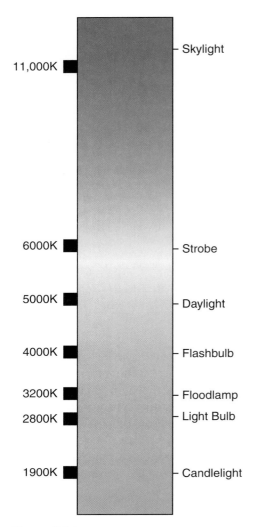

	Skylight
11,000K	
6000K	Strobe
5000K	Daylight
4000K	Flashbulb
3200K	Floodlamp
2800K	Light Bulb
1900K	Candlelight

Figure 5-34

Kelvin scale indicates color temperature.

film exposed in tungsten light with an 80A filter would require exposure of two more stops to account for the density of the filter. Those two stops effectively reduce ISO 100 film speed to ISO 25. In the same circumstance, a digital camera would be set to a white balance/color temperature of 3200 K while maintaining ISO 100.

A feature found on many digital cameras is a form of automatic white balancing. This setting calls for the camera to determine the best color temperature rating, which effectively engages yet another automatic feature that naturally will have gaps in accuracy. The autowhite balance (AWB)

can supply a range as wide as 2500 K to 10,000 K. A camera's AWB can receive information from more than one input source in addition to the sensor. Many cameras will allow the photographer program in one's own selected white balance settings for consistency in repeated, identical lighting conditions that may happen in studios where the light changes rarely.

For photographers who work in a variety of lighting conditions, there are other methods for assuring an accurate white balance. Makers of diffusion panels that attach to the lens, such as the ExpoDisc, intend for their products to be solutions to the numerous foibles commonly associated with AWB. Essentially turning the exposure system into an incident meter, the diffused panel accepts an incident reading not only for exposure but also for determining white balance.

Most photographers will work to get the exposure and balance correct at the point of capture. However, the utmost flexibility exists when capturing digital images in the RAW mode. A RAW or unprocessed raw data image file, before any image processing takes place, does not have the white balance set regardless of camera capture settings. The photographer can set the white balance *after* exposure during image editing without any degradation of the photograph.

Film and Filters

Conversion, light-balancing, and color-compensating (CC) filters are required, however, for those photographers who are using film and working in a variety of lighting conditions. These three basic categories of filters are among the most common in color photography. When compared with exposing an image in digital RAW, balancing potential filtration and light is much more critical in analog film capture. The elements of discipline required for managing color correction with film will provide the basis for a greater understanding of what is possible with digital capture.

Conversion filters allow the photographer to use a film under lighting conditions that are inconsistent with the film's original color balance. To understand the conversion, simply consider that a daylight film will need to be *converted* when used under tungsten lighting. Without a filter, the image will be deep orange in tint; thus, the converting filter will need to be blue. The opposite will apply when using tungsten film in daylight conditions. Without a filter, the tungsten film will be quite blue, but converted by an orange filter, a near neutral response will result. Citing the typically slower speed of tungsten film, the 3200 K-rated film is often described as daylight film with the filtration built in. Table 5-4 provides the specific filters that are traditionally used for color conversion.

Another scale exists for gauging and tracking alterations in reaction to color temperature. In film exposure, the Mired scale is often implemented when deciding on light-balancing filtration. The Mired scale (a term shortened from microreciprocal degree), is typically discussed after photographers have become acquainted with the Kelvin scale. In the photographic tradition of positing applications that are opposite, the Mired scale is inverse to the Kelvin scale, with the cooler colors registering numerically lower than the warmer colors. The Mired scale contains units that are determined by dividing the temperature into 1,000,000. Tables 5-3, 5-4 and 5-5 review the comparison between the Mired scale, the Kelvin scale and the effects on filtration.

The Mired scale is preferred by certain photographers, filter manufacturers, and camera designers because the Kelvin scale can produce inequalities depending on where the light color falls on the Kelvin scale. A 1000 K change between 2000 and 3000 K is considerably greater when compared with the same difference between 5000 and 6000 K. A 10 Mired shift creates the same amount of visual change throughout the entire Mired scale. The Mired designations are the reciprocal of the Kelvin numbers, derived from using the basic formula. The ability to determine the correct light-balancing filtration becomes much more accurate because the corrections are

Figure 5-35

Exposure made with an Elinchrome 400BX multivoltage flash unit, seven-inch reflector, and no filtration.

Figure 5-36

Image made with a one-quarter CTO filter on the strobe unit. This cut 1/2 stop of light, which mandated an increase of flash output and the aperture, remained the same as figure 5-35. The effect of a warming gel filter, or any filter, will be more apparent with lighter toned subjects. Note that the wood also warms up considerably in this example.

typically made in the higher Kelvin or lower Mired readings.

One camera maker, Nikon, has designed a manual white balance control that uses both scales in conjunction to achieve greater evenness of change. Each shift within their 2500–10,000 K scale is designed to achieve a standard 10 Mired difference. Canon, Nikon, and others also feature white balance autobracketing. The feature allows the photographer to initiate a sequence of up to nine exposures, each having an incrementally different white balance. Depending on the maker, the increment options may include 5, 10, 20, or even 30 Mired shifts for each exposure.

Figure 5-37

Assistant Chief Operating Engineer and Chief Operating Engineer Henry Marks by Daniel Overturf. In the subterranean pump house of Chicago's Calumet Water Reclamation Plant, 350 feet below the ground, the existing light is an intense mix of tungsten and mercury vapor. The two men were lit with a small, battery-powered 400-W flash head that was equipped with a ¼ CTB filter to heighten the color difference. The color variation emphasized the separation between subject and background.

Figure 5-38

Exposure made with a daylight camera setting under florescent lighting. Note: a Kodak Q-14 color bar has been included for reference.

Figure 5-39

Image made with the camera adjusted to correct for flourescent light sources.

Many color meters will display Mired readings. In figure 5-40, the photographer is using daylight film that has a Mired value of 182 (5500 K). The light source is reading –345 Mired (2900 K). Subtract 345 from 182 for a light-balancing number of –163. Minus numbers call for blue filtration, and positive numbers require yellow/amber. The Mired indication for what is commonly known as an 80A conversion filter is –131, and –32 is the Mired shift value of an 82B light-balancing filter. The two filters stacked will provide a neutral response under the strong tungsten illumination.

Color-compensating or CC filtration is also designated on color meters. CC filters are available in all of the additive (blue, green, red) and subtractive (yellow, magenta, cyan) colors. Most color meters are designed to indicate color compensation for the green or magenta casts, whereas the light-balancing/Mired indications attend to the blue/yellow range. The color compensation numbers indicate smaller, more precise adjustments that allow for casts in lighting that can exist in natural or artificial lighting. Their use is quite common when planning to neutralize the color of a florescent light tube. In the latter example, a color compensation filter is often stacked with a light-balancing or conversion filter to register a neutral response.

For a hypothetical florescent lighting correction, see table 5-6. The Mired shift is the same as a standard 5500 K material to 3200 K lighting conversion. The additional 25 cc magenta is indicated by the meter to further correct for the green present in the florescent tube's phosphors. The 80A (Mired, –131) filter would be stacked with a magenta filter to absorb the green cast from a fluorescent light. The combination of the two filters would most effectively counter the cast being created by the discontinuous light source.

Table 5-3

$$\text{Mired value} = \frac{1}{\text{Kelvin Temperature}} \times 10^6$$

Table 5-4

Conversion filter	Film	Temperature change	Mired shift
85	Tungsten	5500–3400	+112
85B	Tungsten	5500–3200	+131
80A	Daylight	3200–5500	−131
80B	Daylight	3400–5500	−112
80C	Daylight	3800–5500	−81
80D	Daylight	4200–5500	−56

Table 5-5

Light-balancing filter	Color	Mired shift
81	Amber	+9
81A	Amber	+18
81B	Amber	+27
81C	Amber	+35
81D	Amber	+42
82	Blue	−10
82A	Blue	−21
82B	Blue	−32
82C	Blue	−45

Color Control: Capture and Postcapture

Understanding color temperature and how to adjust the color in the capture on film or digital will provide the photographer the overall control of that facet of the image. The established method of matching film, filter, and light source will allow the photographer to achieve neutrality or to tweak the color for desired and controlled affects. Digital capture, from the most advanced digital SLR to camera function on a cell phone, will provide the controls that can lead to a neutral color rendition or other experiments with the color response of the sensor (fig. 5-41). These controls were at one time, especially when working with transparency film, the ultimate tools available to the photographer. However, in contemporary applications, nearly all images are finalized in a postcapture computer program before printing or publishing. So, how much influence does postcapture image manipulation have on the exacting nature of color control when making a photograph?

Whether an image originates from scanned film or a digital capture file, post-capture color control with imaging software has become commonplace. Once a neutral gray or standardized color target has been photographed under identical lighting conditions, the color-balancing function in the software (*Curves* in Photoshop or *Develop-Temp* in Lightroom, for instance) can produce neutrality. A photo filter or similar editing option essentially reproduces the filtration effects described above by allowing the user to apply a selected 80, 85, and other familiar photographic filter designations. As previously mentioned, images created in the RAW mode have the ultimate flexibility for color control in the postcapture stage.

Most professionals would agree that it is critical and efficient to get the exposure correct at capture. Although one can adjust and refine an image that was not shot with the correct color temperature, there can be downsides. Too much alteration in Photoshop to correct an incorrectly exposed image can lead to a loss of information and a potentially inferior final image. An image that is captured correctly allows for finer adjustments to be considered earlier in the digital image processing, which means greater efficiency and quality.

In practice, especially when on location, many photographers simply accept the color temperature of the light in a photograph. There may be adjustments made in postcapture processing, but critically adjusting at the time of capture may seem onerous if one is going to refine the image later. There are instances, though, when a critical degree of adjustment will be beneficial while exposing the image. Many

Figure 5-40

Figure 5-40

A color meter reads ambient tungsten light on location. The illumination is from a standard household bulb reading at 2900 K. The correct filtration would be to combine 80A (Mired shift, −131) and 82B (Mired shift, −32) filters, which results a combined Mired shift of −163 for balancing the light to daylight exposure. The light-balancing/Mired shift requirement is shown on the meter.

Figure 5-41

A meter reads the output of an advanced imaging device's lighting unit. In this tongue-in-cheek illustration, a mobile phone's light unit is "measured" by a flashmeter. Actually, modern cellular phones claim to have "flash" units that are actually small continuous sources that simply turn on and off quickly but do not actually constitute a real flash unit.

Table 5-6

Circumstance:			
Florescent light color meter reading:			
Film	Light	LB/Mired	CC
5500	3190	−131	25M

Filter solution:

Filtration for a neutral balance: 80A + 25 cc magenta wratten filter

architectural photographers will "dial in" their exposures when photographing interiors. The reading of color temperature allows the photographer to match upholstery and floor covering materials regardless of how the lighting treatment changes. Other examples could include projects that require the careful matching of clothing fabric, a single drapery tone installed in a variety of locations, a car finish photographed in a range of light, and so on. By reading the color temperature and making the adjustment at the capture stage, later adjustments will be diminished.

Summary

For most photographers, the uses of different types of meters in photography remain a mandatory part of the photographic experience. From the handheld light readings made with a professional meter to the program mode readings that create exposures with the most automatic camera, the meter initiates all exposure settings. In other words, meters are at the start of every photograph. Artificial light photography will reveal the importance of intensity and color temperature information when exploring a photograph's technical solutions and creative potential.

Lee Buchsbaum

Lee Buchsbaum, from Boulder, Colorado, is an editorial and commercial photographer for mining, rail, coal, and energy publications and affiliated corporations and public agencies. Also a writer, he contributes feature articles and images to *EnergyBiz*, *Trains*, and *CoalAge* magazines in addition to serving as the Editor and Chief Photographer for *Coal Transporter* (www.lmbphotography.com).

Title: **Foundation Coal Holdings, Cumberland Mine, 600 Feet under Waynesburg, Pennsylvania, June 2006**

This image was made while on contract assignment for Foundation Coal Holdings, one of the larger coal producers in the United States. For many years, I've worked with coal and energy-related subjects. I specialize in photographing underground in coal mines and other challenging industrial situations.

For this image, I was tasked with photographing the mine's long wall cutting head, part of a $35 million mining system. Exclusively for my photograph, the company had a scheduled a downtime window of 20 minutes. I set up a Calumet/Bowens 750 w/s Travelite to my left. The head was fitted with a small softbox that, thanks to many trips underground, has a front panel that can hardly be considered white or translucent anymore. I positioned a Canon EOS 5D on a geared tripod head with its legs sitting in about 12–14 inches of murky water. I slaved the head to a Canon 580 EX II on-camera flash and began doing a series of timed exposures and shutter drags. The on-camera flash is also used as a focusing aid in the dim underground locations.

Other than specific work areas, a mine is as black and dark as one can imagine. I try to use whatever light is available, especially to get a sense of depth. Underground, you generally only have two "ambient" sources. The machinery is usually outfitted with working lamps, and the second source comes from the miners' headlamps. The former

Figure 5-42

Foundation Coal Holdings, Cumberland Mine, 600 Feet under Waynesburg, Pennsylvania, June 2006. Courtesy of Lee Buchsbaum.

Figure 5-43

Lighting diagram for *Foundation Coal Holdings, Cumberland Mine, 600 Feet under Waynesburg, Pennsylvania, June 2006.*

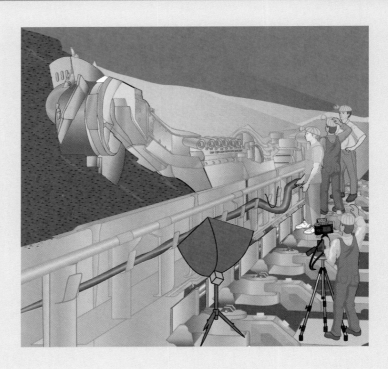

Figure 5-44

Lee Buchsbaum. Courtesy of Lee Buchsbaum.

may have a wide Kelvin range of color temperatures that each record differently. However, the miner's lamps consistently provide a nice warm glow in a rather distinct circle of light. For this

image, because most of the longwall crew was idle, I asked them to help me paint the machine with light.

Behind and next to me, in very tight quarters, six miners were rotating their headlamps in a circular pattern projected on the longwall head while I counted aloud to 5. Another miner, standing in front of the *subject miner*, leaning so he was hidden from the camera, pointed and slowly rotated his helmet light back at both the subject miner. This source created a light-painted backlight and at the far side (from the camera) of the longwall drum. The subject miner turned his light off and was asked to hold very still. Incidentally, I've found that I have to shut off my own "bug light" when I make the exposures. If I forget, there will be a big, overexposed circle in the middle of my frame or wherever I happen to have my head pointing.

Josh Sanseri

Josh Sanseri, from Los Angeles, California, is an editorial, advertising, and fine art photographer whose work has been published in numerous magazines and exhibited both domestically and abroad. Sanseri also teaches photographic workshops in Santa Fe, Los Angeles, and Venice, Italy (www.sanseri.com).

Title: Brett Magdovitz, Owner, Butler Street Bazaar, Memphis, Tennessee

This photograph was made as part of an ongoing personal project documenting small business owners. The series is made up of editorial style documentary portraits of men and women from around the United States and Australia.

I decided to make this photograph at night to take advantage of the available light Brett had hanging from the ceiling. If I made this picture during daylight hours, those lights would have had much less character.

I used two lights in this photo. The main light is an Extra Small Chimera soft box equipped with a ¼ CTO (color temperature orange) gel and a fabric grid attached to the front. The second light was placed directly behind Brett, just within his warehouse. This light utilized an open reflector with two full blue gels (CTB) attached to the front.

Each light is powered via its own power pack, and the back light is triggered using a Pocket Wizard. The main light is then triggered with its built-in slave cell. The camera's exposure was set at f4 2/3 with a shutter speed of 2 s. Once the flashes fired, the shutter remained open for the remainder of 2 s, thus burning in the available light that is illuminating the two characters behind Brett. Because Brett was sitting in nearly total darkness, the single flash exposure on him was not altered by any additional illumnation in the background during the entire 2 s exposure.

Equipment used: Mamiya 645AF w/Kodak Proback 645, Profoto Acute 2400w pack and Profoto Acute 600w pack, two heads, 16- × 22-inch Chimera, fabric grid, Pocket Wizard, CT Gels.

Figure 5-45

Brett Magdovitz, Owner, Butler Street Bazaar, Memphis, Tennessee. Courtesy of Josh Sanseri.

Figure 5-46

Lighting diagram for Brett Magdovitz, Owner, Butler Street Bazaar, Memphis, Tennessee.

Profoto head, 2400 watts, fixture laying on the floor, CTB gel, with Pocket Wizard

Profoto head, 600 watts, on 11' stand, with 1/4 CTO filter, with Pocket Wizard

Mamiya 645 AF w/ Kodak DCS digital back

Figure 5-47

Josh Sanseri. Courtesy of Josh Sanseri.

CHAPTER SIX

LIGHT SOURCES

Figure 6-1   A contemporary xenon flashtube is only one of many photographic artificial light sources.

The decision to make a photograph with artificial light requires the knowledge of a fairly large range of additional equipment to be used in conjunction with a camera. Artificial light inevitably forms the basis of a new set of considerations and options. The possible lighting approaches are multiple, and the number of solutions for creating the light is even greater. There is a vast amount of historical and technical information available to guide one through the options. The potential of the image can be thoroughly explored if the photographer understands the available lighting applications.

From the very basic to the utmost in sophistication, lighting devices are fundamentally simple to understand. The photographer who spends the time experimenting and gaining experience with lighting options will eventually form a baseline or a set of technical starting points. That knowledge base will expand over time as the photographer tackles each new project with greater confidence. A critical step toward forming a consistent ability to assemble a lighting arrangement is to understand light sources and the power required to create them.

Photographers have traditionally made images with both flash and **continuous light** sources. Many so-called still photographers are transitioning into time-based or moving images. A project might call for a combination of still images and film/video capture. In some cases photographers are revisiting their earliest experiences with continuous lighting. Indicative of the development of moving image applications are hybrid cameras that feature both still and video capability. Flash will remain popular with the still photographer, but only continuous lighting will do for moving images. The contemporary photographer will often be held responsible for a very broad and deep understanding of all forms of lighting, to be employed in an unlimited array of imaging applications.

Equipment Planning and Preparation

Artificial light, natural light, or a combination of both will dictate the look of the image. The equipment necessary for an artificially lit image can be very complicated or absolutely straightforward. Moreover, a photographer may design an intricate lighting scheme only to ensure that the image looks "natural" or not artificially lit at all.

Of all the possible accessories that a photographer may use to create an image, the choice to light a subject may be the most complicated and time consuming to arrange. In many photographic projects, lighting equipment will far outweigh and dominate the amount of required camera equipment. On many elaborate photography assignments, the photographer, perhaps with the aid of assistants, will be working out the details of the lighting equipment for a decidedly longer time period when compared with the camera decisions. The requirements of **preproduction**, a term shared with filmmaking, will facilitate the photographer's visual goals. The amount of effort required to fine-tune the lights to create an image confirms the adage, once again, that light does indeed make the photograph. For a truly elaborate example of preproduction, see the "Photographer at Work" segment featuring Richard Sands and Gregrory Crewdson at the end of Chapter 7.

The photographer will plan out the number of fixtures, types, and arrangement with a lighting diagram during preproduction. This starts with a previsualized version and a list of the equipment that will be set up for the initial attempts. Depending on the photographer's working process, this can be carefully scripted in written or sketched form. In other cases, the experienced photographer will quickly visualize the plan, based on previous knowledge of equipment and subject. Without exception, the initial setup will be at least slightly adjusted and sometimes even totally scrapped. Most photographers do not consider their early, perhaps abandoned, attempts as a waste of time. They see the early stages as necessary work that will lead to discoveries and, ultimately, an effective solution.

Power Sources: Alternating Current (AC) or Direct Current (DC)

All lighting units have a bulb or flash-tube located in the unit's head. The bulb or tube is powered by one type of source or another, a battery (**DC**) or through a standard socket (**AC**). Portable flash units, such as speedlights that attach to smaller cameras, are predominantly battery powered. Technological advances in many portable electronic devices have led to increasingly sophisticated, efficient, and smaller flash and battery units. The standard AC wall outlet can be found in every photography studio and also in many locations chosen for photographs. The photographer will usually choose either AC or battery power exclusively, depending on the circumstances of a single project.

AC: Power from the Outlet

AC power provides the option to use both continuous and/or strobe sources. Regardless of the photographer's lighting choice, the amount of power being drawn by the chosen lighting setup is critical knowledge. Any artificially lit project is dependent on the photographer understanding the power limitations in a given situation. Preshooting or performing a test of the lighting setup and related AC power supply is highly recommended before the actual photograph is made.

Most studios have specialized boxes with multiple outlets that are connected to dedicated circuits in the studio's electrical system. Semi-portable and with the ability to be relocated within a set, the boxes are designed for the heavy amperage levels that are required by certain studio flash systems. These are sometimes called **spider boxes** because of the vast amount of wires involved in the single panel, as seen in figures 6-2, a and b.

A flash burst puts an immediate, and sudden draw on a circuit and the associated breaker as the flash's power supply begins to **recycle**. A typical breaker found in a common household breaker box will be the 20-A size. This nominal size also applies to the basic circuits found in many studios created in spaces that are simply co-opted for photography. Most people have a healthy respect for electricity, but caution needs to be strictly exercised when working in spaces that have not been evaluated by a licensed electrician. Some flash units will tax older

Figures 6-2 a and b

A spider box is used in many studios as a central power source. This version features erasable labels for designating outlets to specific equipment. There are nine total outlets on this spider box. The outlets are wired into three separate circuits in the box, providing three outlets per line. The outlets alternate to prevent one line from being overloaded. In other words, outlets 1, 4, and 7 are on one line, whereas the other two consist of outlets 2, 5, and 8 and 3, 6, and 9. There is one 50-A breaker at the top of the box, and each outlet is rated at 20 A.

breaker boxes and may even trip a breaker, especially if the **recycle rate** is variable. Power packs with variable recycle options, for instance, will have a greater draw when the recycle rate is set to the faster option.

A **model light** is the continuous quartz or tungsten light built into most studio and some portable flash units. Usually located within a round flashtube, the model light immolates the direction and quality of the flash. A model light can also be a large draw on an electrical breaker box, especially if multiple heads are connected to a power pack and used at full power. To accommodate the large power demands, commercial photography and video studios rely on industrial-grade electrical panels, as shown in figure 6-3.

DC: Batteries Go (Almost) Anywhere

Photographers understand the basics about batteries and portable power supplies long before they become photographers. Batteries power any flashlight, radio, or portable electric device. Upon using a flash for the first time, the photographer can certainly grasp the concept of a fully charged battery versus one that is depleted. That difference, although very obvious, is most critical in beginning to understand the advanced levels of portable power supplies.

The flash system found in the simplest of cameras, including disposable snapshot

models, run on some type of battery power. Many cameras, especially older ones, can operate without a power source. However, batteries are required to power the flash units that may be used with those older cameras. A flash unit will run on rechargeable batteries or multiple disposable batteries, usually one of the ubiquitous AA or AAA sizes.

What else must be learned about batteries beyond their charge status? Depending on the system, there could be many intricacies regarding the connections, recharging, and battery life that will be necessary for working with a portable flash unit. Moreover, technological advances made in recent years that have added more power, longer battery life, and flash head versatility to portable systems.

There are three basic categories of portable flash. The general divisions also indicate size and, in some cases, level of sophistication. A variety of portable flash units are shown in figures 6-4, 6-5, 6-6 and 6-7.

1. Flash unit built into a camera
2. Flash unit or speedlight that attaches to the hot shoe of a camera
3. Flash unit that attaches to the camera via a sync cord, usually mounted on a bracket or other support

There are essential preventive measures that should be followed when using portable, battery-powered flash units. The following list entails a basic overview.

1. Never allow a battery system to get wet unless it is designed for that purpose.
2. Always use a power supply that is specially designed for the flash unit. Do not attempt to mix batteries, power supplies, and flash units that are not intended for such adapting. There are non-original equipment power supply sources that can be adapted to a variety of flash units, but those require at the very least a dedicated power cord and, in some cases, a dedicated module.
3. Make certain that the units are recharged and ready when not in use. Most contemporary recharging mechanisms include

Figure 6-3

Photography studios use industrial-grade power panels. All studio personnel should be required to know the basic functions of the box in case of emergency. Each breaker switch on this studio panel is rated at 60 A, three times the average household circuit breaker.

Figure 6-4

A later Fuji 6x4.5 roll film camera, equipped with a "pop-up" flash unit located beside a hot shoe.

Figure 6-5

Grouped for illustrative purposes, are a cluster of cameras shown with different flash units. Left to right, Nikonos V camera with Novatek underwater flash unit, Boy Scout camera and flash bulb unit, Hasselblad Xpan camera with an Interfit flat-panel flash unit, and Zeiss Super Ikonta IV camera with Vivitar 283 flash unit.

a limiter that will not allow the battery to be overcharged, but overcharging still remains a concern for certain units.

4. On location, some photographers power small AC flash units with DC to AC automotive inverters. **Power invertors** for automotive use have become more common and sophisticated. Especially useful when traveling between locations, the invertor can be used to recharge the battery while driving. Invertors are produced in various sizes and capacities with different methods of installation. Minimal research will be required to select the model that is best for your vehicle and equipment.

5. As a matter of insurance, always carry a duplicate or spare battery, **Prontor-Compur (PC) cord,** and even flash unit when going on location. Entire battery-powered systems have been known to mysteriously die on the way to or during the making of a photograph, although that rarely happens when the photographer brings a spare.

6. The photographer will need to fire the flash system to test for basic function and to determine exposure. Depending on the battery supply and the unit's power consumption, this can drain the battery while not making a single photograph. Be sure to use as little battery life as possible when testing.

Continuous Light Sources

All nonflash forms of artificial light, photographic or available, can be considered continuous sources. There are three broad categories in photographic applications, **incandescent**, **quartz halogen**, and **hydrargyrum medium-arc iodide (HMI)**. There are, however, striking differences between the different types of continuous and/or **tungsten lighting**. Despite advances and improvements, one type has not supplanted or replaced the other. Photographers continue to implement a wide array of continuous lighting options, from simple (fig 6-8) to sophisticated, to match the needs of the image.

Tungsten Lighting

The tungsten light category consists of either quartz halogen or a standard incandescent bulb. Another distinction typically

Figure 6-6

The Metz Mecablitz 76 MZ-5 is a later version of the handheld flash that, despite the extra bulk, holds a considerable power advantage compared with many hot shoe-mounted speedlights. Most modern flash systems offer dedicated modules, like the one featured in the top left. Note also the four voltage adapters that indicate that the charger unit can be used worldwide. The battery, encased in green at lower right, is rated for 135 flashes at full power.

Figure 6-7

The Norman 400B is an example of a professional grade portable flash unit. Shown are the recharger, two batteries, flash head, and power supply/battery compartment.

drawn in tungsten lighting is between the two extremes in respect to the shape of the light. Generically, these two extremes are the flood (broad) or spot (narrow) source. Some units will have a variable pattern that can shift the shape of the light from one extreme to the other. Tungsten sources range from the simplest single light bulb plugged into a wall outlet to the very elaborate, high-powered source. The more powerful continuous sources require greater care and attention to the electrical supply.

Many photographers begin their photographic artificial light experiences by using a continuous source. The ability to see what the continuous light has created or how the light is changed though adjustments makes learning about lighting easier for some when compared with understanding a flash system. The bias toward using a continuous light to learn the fundamentals of lighting has diminished, though, because students can now inspect a flash-lit digital capture almost immediately. The continuous source

remains a valuable learning device in some programs because students still find valuable the ability see the changes occur gradually and in real time, not just in the capture from a momentary flash.

Interestingly, it was the early period of digital capture that brought a resurgence of continuous lighting. Many of the first professional-level digital capture systems were called triple capture units. The cameras required three separate exposures—blue, green, and red—records of the same image. The systems combined the three exposures into a single capture. The inability to capture the individual moment, especially with live models, led to the improvement of single-capture digital camera systems that have been the norm for some time. Certain commercial studios still prefer the quality of the triple capture and retain the systems for various static subjects.

Tungsten light is not often thought of as a portable, DC lighting source. However, as many photographers have discovered, the common flashlight can be used as a small tungsten-balanced source. The Mag-Lite company, which produces an entire range of flashlights, is perhaps the best-known flashlight, and this company has made its technical specifications available for photographers to use during planning. Mag-Lite states that their small incandescent bulbs are nominally rated at 2900 to 3000 Kelvin, whereas their light-emitting diode models are rated from 3100 to 3200 K. The Mag-Lite, shown in figure 6-9, is often employed as an excellent tungsten-balanced lighting instrument for what is popularly known as light painting.

"Painting with light" is one literal interpretation of Sir John Herschel's term "photography" coined in 1839. "Painting" can also apply to any image made with a long exposure where a single lighting instrument is used to illuminate multiple areas in an image, as shown in figure 6-10. Photographers have long used this technique to fill in large areas of an interior during a long exposure. Assistants, traditionally dressed in black, are asked to move through a set during a very long exposure and point a light source toward areas that would otherwise be lost to shadow. (See Lee Buchsbaum's photograph after Chapter 5 for a most unique application of on-site personnel for light painting.) Facilities such as a restaurant with multiple booths or a theater with many rows are the types of spaces that might be candidates for light painting. By painting light into the nooks and corners of a space, the image looks as if there have been as many lights employed as there are dark areas, instead of just one that was moved around. Continuous lighting is typically used for painting, but others have used multiple flash pops to light small portions of large spaces, too.

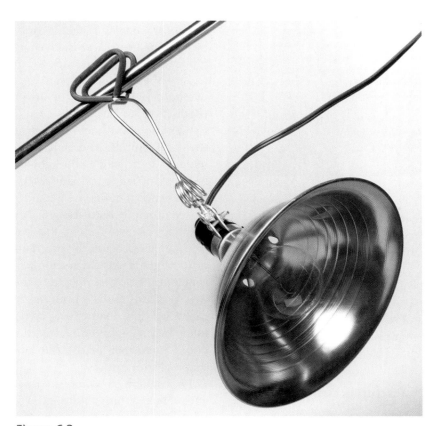

Figure 6-8

Simple incandescent light fixtures placed into large aluminum reflectors have long been used in workshops. They are also the first artificial light sources of many photographers. The basic fixtures accept a range of typical household bulbs, and some are even rated for higher wattage bulbs; some are rated as high as required for a photoflood bulb.

Figure 6-9

The flashlight is a continuous light source that can be a rudimentary, though sufficient, light instrument for photography.

Figure 6-10

A flashlight illuminates a laundry line at late dusk. Exposure time was 30 seconds at ISO 160, with Fuji NPL film. The small bulb is rated at nearly 3200 K, so the tungsten-balanced film was the correct match.

Quartz Halogen

Most professional tungsten lighting begins with a quartz bulb in a heatproof housing (figs. 6-12 and 6-13). The term **quartz** refers to the glass that is used to enclose the bulb. The term **halogen** refers to a reversible chemical reaction that occurs within an inert gas contained in the bulb that protects the tungsten filament.

Quartz characteristics include:

1. Color temperature: 3200 K, matched to tungsten films and tungsten settings for digital capture.
2. Color consistency over the life of the bulb can be 2,500 hours, which is better than a regular tungsten light bulb. There will, however, be some color shift as the quartz bulb ages.
3. Expense: relatively inexpensive, especially when compared with the HMI.
4. Heat: Quartz lights are also well known as hot lights, for good reason.

Fresnel Lights

The **Fresnel** light (figs. 6-11 and 6-14) is a unit designed with a lens to control the shape of the light. Invented in 1822 by Augustin-Jean Fresnel for lighthouses, the lens is a relatively thin optic that uses concentric circles to focus the beam of light from a bulb. For photography studios and location work where lights are mounted on a basic light stand, the unit's bulb can range from low wattage (100 W) to much larger units (5000 W). The 100-W unit may have a Fresnel lens as small as 2 inches in diameter, whereas a 5000-W unit will often be equipped with a 10-inch lens. Industrial-grade Fresnel units up to 24,000 W (24-inch Fresnel lens) can be found on overhead lighting grids in film and video production studios.

Common to almost all Fresnel units is the basic lamp head design. The outer unit remains static while the light fixture with bulb is moved back and forth from the lens, as shown in figures 6-15 and 6-16. The closer the bulb is to the lens, the broader the light. Repositioning the bulb further from the lens creates the pronounced beam or spotlight effect. The resulting beam's size is determined by the length of the housing, which in turn sets the limit on the travel of the unit's light fixture away from the lens. Many Fresnel lights come with a set of barn doors to further adjust the amount and shape of the light.

Photographers who use Fresnel lights will select a range of lights from their inventory, from lower to higher wattage, for different locations in the set or on location. The size of the spot can be adjusted (fig. 6-17) and intensity controlled by distance to the subject. Using different sizes of

Figure 6-11

Shown are two very different continuous lighting sources, although both are rated at 3200 K. The Arri 1000, left, is a 1000-W Fresnel lens-equipped spot source. The Mole-Richardson Softlite on the right provides a broad, soft source. The two cords on the 2000-W Softlite indicate that there are two lighting fixtures and bulbs in the base of the unit that combine within the large, cove-shaped white reflector.

Figure 6-12

Lowel-Light Manufacturing, Inc., started by Ross Lowell, has created many uniquely portable and efficient tungsten lights for the creation of still and moving images. Shown here are examples of a 250-W V-Pro, a Caselite with two 55-W fluorescent bulbs, a 500-W Omni with barn doors, and a self-contained softlight called a Rifalite, shown with the woven glass front diffuser so the 500-W fixture is revealed.

Figure 6-13

The Lowel Tota-Lite is one of the most compact tungsten sorts available to photographers, filmmakers, and videographers. Shown here, the Tota-Lite is shown closed up for transport (left), completely open with its 750-W bulb (top), and completely open from the rear (bottom).

Figure 6-14

An Arri 650 is shown with barn doors attached.

transitioning into a digital capture workflow used and still work with HMI units. The HMI design employs a mercury-halide gas to discharge an arc between electrodes that creates a continuous light source rated at approximately 5600 K, or close to daylight. HMI units are designed around a ballast, similar to the basis of a common fluorescent light fixture. The electronic ballasts on the later models of HMIs have provided flicker-free illumination, especially critical for film and video. The HMI design produces a much more efficient source than a tungsten filament unit. There are important differences between the HMI and other tungsten sources, as detailed below.

The HMI source has unique characteristics when compared with other continuous lighting options:

1. Color temperature: 5300–5600 K (close to daylight films and digital daylight capture settings).
2. Color consistency over the life of the bulb: One HMI bulb will last typically 6,000–8,000 hours.
3. Heat: One of HMI's chief advantages is very little radiant heat.
4. Expense: Much more expensive than other continuous sources; many photographers rent HMI units as needed.

Fresenel units will provide a wider range of options for the photographer. For instance, small Fresnel units can be placed to fill in shadows. On the other end of the size spectrum, large Fresnel units are sometimes used to mimic sunlight. Placed high up and far from the set, the sharp-edged shadows can imitate the look of the sun.

HMI

HMI sources are a specialized subcategory in the continuous lighting division. Many studios that were on the leading edge of

Electronic Strobe/Flash

After continuous sources, electronic flash or strobe is the next type of photographic lighting for discussion. An electronic photographic flash is most common today, but the developments in this area started long ago when using artificial light with a handheld camera and/or capturing moving objects became priorities.

Robert Wilhelm Bunsen, the German chemist of Bunsen burner fame, and Sir Henry Enfield Roscoe of England have been credited for the first experiments with igniting magnesium for momentary photographic illumination. That was in 1859, and by 1864, magnesium was being marketed to photographers as the best method

Figure 6-15

The Arri 1000's
1000-W bulb, with bright
silver reflector located
immediately behind the
fixture, is moved forward to
create the broadest beam of
light when passing through
the Fresnel lens.

Figure 6-16

The Arri's bulb is moved
backward to create a
narrow beam of light or
spot when passing through
the Fresnel lens.

The Arri has a single control on the rear of the housing to change the position of the bulb and, thus, the size of the beam emitted from the Fresnel lens.

Figure 6-18

The Milk Drop Coronet, 1957, by Harold Edgerton. © Harold and Ester Edgerton Foundation, 2008, Courtesy of Palm Press, Inc.

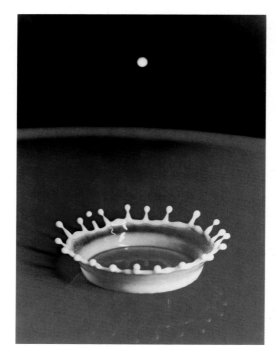

trapped any resulting smoke. The modern version of the flashbulb used aluminum or zirconium wire in oxygen. Because the resulting color was closer to tungsten, the bulbs were usually coated blue to balance with daylight film.

Thanks to Dr. Harold Eugene Edgerton (fig. 6-19), who refined the stroboscopic light and paved the way to many modern applications, we are able to work with a unique photographic tool that is known as an electronic flash or strobe. Edgerton's research in the area is well-known and documented. His 1931 electronic flash began the developments that led to the virtual demise of the flashbulb. Bridging very different fields of endeavor, Edgerton's photographs are hung in museums as art, and at the same time, the images are used to illustrate technical scientific research.

One well-known example of Dr. Edgerton's photographs of arresting motion is *Milk Drop Coronet*, 1957, figure 6-18. The flash duration for *Milk Drop Coronet* was reportedly less than 1/10,000th of a second. Edgerton's photographs evidence the power of the extremely short exposure that was only possible with the strobe he invented. The images he created remind us of photography's ability to show the unseen.

The *Milk Drop Coronet* image is one of the better known photographs in the widely respected Edgerton portfolio. In the interest of accuracy, students should note that Dr. Edgerton had predecessors from a much earlier time in the field of splash and stop-action photography. The lesser-known, but quite accomplished, A. M. Worthington was the first to announce his serious interest in 1876 by giving a paper called *On Drops*. His first photograph was made in 1894, and his first complete book of photographs on the topic was called *A Study of Splashes*, first published in 1908 and then again in 1963. Although Edgerton's work was based in electronic strobes, Worthington's images were made with a forerunner of modern lighting equipment called a Leyden jar. The device was invented in Leiden, The Netherlands by Peter van Musschenbroek and included the

for creating nearly instantaneous light. In the 1880s, flash powder, a mix of magnesium and potassium chlorate, became the next advancement in the field. Paul Vierkotter of Austria filed a patent in 1925 for the first flashbulb. The flashbulb was engineered around the established ideas of igniting magnesium. A wire coated with magnesium was ignited inside the bulb that provided a closed atmosphere and

Figure 6-19

Prominent figures in the specialized field of high-speed photography, William Hyzer (left) and Harold Edgerton (right) were photographed in 1982 at the 15th International Congress on High Speed Photography and Photonics, held in San Diego. Photograph by Professor Andrew Davidhazy, Courtesy of Rochester Institute of Technology.

original issue of the capacitor, an essential component of all of the modern electronic strobes.

Also participating in the early efforts to photographically capture what could not be seen were British scientists C. V. Boys and Lord Rayleigh, who helped invent the devices that would allow Worthington to arrest splash motion. Another figure in the early days of high-speed photography was Ernst Mach, who worked to capture an image of a flying bullet starting in 1887. His name would later be lent to the measurement of supersonic speeds.

Edgerton's forefathers in high-speed photography based their experiments in the development of mechanical means to create a stop-action image. Edgerton's developments in high-speed photography were rooted in the advancement of the strobe, which is why he remains the seminal figure when discussing the invention of the electronic flash.

Flash Power: AC

As described earlier, the source of power for a flash unit can be either AC or DC. Studio photographers will use AC power almost exclusively. Battery or DC power is often used on location, but many photographers will also prefer to use AC power while away from the studio if possible.

A portable power generator is the preference of some for powering flash systems on location, but many others rely on available power and multiple extension cords. Both solutions have drawbacks. Generators produce power that is not as consistent or reliable as a fixed outlet in a building. Certain power packs work poorly with generators that are not specifically rated for this purpose. The general guide is to make sure the power pack's output level is well below the generator's rating to facilitate a consistent power level for the flash system. However, a photographer would be wise to contact the flash manufacturer before attempting to connect a photographic power supply to any generator.

Whether used with a generator or an outlet, the extension cord must be heavy gauge and long enough to accommodate the desired setup. Linking one cord to another to make a longer run can seriously endanger the power pack because the resistance is greater than using a single cord of sufficient gauge. A power or extension cord should always be completely uncoiled, no matter the length, because a coiled line will also diminish efficiency.

AC will power two major categories of flash units. The first, the **power pack** (fig. 6-20) and flash head combination, uses one power cord and can operate many flash heads, depending on the power pack capacity. The second, **monolights** (fig. 6-21), are individual and require a power cord per flash unit. Many photographers use both types simultaneously, depending on the requirements of the image, the location, and how their lighting system has been accumulated.

AC: Monolights and Power Packs

Typically, studio photographers will choose the power pack and head system for greater power and expandability. Functionally, both the monolight and the pack/head combination are portable, as long as an AC outlet is available. The monolight is often considered to be an ideal choice for location work because its power source and head are self-contained. However, the power pack and head system can perform just as well on location. There may be an advantage to the pack/head choice because the photographer can use a pack to power multiple heads. Depending on the light rigging required

for the photograph, flash heads that are powered by a pack can be easier to position within a set because they are usually smaller and lighter than a monolight.

One advantage of the monolight is that the starter studio can buy light units one at a time for greater convenience and economy. A photographer can begin making flash-lit images with just one monolight. If more than one unit is used and because each runs on a separate AC cord, the photographer can utilize separate electrical circuits if the AC power supply is old or questionable. The downside of this trait is that one *must* have an outlet for each unit, which can sometimes be a challenge to find on location. Using multiple outlets on a single extension cord is not advised unless the gauge of the cord is sufficient to handle the large power draw created by more than one monolight.

Monolights may also be advantageous when traveling, because only necessary, specific lighting can be packed for a given project or location. Because monolights come in various power levels, some units with less output are much smaller and more convenient to pack. Monolights can range from 100–1000 W or more, and the weight can run from 2–10 pounds. Another advantage to most modern monolights is the built-in photo eye. The photographer needs to connect the camera to only one monolight, and the other units will be linked to the wired light via the photo eye.

Flash Power: Battery

A photographer's first experience using a flash unit will likely be the small flash built into a simple point-and-shoot camera. That tiny light source is meant to illuminate snapshots in dark locations and perhaps provide adequate fill flash for close subjects in bright sun. The controls are typically integrated into the overall exposure system of the camera. The camera's built-in flash can usually be programmed to create a flickering light that, theoretically, diminishes the *red eye* effect that occurs when photographing people in low levels of ambient light. The flash system in a point-and-shoot camera

Figure 6-20

Power packs supply the power to flash head through a heavy-duty cable that connects with a locking mechanism. The controls on the top of a Calumet Elite 2400 power pack indicate two channels, with two flash head connections per channel, shown above the handle in this instance. The channels provide separate controls for each head, each of the model lights, and other features. Each brand of power pack will have similar features, but the layout may be completely different from model to model.

can be altered in a variety of ways to provide an exposure alteration within the photograph. Based on the intricately convenient nature of these automatic exposure systems, the battery-powered flash capability of a point-and-shoot camera is among the most advanced in photography.

Sophisticated portable flash systems, at one time only found in the studio, can now run on battery power in almost any location (fig. 6-22). For some time, location photographers have been able to use flash equipment that resembles traditional studio equipment, complete with many accessories. Many major flash companies have a portable, battery-powered option in their systems.

The amount of flashes that will be available relates directly to the amount of power or flash intensity that is chosen by the photographer. Battery capacity is finite, and that limit will determine how a photographic session should be planned. The higher or stronger the intensity of individual flashes, the less number of flashes will be available. There are compromises inherent to using a complete flash system that runs on battery power. The recycle time may be slower between exposures. Some systems will require up to 3 hours before a large battery will be fully recharged. Another variation is that some of the battery systems will run units that can also be used on AC circuits, whereas some use dedicated heads that can only be connected to battery power.

The power packs available for standard AC outlets outnumber those available with battery versions. The battery units are limited when compared with an AC power pack's higher power levels, faster recycle times, and versatility in general.

Flash Synchronization

The camera's shutter type, either focal plane or leaf, will determine the shutter speed limitations when synchronizing, or **syncing**, a flash unit to the camera. Found on many roll film and view cameras, a leaf shutter will be synchronized at all shutter speeds through their top speed of 1/500th of one second.

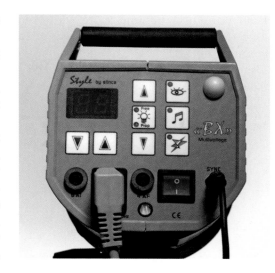

Figure 6-21

Like all monolights, an Elinchrom FX has all of the controls onboard. The control panel will allow adjustments within a five-stop power range and alter the model light and other aspects of the output.

Focal plane shutters, found on most of the later 35-mm film cameras and contemporary small format digital cameras, typically have sync speeds of 1/60th, 1/125th, or 1/250th of one second. If a shutter speed is set faster than the camera's sync speed limit, as seen in figure 6-23, the image will be only partially exposed.

Older cameras will have two flash contacts, which was standard years ago when flash bulbs were still in use (figure 6-24). Be sure to note that the sync connection between the flash and the camera is for firing the flash only and contains no electrical charge.

Many generations of cameras have been built with different forms of **accessory shoe**. Eventually, the norm was to make the shoe with a flash contact that would connect to the contact on the base of a flash unit. For obvious reasons, the term for the accessory shoe that has the syncing contact is a **hot shoe**. Hot shoes have a single contact point to fire the flash without a sync cord. The hot shoe's connections became more elaborate when the dedicated flash unit was created. Through additional pin contacts, each camera manufacturer engineered further relationships between the flash and the camera (figure 6-25). As one or more automatic exposure modes became the norm on cameras, dedicated flash units also became more common. The sensor on the flash unit works in conjunction with the camera's metering system to provide an optimal amount of data with which to regulate the flash power and, thus, the overall exposure made by the camera.

The digital single-lens reflex has created new and different wrinkles in flash sync specifications. Digital cameras employ focal plane shutters to create their exposures, much like their film counterparts. The shutters are used in close association with the sensors that accept the information as the image enters the camera. However, the **charge-coupled device (CCD),** shown in figure 6-26, and **complimentary metal oxide semiconductor (CMOS)** sensors each have unique flash sync and exposure characteristics.

On CCD sensor-equipped cameras the shutters are timed up to 1/125th of one second, and the chip would be charged with time to match the shutter. Faster than 1/125th the focal plane shutter would continue to fire

Figure 6-22

A long way from an outlet: A battery-powered control pack and flash head are shown on location.

Figure 6-23

This example shows the partially exposed image that is the trademark of a flash photograph made by a focal plane shutter set too fast or beyond its maximum sync speed. This image also shows the direction the shutter travels during the course of an exposure. A shutter curtain that travels vertically or, as it is sometimes called, a vertical curtain is evident when the unexposed portion of the image is horizontally oriented or across the length of the frame. The opposite would be true with the so-called horizontal curtain when the image is partially unexposed across the short space or one end of the rectangular image. This is an example of the horizontal shutter curtain. Although a traditional practice when acknowledging the distinction between shutter directions, the orientation terminology is really only accurate when the camera is used in the horizontal or landscape position.

Figure 6-24

A PC cord is inserted into a camera flash contact. Many small format and digital cameras have both a PC connection and a hot shoe. The hot shoe allows cordless connection for a top-mounted flash unit. The separate PC connection allows the camera to be connected to most any electronic flash unit. This camera, a Leica MDa, has two PC sockets, one for electronic flash (left) and the second for flashbulb units (right). The camera is equipped with an accessory shoe to attach a flash, but there is no flash contact, so it is not a hot shoe. Many older cameras do have a hot shoe, so the PC cord connection is mandatory for flash use.

Figure 6-25

Two examples of hot shoes found on the top of smaller format cameras. The camera with dedicated terminals on the shoe (left) accepts a specifically designated flash unit or attachments to connect into the camera's overall exposure system. The second hot shoe example has a simple single-contact hot shoe connection, located in the center, to fire the flash unit. Note that the center contact is identical. Both cameras will be able to fire a single contact or generic flash unit, but only the camera designed for a dedicated unit will able to engage all of a dedicated flash unit's automatic, interconnected modes.

at 1/125th, but the sensor is only charged for the set shutter speed, up to 1/8000th of one second. Flash sync speeds are commonly synced at 1/500th on CCD cameras.

CMOS sensors are considered to be a bit slower to charge than the CCD. However, many manufacturers decided to replace their CCD sensors with CMOS technology. CMOS sensors are completely reliant on the focal plane shutter at all speeds. That relationship has led to a sync speed of 1/250th on most CMOS cameras.

One last note on digital capture and flash sync speed is relative to the Canon Speedlight (fig. 6-27) and Canon digital single lens reflex (DSLR) bodies. Because of the unique interrelationship between dedicated flash unit and camera, Canon claims that their DSLRs can achieve a flash sync of their top speed, 1/8000th of one second, when coupled with their dedicated Speedlight.

Flash-Triggering Devices

There are four basic methods for triggering flash units. Cameras and flash units are conjoined through methods of **synchronization** to make a flash connection. Aligning the camera and the flash requires specific equipment and an understanding of the purpose of each specific type of connection.

One of the most significant developments in flash triggering of the last two decades pertains to the sensitivity of delicate circuitry in modern cameras. Understanding the circuitry found in modern cameras is particularly important when considering a triggering method for a flash system. Even before the advent of digital capture, certain film cameras contained electronic systems that did not mesh with older flash systems, especially high-wattage studio strobe units. Although many safeguards and updates have been introduced in recent cameras

Figure 6-26

The bare CCD sensor on an Imacon FlexFrame medium format 4040 digital back is shown with a Mamiya RZ-67 mount. The FlexFrame's sensor is 36.9 mm × 36.9 mm and creates 8-bit files of 48–192 Mb or 16-bit files of 96–384 Mb. There is also a live video feature.

Figure 6-27

Canon's high-speed sync potential, up to 1/8000th, is only available with a dedicated flash.

Equipment design required photographers to use a sync cord between the flash and the camera in the period after flash powder fell out of fashion and before the hot shoe was invented. Still used by many photographers, a sync cord is the standard choice for hard-wired flash connection. The most common sync cord is the PC, which is an acronym for Prontor-Compur, a prominent manufacturer of camera leaf shutters. The cord began to replace existing designs during the early 1950s. There are a few alternative designs for sync cords, but the PC remains the industry standard.

There are sync cords available in Y designations for simultaneously connecting a light meter and a camera to the flash unit. Other Y cords are manufactured to connect multiple flash units, even with different flash connections, or multiple cameras to a single flash unit. Photographers will also design special-purpose, custom cord applications for specific projects. Depending on resources and expertise, these can be either custom-made or homemade cords.

Shown in figure 6-28, the three most common flash sync cord types are the household, the 3.5-mm plug, and the TRS (1/4-inch phone plug). More universal is the camera end of the sync cord, although there also have been dedicated versions of camera connections. Shown in figure 6-29 are the standard PC-to-camera connection and the older standard, the bi-post. It should be noted that in later years, the PC designation had led to confusion because the acronym also stands for personal computer. Many digital photographers, without previous PC flash cord experience, have mistaken a camera's PC outlet as a possible computer connection port.

Another syncing accessory, the photo eye, or slave, is a triggering method that relies upon another flash source. These are used to set off the additional flash units without a cord. As discussed previously, a modern commercial flash power pack or monolight will often have a built-in photo eye. Also common is the small slave unit that plugs into a flash, available in different

and flash systems, photographers should always research the compatibility of their equipment before connection.

As previously mentioned, the hot shoe is a U-shaped fitting for flash units located on the top of a camera. Reports indicate that the hot shoe came into existence during the late 1930s. Common on 35-mm camera designs since the 1970s, the hot shoe is the most common method of triggering a flash for small cameras and small flash units. A hot shoe can also be outfitted with an adapter to connect the camera to a sync cord, which is especially useful when a small camera does not have a separate sync cord socket.

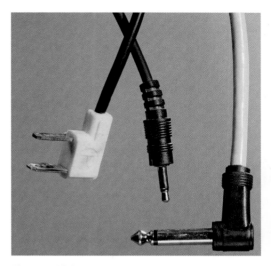

Figure 6-28

Household, miniphone, and TRS sync cords ends that connect to flash units. The miniphone connection is featured on radio transmitters.

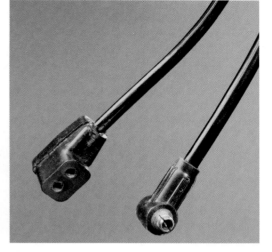

Figure 6-29

Sync cords ends: Camera sync connections for standard bipost and PC type outlets.

designs and degrees of sensitivity. There are limitations to a slave's ability to *see* the original flash. Sometimes, in a complicated set, slaves will be attached to a PC cord and placed in full view of the original flash to ensure a positive trigger. Unimpeded by physical obstructions, professional photo-eye units claim to be able to read the flash from a maximum of 3,000 feet away.

The **radio trigger system** requires two or more units to cordlessly synchronize the camera to the flash unit, as shown in figure 6-31. The camera is connected to the transmitter unit. Multiple receiver units can be placed on the same transmitting channel and may be placed as far as 1,600 feet away from the transmitter. A radio unit is connected by a signal, unlike a photo eye. The radio transmitter/receiver does not rely on sensing an original flash, thus enabling radio units to read each other around corners and through other physical obstacles. The transmitter is connected to the camera by a PC cord and/or a hot shoe, depending on the design. Some units can be switched to function either as transmitter or receiver. The radio transmitter is quite popular with sports or other event photographers who may be working alongside colleagues in the same location. Radio

units have multiple channels that provide isolation for the photographer's signal in the event of overlapping equipment and signals. Radio trigger units are popular for anyone who does not wish to be tethered to a flash unit by a PC cord, regardless of the circumstances.

Flash Heads

Flash heads constitute the business end of the flash system. Power, kept at a high voltage, is stored in a capacitor and then transferred to the head, where the flash tube is set off. Whether the power source is a battery or a wall socket, a power pack, or within a self-contained unit, the capacitor-to-flash tube relationship remains consistent. After a flash is discharged, the power source automatically begins to recharge the capacitor for the next flash.

The flash tube is constructed of very few essential components but built to exacting specifications in an array of dimensions and shapes. The essential relationship of xenon gas, enclosed in a glass tube and triggered by a high-voltage discharge from the capacitor, exists in all flash heads (fig. 6-33). Additional gases are added to form the correct color of flash, usually slightly cooler than daylight at approximately 6000 K. The common design

Figure 6-30

A photo eye or slave, shown with a coin for scale, can be attached to a flash to cordlessly trigger the flash unit. This model is designed to use either the household connection or a standard PC terminal.

Figure 6-31

Two radio units connected to a camera and a flash power pack. The units are identical, but to operate this arrangement the camera's radio unit is set to transmit, and the flash unit is set to receive.

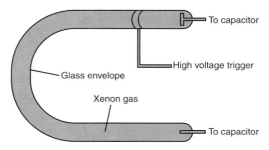

Figure 6-32

Broken down to the utmost basic components, the xenon flash tube is a simple device.

Figure 6-33

A close view of a contemporary xenon flash tube.

of a xenon tube, as shown in figure 6-32, is altered to suit a variety of applications. Indeed, the smallest 1.3-mm xenon flash tube found in some mobile phones and the twin flat tubes in a 6000-W Elinchrom head use identical basic technology.

Most flash heads have similar components, as seen in figures 6-34 and 6-35. One typical feature is the modeling lamp which is a continuous source that mimics the quality of light emitted from the head. However, each brand of flash head has individual features. Different companies, various intended purposes, cost, system compatibility, accessory range, durability, and other factors face the photographer when choosing a system or systems. This information is highly valuable to an aspiring professional assistant. A freelance assistant who works at a variety of studios will be required to understand the characteristics peculiar to a myriad of flash systems.

Producing a variable focus flash head provides one example of how two companies differ in design and function. Shown in figures 6-36 and 6-37, the Balcar (upper) changes from spot to flood by moving the flash tube further in or out in relationship to the reflector. The Speedotron 202 head features a threaded reflector mount that allows the reflector to move in relation to the fixed flash tube. Flood positions for both heads are shown in figure 6-36. The spot position

is shown in figure 6-37. The ability to switch from flood to spot is not available in all brands and serves as another example of the wide range of differences in flash head design.

A lighting company's manufacturing and technical service location is another, often neglected, factor that should be considered when choosing lighting equipment. Unlike cameras, which are now chiefly built in China, flash systems are built around the world. Included are domestic companies such as Norman in Minneapolis, White Lightning in Nashville, and Speedotron in Chicago. Each instance of domestic manufacturing ensures that the technical service will be performed not far from the manufacturing facility. Bowens manufactures Calumet's equipment in England, so they have an extensive service center in Chicago and other major cities to service all of the equipment that they sell under their name. Elinchrom is Swiss, although distributed and serviced through Bogen in the United States. Balcar is French, although sold and serviced by Calumet in the United States. Broncolor is Swiss and serviced along with the Sinar camera line in New Jersey. Profoto is Swedish and is serviced through Mamiya in New York. In addition to these well-known brands, there are many

Figure 6-34

Most flash heads are designed with the same basic components.

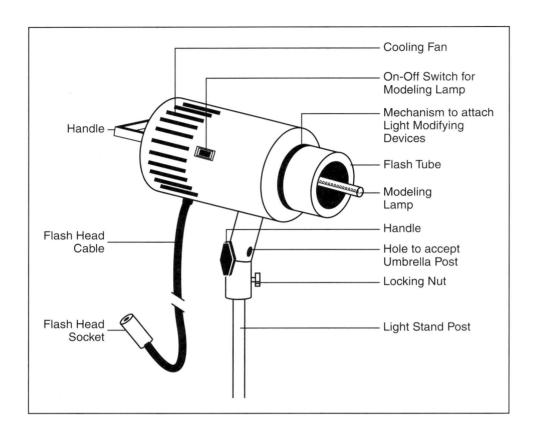

Cooling Fan

On-Off Switch for Modeling Lamp

Mechanism to attach Light Modifying Devices

Flash Tube

Modeling Lamp

Handle

Hole to accept Umbrella Post

Locking Nut

Light Stand Post

Handle

Flash Head Cable

Flash Head Socket

Figure 6-35

Weighing less than 2 pounds. and rated at 2400 W, the Calumet Elite is an example of a lightweight contemporary flash head.

used in studios. Professionals report that this form of *flash regionalism* has somewhat broken down. Profoto, for instance is a respected and popular brand from New York to Los Angeles.

Lighting Equipment Repair

There is one certainty under which all photographers operate: Sooner or later, equipment will be in need of repair. Gear can become damaged during a project, such as the flash tubes in figure 6-38, or simply fail to function. The equipment might have just failed due to age or even from a *lack* of use. In most major photo market cities, repair technicians regularly fix power packs, flash heads, and other components.

Photographers bring their equipment to a trusted repair staff that usually knows the equipment far better than the owners. The relationships that build between photographers and repair/rental facilities are critical to the success of both parties.

independent professional lighting equipment repair and service operations.

There was a time when a region or even a city was known to use a specific brand. A city might be known as "Broncolor town" because that might have been the predominate brand

Figure 6-36

Balcar and Speedotron heads in *flood* position.

Figure 6-37

Balcar and Speedotron heads in *spot* position. Balcar's head is rated to provide a range between 50° and 120° when adjusting the focusable head and basic reflector.

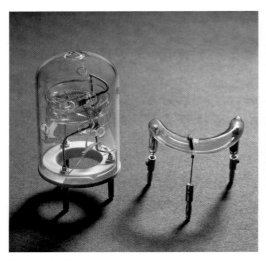

Figure 6-38

Flashtubes are fragile and can be damaged if abused. The two tubes shown here, a Speedotron and Norman, were damaged when the flash heads were dropped in the studio.

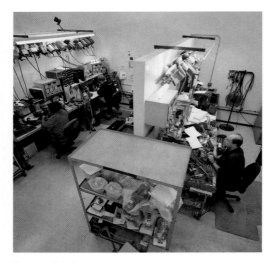

Figure 6-39

Three technicians repairpower packs, flash heads, tungsten light units, and other assorted equipment at Calumet Photographic in Chicago.

At the Calumet repair facility in Chicago (fig. 6-39), Repair Manager Debbie Ball had this to say about the topic: "Photographers rely on us to make sure their equipment is repaired quickly and expertly. We rely on the photographers to always need us. The relationship works pretty well."

Summary

Light sources, both flash and continuous, continue to evolve in sophistication. The capabilities of contemporary equipment grow similarly as photographers demand greater flexibility in power supplies and head design. The creation of new versions of traditional lighting equipment can enliven the most experienced photographers as long as they remain open to new approaches. Photographers who choose to explore the multiple possibilities available will find their choices can lead to alternative solutions and new images.

Peter Z. Jones

Peter Z. Jones, from San Francisco, creates fashion, travel, and editorial photographs for clients and gallery exhibitions (www.peterzjones.com).

Title: *Football* Training Day

This photograph is part of a series that I did for my fashion/editorial portfolio, not for a client. I had initially planned on using only natural light, which I had predicted was going to be overcast. I wanted the look of the images to remind people of a cloudy, cool day in England. The day turned out to be very bright and sunny, so I had to devise a very different look and feel.

I understood that I was not going to be able to approximate a dreary day in the United Kingdom. So I went the "other way" with my lighting. The intensity of the flash effect was adjusted by controlling the balance between the aperture setting and the shutter speed, both of which were set in reaction to the existing light. I placed two electronic flash heads in the soccer field and used only open, seven-inch reflectors. Bracketing with my shutter speed, I dialed in the tonality of the sky to be sure to render the figures slightly brighter than the background.

Figure 6-40

Football Training Day. Courtesy of Peter Z. Jones.

Figure 6-41

Lighting diagram for *Football Training Day.*

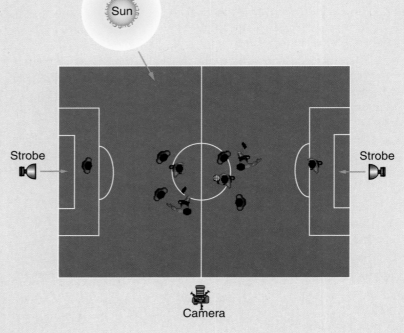

Figure 6-42

Peter Z. Jones. Courtesy of Peter Z. Jones.

Chris Walker

Chris Walker, from Auburn, Alabama, is an Assistant Professor in the Department of Communication and Journalism at Auburn University. Walker, a professional photojournalist in a previous life, now specializes in personal documentary projects and platinum/palladium printing (www.chriswalker photo.com).

Title: Mary, Orle, and Odocoileus; 1999, 4 × 5-Inch Platinum/Palladium

Mary was my paternal grandmother, who owned the chest; Orle is my mom's brother, who killed the deer; and *Odocoileus* is the genus of the deer. The narrative tableaux image is from a series exploring the notion of resurrection for beings other than humans. Are deer really soulless? Dogs? I think not. Then what of clams and centipedes? Does a line get drawn somewhere? What happens to them when they die? Really, is it automatic that sheep go to heaven and goats go to hell?

Most of the image was not light painted, in the traditional manner of the process. The photograph was layered together, from a total of 15 different exposures.

1. The base exposure on the trunk and antlers is from a single tungsten bulb, diffused with wrapping plastic, out of the frame, at the top right of the picture. The exposure was about 2 minutes.

2. The distant wall, at left, through the stanchions, was lit by exposures from two separate bulbs, the normal lighting on that side of our barn. The lights were dim from wattage and the distance, so that exposure was longer, probably about 10 minutes.

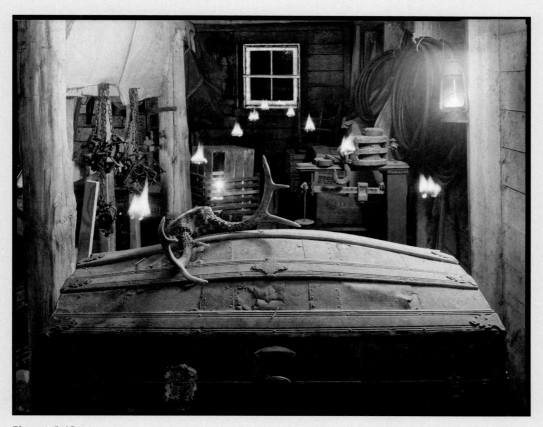

Figure 6-43

Mary, Orle, and Odocoileus. Courtesy of Chris Walker, Auburn University.

Figure 6-44

Lighting diagram
for *Mary, Orle,*
and *Odocoileus.*
Courtesy of Sean
Kelly, University of
Florida.

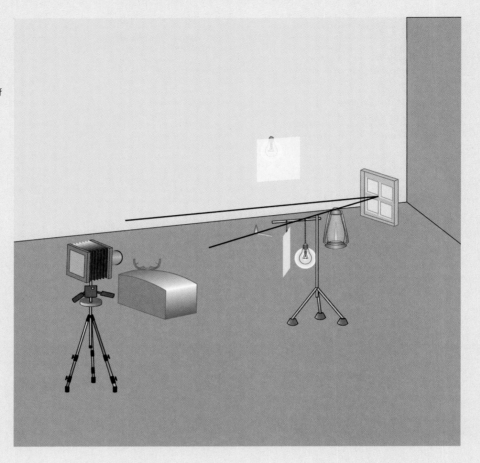

Figure 6-45

Chris Walker.
Courtesy of Sean
Kelly, University of
Florida.

3. The distant window, the only thing actually painted here, was painted with a snooted Mag-Lite, slowly (albeit unevenly) tracing its path around the frame.

4. The point source on the candle in the fish crate lasted about six minutes.

5. The lantern, my maternal grandfather's, was lit and burned for about five minutes. The lantern was so dim it did not light anything

but itself. Fortunately, I could see that this was going to happen, hence step 1.

6. The 10 floating flames are matches, each of which was exposed for about a half a second, individually. The shutter was then cocked again, and the next one was exposed. Their positions were marked by stringing a pair of wires through the image and attaching fishing *split shot* every *x* many inches, to keep them more or less paired and on a similar level.

In total, there are 15 individual exposures here, ranging from 1/2 s to about 10 minutes. An additional side note on technique: In an effort to be the barometer in obsessive-compulsive photography, I based the film development on the reciprocity failure shift. I started with the longest exposure time and made adjustments to the other exposures so that they would all balance out evenly in the negative during processing.

CHAPTER SEVEN

MODIFIERS AND ACCESSORIES

Figure 7-1 Reflectors are the most common light modifier. They will produce a light pattern that indicates the attachment's surface, shape, and size. The four reflectors shown here all have different physical properties. Smaller reflectors are often considered umbrella reflectors because they will allow the umbrella's rod to pass *by* the reflector (far left). Some companies will allow the umbrella's rod to insert *through* the reflector (lower). The reflector in the rear is 20 inches in diameter and casts a broad light. Balcar claims that the FX 60 (lower right) will provide no hot spots because of the faceted construction of the surface. Although most photographers will use the reflectors manufactured for their flash head, some have been known to adapt and cross brands to achieve a desired light pattern or degree of output efficiency.

Modifying attachments and accessories for lighting instruments are available in great numbers and variations. The photographer can choose from a dense array of options, from the commonplace to the very specialized. A case could be made that suggests that the characteristics of a photographer's work are defined

Figure 7-2

The pins of the Elite head's six-inch reflector are shown at the point of locking into the head. All flash heads are equipped with an interlocking point for modifier connection.

by how the light is modified as it leaves the lighting instrument. Many items may be universal in nature, such as the collapsible **soft box** attachments that became ubiquitous decades ago. What follows is an overview of the multitude of attachable **modifiers** that will individually change the quality of the raw light emitted from light sources.

Reflectors/Backlight Reflectors

A reflector is the most basic and efficient modifier for a flash head or continuous light source. Usually the simplest attachment, the reflector will often come as standard equipment with a head. All brands have refined their version of this most basic accessory, and each has statistics for the efficiency, versatility, and other performance features. Some reflectors are interchangeable between companies, but most are not. If the reflector mounting design will work between systems, most other modifiers should as well (fig. 7-2).

During storage and travel, reflectors can also function as basic protection for the delicate flash tube and model light. Certain brands include separate flash tube protection covers that make the flash heads smaller and easier to pack, leaving the reflectors to be safely stored on their own.

Reflectors are available in different sizes and shapes. The usefulness of the several variations depends on the diversity of projects confronting the photographer. Most reflectors are lined with a bright silver surface, but there are exceptions to that common trait. The reflector that is designed exclusively for use with a black **snoot** attachment is painted flat black inside. The reflector attaches to the head, and the snoot then fits on the end of the reflector. (The snoot will be further described in this chapter; for an example of black reflector and snoot illumination, see also fig. 7-22.)

Tapered or elliptical reflectors, attached to flash heads, are placed behind the subject to create an oval shape on the background (fig. 7-3). Photographers have been known to form a **background reflector** by employing a standard reflector with a small flag or other handmade alteration to create the taper.

Other modifiers are attached to the reflector, which compound the modifier's functions. The reflector may have a **grid spot** inserted into the front edge. A **polarizer**, diffusing sheet, or colored gel might be clipped to the outside edges. A reflector is nearly indestructible, but care should be taken to leave the round front undistorted to ensure that accessories can be easily fitted.

Grids, Snoot, and Barn Doors

Grids or grid spots are used to control the size of the beam of light. The output of a head fitted with a grid is dependent on the size of the honeycomb pattern, as seen in Figure 7-4. The grids are inserted into the front edge of the strobe head's reflector or sometimes clipped on the outer edge. A 10° grid has a narrow beam of light, versus the larger beam from the 40° grid. A typical set also will include 20° and 30° grids. A grid of appropriate size can be fitted to larger reflectors, too, which creates a bigger, though still concentrated, beam. Where the smaller, 7-inch grids may be used as accent spots or for a hair light, a 20-inch reflector with a 30° or 40° grid can be employed as a key light. The attached grid will affect the amount of emitted light, although the center of the tighter beam will retain much of the original intensity. Photographers may also place a grid spot in front of the center of a soft box to combine the qualities of these dissimilar sources, as shown in figure 7-5.

A snoot is essentially a conical tube placed on the end of a reflector (fig. 7-6). A snoot is used to pinpoint with light a small portion of the image. The light beam's alteration depends on the length and diameter of the snoot and the reflector type. The snoot and reflector should be matched for the desired effect. A black reflector will produce light with a cleaner edge, although the dark surface considerably diminishes the head's output. The more efficient silver reflector will produce an effect that is more erratic because of the reflections created by the combination of snoot and reflector surface.

Flash heads and continuous sources can be equipped with a set of **barn doors**, a modifier that is very effective in delineating a somewhat definite edge to the illumination. Typically, there are four metal blades that bend in and out to block and shape the light right at the source.

Gel Filters, Polarization Material, and Scrims

Placing a **gel filter** in the light's path will modify the effect of the open reflector. As shown in figure 7-7, a gel holder can be used to position the filter in front of a flash or continuous light head. Care should be taken to not melt the gel filter when used with a continuous light source. If the model light is not left on, a flash head will stay cool enough that gels are sometimes clipped to the edges of reflectors.

Rosco, Bogen, and other companies offer an impressive inventory of different colors and shades. Depending on the company's organization of the available colors, the filters may also be designated as a conversion

Figure 7-3

A version of a flash head fitted with a tapered back light reflector. The head is designed to be placed low. This head is clamped to a leg of a C+ light stand's base, called a turtle base.

or correction type. The wide range allows the photographer to choose filters as one might choose shades of paint. For instance, Rosco offers both a "Surprise Pink" and a "Pale Rose Pink," which are most assuredly different in their shades of pink. Convenient and complimentary, gel swatch booklets are offered to photographers to continue the paint selection analogy.

The polarization filter for lighting equipment appears very similar to a gel filter. Usually the same size and attached to a head by a gel holder, the polarizer is as different from colored gels as a camera polarizer is different from color filters. The **polarization material** is designed to reduce obvious glare from surfaces such as glass, acrylic material, and liquids.

A photographer can use a combination of both a camera lens polarizer and polarization material on the light source. Often employed to photograph highly glossy objects, the **double polarizing** method will effectively reduce the subject's glare, despite where the camera may be placed. Figures 7-8 and 7-9 compare single and double polarization.

The photographer must remember when double polarizing that the filters will seriously reduce the light intensity. Combined with the filtered lens, the overall intensity is cut by nearly four stops. Four stops, which

Figure 7-4

Grids are usually available as a set, with the honeycomb pattern typically ranging between 10° and 40° beams. Shown here are the 30° (left) and 10° grids. Tabs are used for retracting the grid from the reflector and also to identify which size grid is being used. The tension provided by a flat metal spring, shown on the rear grid, holds the grid in the reflector.

Figure 7-5

The soft box provides excellent soft light, and, placed directly in front, the grid spot adds a spot source. This example shows a combination used by some photographers to wrap a soft source around the subject but also add a spot source to a specific area of the image. The emphasis of one source or the other is varied by the power level of each flash head.

is a filter factor of 16×, might be difficult to accommodate without a strong power source. Considering how the filter factor can be applied to the power source will help the photographer determine whether double polarizing will be possible. For example, the 16× factor equates to starting with the full output of a 2400-W power pack and then applying the four stops or 16× factor caused by the filtration. The output of the 2400-W pack is now functionally reduced to 150 W of power after the filtration is factored. The amount of effective power that is reduced in this equation explains the need for a large amount of initial flash power which may be required to achieve a desired aperture.

A **scrim** is a flat, mesh-covered device that comes in different shapes and sizes (fig. 7-10). Between a light and the subject, the scrim forms a neutral color method to reduce the intensity of a single light. The construction of the scrim mesh material, appearing like gray screen in various densities, will depend on the light source. Synthetic fabric can be used with flash heads, but metal must be used with continuous lighting. Scrim material, stretched in a small wire frame, is a commonplace shading method for the portrait photographer. In portrait applications, a U-shaped scrim can be fashioned to shade the face right below the jaw line and thus make the face's edge more dramatic.

Umbrella, Diffusion Panel, Soft Box, and Omnidirectionals

Balcar first introduced the umbrella in the 1950s to function as a soft light modifier. The soft light is created by pointing the head away from the subject and into an open umbrella, which wraps the reflected light around the subject. A photographic umbrella is presently available in a variety of forms for as many different effects. Umbrellas come in different surfaces such as white, silver, gold, or striped (a mix of gold and white, for instance). Other models are available in

Figure 7-6

The snoot snaps onto the outer edge of the reflector. The reflector can be either silver-lined or black, as shown here. See figures 7-21 and 7-22 to compare the effects of the different reflectors attached to an identical snoot.

Figure 7-7

A standard gel holder is approximately 11 × 11" inches. The holder slides onto the stand below the head mounting apparatus and can be positioned at different distances to the head. The variable placement allows for different reflector sizes. Because a gel filter can be melted, the hinged gel holder also provides for swinging the filter in and out of position when using a continuous source or extended use of a flash head's modeling light.

sheer diffusion fabric for pointing the light head through the umbrella. Umbrellas can be used with continuous sources, provided that enough space is allowed to protect the umbrella from the hot lamp. Umbrella sizes currently range from 27 to 60 inches.

Diffusion panels create large, soft light sources and will work with both continuous and flash lighting. Materials used for diffusion vary in durability and color, from fragile paper vellum to sturdy sailcloth. The variance of color in the diffusion material should be taken into account when planning for the eventual color response by the

Figure 7-8

Two flash heads are reflecting in two sheets of Plexiglas. The right flash head is equipped with a polarizing filter, but the camera does not have a polarizer on the lens; therefore, the light head is evident in the reflection.

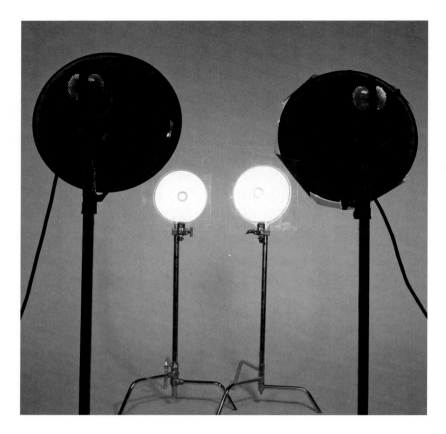

Figure 7-9

The camera has a polarizer on the lens, making the reflection of the right flash head mostly disappear. The polarizing material does not cover the entire reflector, and the uncovered parts of the reflector can be seen. Double polarizing can make most reflections disappear.

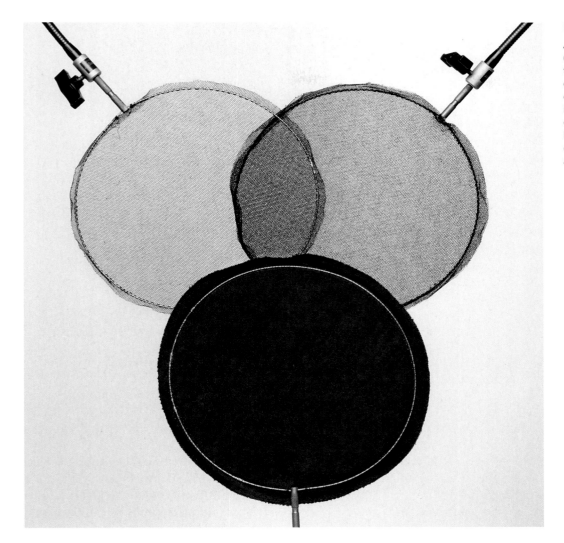

Figure 7-10

A six-inch, one-stop scrim (top-left) and a six-inch, two-stop scrim (top right) can be used to neutrally diminish a light source's intensity. The opaque dot of the same size is shown below the scrims. An opaque dot is also known as a round gobo or flag.

film or capture sensor. The diffusion material's transparency also varies, which affects lighting efficiency. Most photographers will use a neutral diffusion material and then employ a gel filter if the color needs to be altered. The same panel frames can be used for reflector panels of white, silver, or gold material (fig. 7-11).

Long considered a standard piece of lighting equipment, the enclosed box with a diffusion panel attachment has been common for decades. Often referred to as a **soft box**, each company that makes one of these soft light modifiers has initiated a variation in their model name. The term soft refers to the type of light, not to the construction of the box. Soft boxes come in both collapsible and rigid designs, as seen in Figure 7-15. To illustrate the popularity of this modifier, Table 7-1 lists the many brands that offer a version of the common soft box for the photographer. There are design differences and material choices that set each apart from the other. Still, regardless of the names assigned, the boxes are all patterned on the same basic concept. A direct source of light is attached to an enclosed chamber, and the light is softened by means of the diffusion material. The number of light heads will vary depending on the size of the box. In extremely large sizes, such as the Chimera F2 shown in Figure 7-12, as many as 48 heads may be installed.

Figure 7-11

Two light panel frames are clamped together; one is a modifier, and the other is a reflector. The left panel is fitted with standard diffusion material that modifies the flash head located behind. The partially shown right panel has a gold reflector surface that is opaque.

Table 7-1 refers to the names that have been given to the square and the rectangle shape categories but do not include the other dimensional variations such as strips,

Table 7-1

Brands	Soft Box Models
Balcar	Soft box
Broncolor	Pulsoflex
Calumet	Nova or Illuma boxes
Chimera	Lightbank
Elinchrom	Rotalux
Larson	Soff Box
Lowell	Rifa-lite (self-contained unit with light source)
Photoflex	LiteDome
Photogenic	Studiomax and Pro Soft Box
Plume	Wafer Rectangle
Profoto	Soft box
Smith-Victor	Soft box
Speedotron	Soft Light Box
Westcott	Westcott Box and Apollo
White Lightning	Soft box

octagon (eight-sided, fig. 7-13), or hexagon (six-sided).

There are soft boxes designed for electronic flash, and others are made with flameproof materials that work with tungsten/continuous sources. The model light in a strobe head is a continuous source, but the wattage is usually not enough to cause a fire hazard in the box. However, if one was to use a soft box that was rated for a flash on a tungsten light source, a dangerous combination would definitely be created that could lead to a fire. Be sure to check with the specifications to see if the soft box is designed for one or the other. This difference extends to the mounting rings. Figure 7-14 illustrates the difference between the mounting or speed rings constructed from the flash-only plastic/metal rings and all-metal versions that may be used with a flash or continuous source.

Based on the Chinese lantern, **omnidirectional** light head modifiers are primarily intended to be soft, overhead area lights. Shown in figure 7-16 and commonly known as a lantern, the broad

Figure 7-12

An extremely large soft box is the ideal solution for creating seamless highlights on large reflective surfaces in the studio or, as illustrated, on location. The Chimera F2 comes in four sizes, from 10 × 20 feet to 15 × 40 feet. The largest size can be fitted with up to 48 light heads or roughly one per five square feet. Chimera recommends using bare-bulb HMI, tungsten, or flash. The photographer, Paul Peregrine, is shown preparing to photograph a vintage automobile at Jefferson County Stadium in Lakewood Colorado. Courtesy of Peregrine Studio.

overhead lighting recreates a ceiling light and provides a controllable fill source for both still and moving images. The Chimera Birdcage, based on lighting devices for cinematography, and the Pancake Lantern can be either hung or mounted on stands. Both the Chimera models are collapsible and portable. Broncolor's Balloon and ProFoto's ProGlobe are similar products, although the European models are basically acrylic spheres with mounting rings.

Light Modifiers Compared

For comparison, a flash head equipped with a series of modifiers was aimed at the same target to demonstrate the results of different attachments (figs. 7-17 to 7-24). The camera exposure settings were altered in certain examples to maintain a nearly consistent degree of average intensity. The head-to-subject distance was identical in each image. The comparison series intends to describe the pattern and, to a certain extent, the character of each modifier. The comparison set is not meant to specifically describe each modifier's intensity effect, though the patterns created will allude to the efficiency differences between each modifier. All modifiers will alter intensity and pattern variably, depending on the purpose of the modifier and the head's design. The photographer can determine an accurate beginning exposure through experience in using different modifiers and careful light measurement.

Fresnel, Optical Spot, and the Cucaloris

The Fresnel lens, found on many continuous spot light units as described in Chapter 6, can also provide a similar form of light control with a flash head. The Fresnel lens-equipped flash head focuses the light beam, much like its continuous light counterpart. Some flash heads accept a fitted Fresnel lens attachment (fig. 7-25). Other makes offer completely self-contained, separate Fresnel flash heads. The photographer can use the flash head's model light to approximately focus the adjustable flash beam (figs. 7-26 and 7-27). The sizes will vary, as will the power ratings and intensity.

Compared with the Fresnel flash head, the **optical spot** head is a step further in sophistication. Often called a projector head, this head contains a lens that allows the light to be precisely focused and zoomed to alter the beam size. The lens can be adjusted throughout a varied range to place a small spot into a photograph (figs. 7-28

Figure 7-13

The Octaplus 57, a seven-foot-diameter light bank, is one example of a large modifier that can be attached to a flash or continuous light head to create a unique light source. The Octaplus is shown with the front diffusion panel partially detached, revealing another diffusion layer closer to the flash head.

Figure 7-14

Light modifier manufacturers design adapter or mounting rings, often called speed rings, for every light available. Aluminum or plastic with a metal mounting ring, each ring has a specific application.

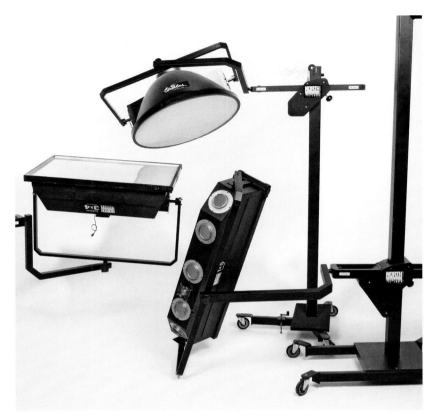

Figure 7-15

Various companies have produced large, rigid soft box units that can be used with different brands of strobe heads. Northlight created the three units shown here: round, strip, and rectangle.

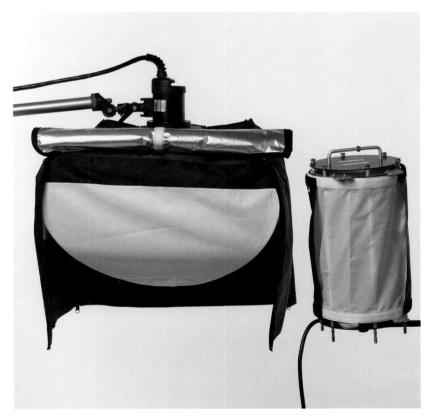

Figure 7-16

Photographers use the Chimera Pancake Lantern and Birdcage for overhead, soft fill light. Both modifiers are also commonly used for video and film.

Figure 7-17

Gray card target: bare flash tube only.

Figure 7-18

Gray card target: seven-inch reflector.

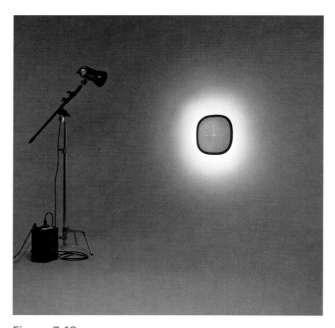

Figure 7-19

Gray card target: seven-inch reflector with seven-inch 20° grid spot.

Figure 7-20

Gray card target: 20-inch reflector with 20-inch 20° grid spot.

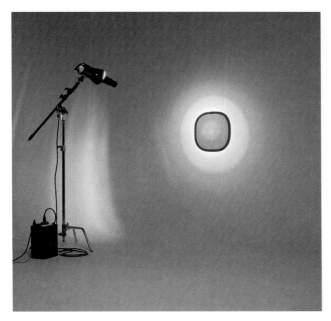

Figure 7-21

Gray card target: seven-inch silver reflector with snoot. The pattern formed is irregular because of the silver surface.

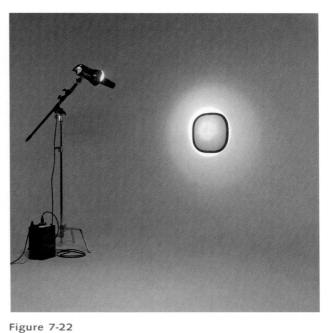

Figure 7-22

Gray card target: seven-inch black reflector with snoot. The pattern formed is much more uniform than one made with a silver reflector.

Figure 7-23

Gray card target: small reflector and 42-inch umbrella, white inside/black outside.

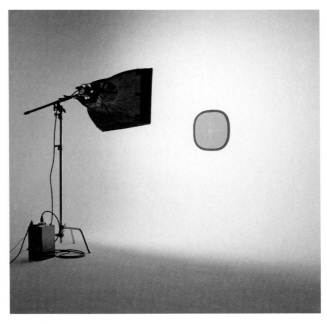

Figure 7-24

Gray card target: 2-foot × 3-foot soft box.

Figure 7-25

Calumet's Elite flash system 200 Fresnel lens is an attachment.

and 7-29). Small metal cutout patterns can be placed into the optical spot head to create relatively hard-edged shapes of dark and light. Figures 7-30 and 7-31 show the ins and outs of focus effects when placing a pattern on two adjacent but uneven surfaces. The patterns are sometimes used to place shapes on a background for specific allusions or just to place irregular forms behind a subject.

Considerably less complex, the **cucaloris** is another method of creating patterns and shapes (fig. 7-32). Alternately spelled cookaloris, cuckaloris, or even cucoloris, the device is a sheet with irregular shapes cut open to allow the light through to a surface, subject, or both. This simple modifier can be used at different distances from the light source and subject to alter the definition of the cut-out shapes. Nicknamed *cookie*, the material used will vary the effect. An opaque cucaloris, usually made of wood, will cast distinct shapes compared with the more transparent, fabric-covered cello cucaloris, which creates more subtle patterns. Photographers will often use a cucaloris to cast a pattern on an otherwise blank wall or floor (fig. 7-33).

Small, Contained Worlds: The Tabletop Enclosure

For certain subjects, such as very reflective and rounded metal objects, managing distinct reflections is a paramount lighting consideration. The riddle includes how to minimize and control the appearance of the

distinctly reflected images of the light sources and the surrounding environment. The latter might include the photographer peering over the camera, the studio ceiling, or anything within the visual range of the surface.

Photographing the odd watch, trombone, spoon, or the traditional object of loathing for the beginning studio photographer, the ball bearing, can all cause frustration and challenges. Placing highly reflective objects in an almost totally enclosed translucent cove solves most of these issues. The rule is simple: the larger the object, the larger the enclosure. In some instances, massive versions of these structures are constructed with surfaces as large as parachutes. Whether large or small, if the actual material is fabric as opposed to a more rigid plastic, the enclosures are often referred to as tents. The units are not totally enclosed, however, because one opening is mandatory for the lens.

Customer demand and contemporary equipment standards have thus led to updating a traditionally homemade photographic device. Following a trend in equipment manufacturing, companies now market clean, "store-bought" versions of the cove, or **tent**. Engineered to be both simple to construct and efficient to light, the manufactured portable, translucent **tabletop coves** are simple solutions for this specialized lighting application. These units are aptly named; for example, Plume/Calumet's *Cocoon* and Laccolite's *Cubelite*, shown in figure 7-34. These enclosures are designed with near-seamless, *infinity* surfaces and are overall sleek versions of their mostly cobbled-together forerunners. Instead of fabricating a tabletop enclosure from foam core and **gaffer's tape**, the assembly process is much more straightforward. The photographer can easily follow the steps required to piece together the durable, frosted plastic panels that connect with zippers. The photographer will aim the lens through the predetermined opening in the prefabricated enclosure, make the desired images, and then disassemble and store the apparatus neatly away.

Small objects, especially those with rounded or multiple reflective surfaces,

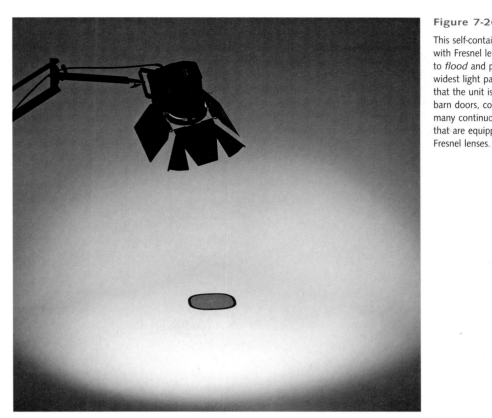

Figure 7-26

This self-contained flash with Fresnel lens is adjusted to *flood* and produces the widest light pattern. Note that the unit is fitted with barn doors, consistent with many continuous sources that are equipped with Fresnel lenses.

Figure 7-27

The self-contained flash with Fresnel lens is adjusted to *spot* and produces the narrowest light pattern.

Figure 7-28

An optical spot head has settings to control the pattern and size of the flash output.

Figure 7-29

In this example, the optical spot head casts a tight triangular pattern. Interior blades create flags to alter the basic shape of the light. The edges will vary from soft to hard by adjusting the focus of the head's lens.

are excellent subjects for an enclosure. The diffused light sources will be virtually undetectable in the object's surface reflections. Photographers can direct lights, almost any amount they feel is best, through any side of the enclosure. The light may even be directed from beneath the object to be photographed by under-lighting through a translucent table upon which the enclosure rests. Gel filters may also be introduced to add color to the illumination. The cove devices are also popular with outdoor photographers who use only natural light as a very effective way to diffuse the sun's direct rays.

The rise of online retail heralded in another very popular use of these enclosed tents or cubes. The increased need for very plain, descriptive tabletop imagery of objects intended for online sale matched well with the even lighting created by a cove. The early days of online catalogs established a specific, plain look for objects to be viewed in the compromised resolution level found on most computer monitors. To date, many of the images of objects for sale are created in a cove and without any pertinent props or styled surroundings. For a direct and efficient presentation on the Internet, the objects are photographed as simply as possible. The brilliant white, simply lit cove environment was the obvious solution to making the process of acquiring images more efficient. Interestingly, the purely high-key approach to photographing objects that continues to dominate online retail photography has considerable precedent in the traditional *knockout* or isolated object employed in many older forms of advertising.

Another contemporary production trend matches well with the cove's simplified use of light. The rise of the tabletop cove has been coupled with the now commonplace digital camera, combined with the occasionally untrained photographer. For instance, there are professional graphic designers who are very skilled with Photoshop and other graphics programs who have become the default photographers for their design project's product images. In many operations, technological advances at many stages of production have fostered a workplace that is often self-sufficient, with everything done in-house. The use of the cove allows both untrained and trained photographers a simple solution to minimizing reflections.

The rise and popularity of the manufactured cove should not indicate the end of the fabricated translucent enclosure. Many photographers still make custom tents and domes to photograph objects of varying shapes and sizes. The degree of adjustment is infinite, as certain photographers will also choose to alter reflections by having a specific amount of lines incorporated for reflections or altering the lens opening to create a certain pattern.

Supports

Light placement/installation is somewhat underestimated in importance to the novice photographer. With everything to comprehend about lighting, flash heads, color temperature, and modifiers, how much attention should a **light stand** require? Considering how critical exact placement of the light head is to the final photograph, photographers soon learn that understanding how the head is positioned is a most serious consideration. Gradually, still photographers took steps toward improving their ability to securely mount their lighting equipment. Some time ago, the motion picture industry's grip equipment purveyors realized that professional photographers formed a somewhat uninformed but potentially profitable customer base. The number of clever and inventive devices designed to meet every possible circumstance grows with each mounting device from Avenger, Matthews, and others. Because this type of equipment is essentially safe from obselence, unlike more transitional aspects of our field, many new companies have also entered the lighting support and grip market.

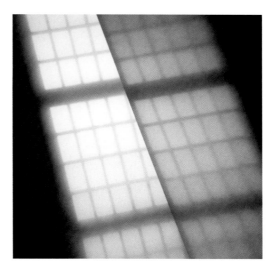

Figure 7-30

Metal patterns are inserted into the optical spot head, which can create a variety of specific shapes. This image shows how the *windowpane* pattern looks when placed upon two adjacent but uneven surfaces. The pattern can only be focused on one of the surfaces.

Figure 7-31

A side view of figure 7-30 shows the separate levels of the adjacent surfaces. The difference explains the clarity and intensity between the two surfaces.

1. Light stands: A light stand can come in countless forms. Folding, rolling, C, C+, different heights, different weight-bearing capacities, telescoping, and other variations allow the photographer to select the correct stand for the intended application (figs. 7-35 and 7-36).

2. **Boom**: A boom is an **arm** or extension that is usually mounted to the top of a light stand. A boom is used to extend a light head into a set or over the top of a subject. There are inherent dangers involved with booms. Care must be taken to properly counterweight the opposite end of the boom to create balance for the stand. The stand, though, is still a single point in this apparatus and can be tipped over. To protect against accidents, the boomed light head should

be placed at the same axis as one of the light stand's legs. Booms come in different gauges and designs (fig. 7-37). One distinctly unique boom has two handles at the counterweight end of the boom that controls the angle of the light head at the opposite end. Often called an articulated boom, the position of the light head can be fine-tuned without any awkward climbing above the set.

3. **Autopole**: A Bogen/Avenger Autopole or Matthews Matthpole creates a sturdy support when wedged between the ceiling and floor of a location or a studio. Spring-loaded clamps press the rubber ends firmly in both directions so booms, backgrounds, and other devices can be safely attached.

Figure 7-32

The wood cucaloris is an opaque sheet with irregular, amoeba-shaped holes cut to allow light to pass. Photographers will construct the cucaloris from thick card stock, a clear plastic sheet with black shapes, or a rigid wood panel, which is more common. Another variation is the fabric-covered cello cucaloris, which is not opaque and provides more a subtle difference between light and dark in the image. Most *cookies* are equipped with a single mounting pin that fits into a grip head and allows for precise placement of the openings and opaque sections of the cucaloris.

4. **Ceiling systems**: Telescoping from a ceiling-mounted rail system, light heads can be positioned into a set while keeping the studio floor clear. There are different varieties of the ceiling systems, but many include the light mounts that raise and lower like a pantograph. Others are simple sliding risers that can support a light head, such as the one shown in figure 7-38.

5. **Temporary mounts**: Lights can be securely mounted while on location using ingenuous yet simple solutions, such as the adapted **putty knife** with a 5/8-inch mounting pin, shown in figure 7-39.

Miscellaneous Accessories

The number of lighting accessories available to the photographer is overwhelming and impossible to list completely here. New devices can be specifically manufactured, adapted from another industry, or even handmade by a photographer. The importance of accessories, though, cannot be

Figure 7-33

The cucaloris forms patterns on the selected surface or subject. Varying the distance between the three elements, light, cucaloris, and subject, will alter the pattern.

overstated. Without the right accessory, correctly employed, effective lighting will not be possible. A few basic attachments will be described in this section. For a more comprehensive list and elaborate descriptions of grip equipment, see Clay Bannister's *Grip Glossary* in Section III.

1. **Shot** or **sand bags**: The bags are used to provide more weight at the base of a stand or panel (fig. 7-40). This may be especially necessary on location outdoors where even a slight breeze can render a head with a large soft box or other lighting instrument almost unusable. Photographers have been known to slip one or more concrete blocks over a C stand riser that, once the block is resting atop the legs, forms an excellent light stand weight.

2. **Cinefoil/Photofoil**: Useful for a variety of purposes, Rosco's black matte Cinefoil and Photofoil is 2 mil (.002in) thick, comes in rolls up to 48 inches wide and can be formed into many useful attachments. Cinefoil is fireproof, which allows use with both tungsten and flash sources. The material, shown in figure 7-41, is quite durable and can be reused in some instances.

Figure 7-34

Four C stands hold up a Laccolite's *Cubelite* being lit by two large reflectors on flash heads. Virtually any light can be used with a cocoon because the device thoroughly diffuses the light source(s).

3. Gaffer's tape: Also known as gaff tape, this standard adhesive tape will be found in any studio or grip bag. The tape is available in many widths and even colors, although matte black is the most common. Used for taping down cords and attaching virtually anything to anything, genuine gaffer's tape does not leave a residue after it is removed. The gaffer tag reputedly stems from the title for the chief lighting technician in a motion picture production unit.

4. **Tabletop reflector card**: Basically a miniaturized version of large reflector panels, a small reflector card can be invaluable when photographing small objects. Often homemade, reflectors can be created from white, silver, or gold card stock with foam core "stands" taped to the back to create the correct angle. Photographers have been known to use small cosmetic mirrors to bounce a distinct reflection back into a small set.

5. **Grip**: A general term that either refers to a person or a wide range of gear. A grip is a term used for an assistant on a film set. The phrase also can refer to the collected lighting gear on a film set, as in "Park the grip truck over there." The word grip is also part of the name for one of the most common light stand attachments, the grip head, which is the device for connecting many elements in lighting (fig. 7-42). When standing behind the stand, the grip head is easily adjusted and set with the larger control handles placed to the right side. The pin of a flag, cutter, finger, etc is placed into the grip head so that the weight of the attachment affects a self-locking clamp by downward pressure. With the spin handles on the left, the grip head's clamping ability is reversed and the attachment might loosen.

6. **Mafer Clamp**: Bogen/Avenger's Super Clamp or Matthew's Mafer Clamp are used to attach many tubular grip elements to stands and to each other. There are many varieties and attachments available for the clamps. One common application connects two clamps by a pin. This enables one end to attach to a pole or stand while the second clamp is open

Figure 7-35

Four basic light stands, all finishing with a 5/8-inch mount for light heads, shown ready for packing: folded roller stand, C+ stand (disassembled into turtle base and 40-inch riser), folded C stand, and folded aluminum stand.

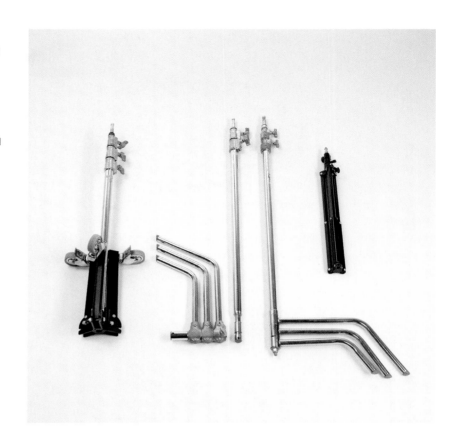

Figure 7-36

The turtle base is the three-legged stand at the bottom of every C+ stand. A C stand has a base and riser permanently combined. Shown are a C+ stand with a 40-inch riser inserted, turtle base without an attachment, detached 20-inch riser, and base of a C stand.

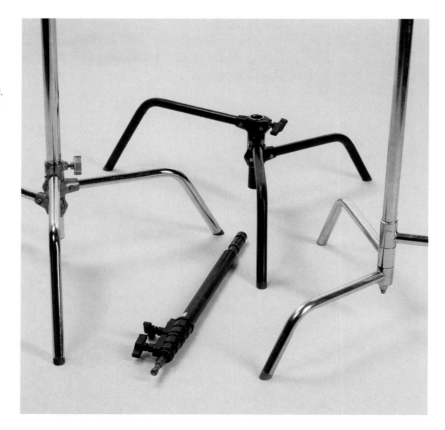

to affix a background pole, short riser for positioning a lightweight light head, reflector card, gobo, flag, and so on.

7. **Gobo** is a term that also originated in Hollywood. Used for blocking errant light from the lens, many forms of the gobo exist. On large film sets, a gobo (or a set of gobos) may sometimes be as tall as 10 feet. Often called a double gobo or folding slider, the large, black wooden panels are found on most film sets. Photographers often use black foam core or thick cards to create a gobo. A smaller gobo is often called a flag (fig. 7-43), and this device can be used to further augment a lens shade by blocking any errant light. The unwanted light can cause apparent flare in extreme cases but can also cause a more subtle contrast diminishment that might not be detected until after the photograph is made. Flags can come in different shapes, but all are opaque (fig. 7-44). A **dot** is a round flag, a **finger** is a narrow, rectangular flag, and a **cutter** is a larger, rectangular gobo. A dot and finger are compared in Figure 7-45.

8. Arm: There are many extension arms that allow other attachments, such as a scrim, dot, finger, or cutter, to be positioned off a stand. The names of the arms often indicate their design: flex arm, broken arm, extension arm, articulated arm, ball and socket arm, and offset arm. The Bogen/Avenger Magic Arm locks all moveable parts with one control.

Safety: Electricity and Common Sense

The equipment that has been described previously comprises an extensive, but not exhaustive, list of the artificial lighting sources available to the photographer. Divisions and subcategories were created to better explain the equipment. However, regarding safety considerations, there are two main equipment categories to consider. There is equipment that is connected to a power source and equipment that is not. Both categories have safety concerns, but

Figure 7-37

The three booms illustrate the range of different sizes and construction available. The tallest is a Red Wing, the next tallest is the Manfrotto with remote articulating controls, and the shortest is the Avenger mini-boom. Note the counterweights and sandbags as they are applied to make the apparatus steady.

Figure 7-38

Looking down into a studio space, flash heads are shown attached to different floor and overhead supports. Note the telescoping hanger, at far left, that makes use of the overhead pipe grid while keeping the studio floor clear.

electrical safety should be paramount. Lighting equipment that runs on AC or battery power requires a basic understanding of electrical safety guidelines. The other, nonelectrical gear used in lighting has guidelines that are governed by principles of common sense.

Electricity on Location

Using electric power while on location typically requires more oversight than in a studio setting. When available, the best resource to use when on location will be a building maintenance or technical supervisor. This person should be notified in advance, their specifications should be noted, and the rules should be followed.

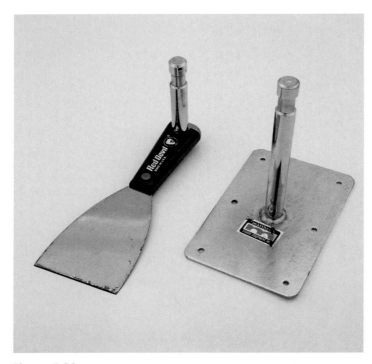

Figure 7-39

Two Matthews 5/8-inch light head mounts; putty knife, for sliding between a door and a jamb; and three-inch baby plate for general mounting applications.

Figure 7-40

Shot or sand bags are placed on the legs of light stands to ensure their stability.

On location, there are many potential dangerous situations that will need to be minimized through preparation, regardless of the size of the project. Many circumstances may have potential for electrical and related precautions. All people near the set, involved or not in the photograph, are the top priority. An assistant or members of a crew, people who are in the photograph, and any pedestrian or passerby could be injured by equipment such as an unsecured light stand, an unattended power pack or a bundle of cords that has been left in the wrong place.

The photographer is liable for any accident caused by the photographic equipment or anything that is associated with the photograph if bystanders happen to hurt themselves. Taping down cords, securing light stands, placing preventive barricades around the set, packing away anything not in use, and all other general safety measures are standard procedures when on location.

The photographer should be sure to leave any location as it was originally found. Returning the location to its original state may actually be a safety factor for those who work or live there. This may include ensuring that all of the existing power cords are where they were found, that any windows that had been opened or closed are returned to their original state, that any heating/air conditioning ducts that had been adjusted are reset, that all furniture has been returned to its intended location, and so forth.

Electricity in the Studio

The studio environment provides a greater degree of security because there are often business codes that regulate the power guidelines for a commercial operation. A studio will follow an internal electrical use policy to ensure the safety of all employees and any visitors. The unknown and dangerous possibilities are certainly diminished when the studio is compared with location work, but the safety of everyone involved is still critical. A thorough understanding of and healthy respect for the limitations of the studio's electrical supply will keep the photographer busy making pictures and not troubleshooting electrical problems.

A photographer should be acquainted with all of the safety factors present when using lighting equipment. Specific guidelines should be followed to ensure that all personnel are safe in the area where the photograph is being made. The photographer is liable for the safety of all parties on the set when making a photograph.

The best approach when learning, or in general if one has specific concerns about safety, is to ask questions until absolutely certain. Ask another, more experienced professional for advice. Ask the lighting equipment manufacturer or a professional retailer. Ask anyone who is qualified about lighting and electricity. Finally, be sure to inquire before attempting any connection or application that may have considerations broader and more complicated than a photographer's experience level.

General safety guidelines are as follows:

1. Acknowledge the limit of the power source connected to the lighting equipment. Do not overload a circuit or a portable generator with a flash unit or continuous source that draws too many amps. If a circuit breaker is tripped or a fuse is blown, inspect the line and amperage limit on the circuit and stay below the recommended amount of amperage draw. Amperage draw also relates to the adjustable recycle time difference featured on some flash units. Adjustable recycle times alternate between fast (draws more amps) and slow (draws less amps). Also, when using more than one lighting source, a preventative measure is to plan to use two different electrical circuits and breakers if possible.

2. Always use an extension cord that is correctly matched to the lighting equipment. All cords are marked with their gauge or wire size. "AWG 14" inscribed on a 14-gauge extension cord denotes "American Wire Gauge 14." The lower the gauge number, the thicker the wire and the higher the tolerances for

Figure 7-41

A 24-inch-wide roll of Cinefoil is shown above a flash head that is fitted with a partial reflector extension formed from Cinefoil.

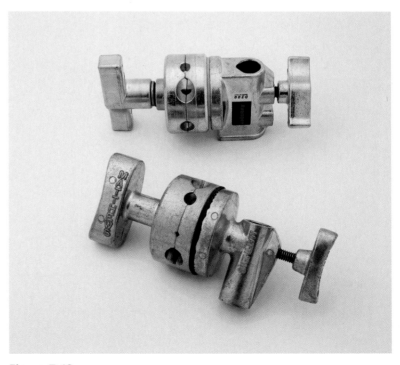

Figure 7-42

Grip heads made by Avenger (top) and Matthews (lower). The small knobs (right) attach the grip head to the light stand and the large handles (left) are for attachments with different pin sizes.

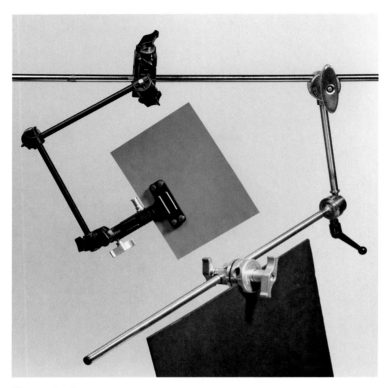

Figure 7-43

Basic grip devices: Manfrotto Super Clamp, extension arm, and lightweight clamp next to a Matthews Broken Arm with a grip head holding a flag.

Figure 7-44

At left is a Matthews folding flag or gobo attached by grip head to an extension arm on a C+ stand. On a C stand, attached by a grip head, is a sheet of black foam core that will perform the same function.

increased amperage draw. Err on the safe side of the equation; using a cord that has thicker gauge wire than necessary is safer than the inverse. Extension cords range in price for a reason. There are cords that may be orange and look industrial but may not be rated to handle the amount of amperage draw a power pack or large continuous source may require. One dangerous aspect to using a *household* extension cord or one that is not rated high enough is that the equipment may be powered and appear as if the cord is suitable. A flash may fire, recycle, and no problem may be apparent. However, a cord that is too small can do long-term damage to equipment. In all applications, use the shortest extension cord possible and unwind the cord completely. The latter refers to the increased, unnecessary resistance that is incurred when keeping an extension cord rolled up during use. The worst scenario would be as follows: using a cord that is too small in gauge, far longer than necessary, and left in a coil.

3. If at all possible, do not touch any photographic lighting bulb without clean cotton gloves. The oil or any other residue left on the bulb from bare fingers can shorten the life of the bulb. Studio flash heads are usually equipped with a flash tube and a model lamp. The latter is usually a 150 or 250-W quartz bulb. Neither the flash tube nor the model lamp should be touched without some sort of glove or a towel. Of course, after one is done making photographs, the bulb can actually be too hot to touch and thus is another type of danger. A continuous lighting sources' specialized bulbs, quartz or incandescent, also requires the same precautionary treatment. Provide plenty of time for flash, and especially tungsten, equipment to cool after use. Most photographers leave fan-equipped flash heads set idle, with the fans running, to cool the heads after prolonged periods of usage.

4. Use only professional-grade gaffer's tape when taping anything on the set, location, or studio. The tape will not stick to the equipment after use and does not leave any residue that could lead to units "smoking" because the heat and residual glue are combined. As discussed previously, always tape down power cords because many people near a set do not understand what may be connected to the cords or the overall danger on a set.

5. Understand the fulcrum principle and the delicate balance that is required when using a boom. The counterweighted nature of using a light head on one end and a dead weight on the other works well until the height or angle has to be adjusted or the head is eventually removed. Often, the best policy is to request help to "spot" the weighted end of the boom when removing a large or even small light source. All related units should be unplugged before this task is performed. Also, some photographers prefer to place a warning flag or tag on the counterweight of the boom because they are often used in dark sets. Injuries have been known to occur from running into a boom weight. At the very least, the lighting setup will be knocked out of position and will need resetting.

6. Never overestimate the capacity of the light stand. There are countless inexpensive stands that may be suitable for holding cards, flags, small gobos or even a very lightweight head, but an undersized stand would not be best for a fully equipped key light. For example, a C or C+ stand would be a safe support for a full sized flash head and a large soft box.

7. Certain manufacturers claim that one will be perfectly safe in disconnecting a switched on flash head from a power pack. A prudent habit, however, would be to ensure the pack is powered down before disconnecting any head or the main power cord. Another holdover from earlier times, one that still makes sense, is to hit the open flash button,

Figure 7-45

Opaque flags called a dot and a finger, with a flex arm, are attached to two grip heads that are connected to a long extension arm.

or "dump" the pack, after switching off the pack. At one time, this was mandatory because packs held enough residual power to fire the flash, even after the switch was turned off.

8. Water is to be avoided at all costs when using artificial lighting. If there is slight exposure to dampness, be certain that the lighting equipment is dry before use or storage.

Summary

The modifying equipment listed in this chapter is designed to assist the photographer in creating desired effects and controls on a wide variety of light sources. With time, different available devices will be added, and current attachments will be altered, but the essential modifying principles will survive. Photographers will also create their own forms of light alterations that will provide a more personal lighting approach. Ultimately, the lighting effects used in a specific photograph are the result of multiple decisions and adjustments that are a reflection of the photographer's personality.

Richard Sands

Richard Sands, from Lee, Massachusetts, is a Lighting Director whose roots are in cinema production. He has worked on 28 theatrically released motion pictures with directors such as Steven Spielberg and Francis Ford Coppola, 47 television movies, over 100 one-hour television episodes, and numerous advertising pieces. He was responsible for many award-winning projects, including three commercials he shot that have won Addy Awards. For nearly 10 years, Sands has created the elaborate lighting for the fine art narrative photographs of artist Gregory Crewdson. Through this unique collaboration, Sands' lighting has been featured in four books and several international photographic exhibition tours. Crewdson on Sands: "I always call him 'the genius of light.' He puts all of the lighting scenes together.... He thinks differently than everyone else I know. He just responds to light. It's remarkable."

Statement

All of my artistic endeavors start by trying to understand every story point that is to be *told* within each specific image. These points start as seemingly incidental areas of narrative that, when combined, become a complex web that maintains a delicate balance within the framework of the story. Once I believe I understand the complete story, my lighting work can begin.

Lighting can easily be compared with music. It must first be *composed,* not on paper but in my head. I envision the exact look of the photograph according to the story, long before I arrive on the set. At this stage, the picture is perfectly composed in my head.

The next step is the *arrangement.* This is the time to put everything into its proper place. "How much gloss on the floor paint?," "How much grading should the scenic artists do to the set walls?," or "How much grading will I do with light"? This arrangement sets up the *conduction of the light.* As the *conductor* of the lighting, I am responsible for the execution of the composition and the arrangement of the piece. I feel that this is where the real fun and challenges await.

No matter how good or bad the set is at the beginning of the project, it will be completely altered by the time of the *finale.* There will be no texture untreated with light. No layers will exist that have not been touched by light. Layers and texture are the fundamentals of light design and are, in fact, created by light or the absence thereof. The composition relies on depth, shape, and balance. Gray scale balance and color balance both, when done properly, lend to an image that will draw one's attention without distraction.

I hold light on a lofty pedestal. Light, for me, is the foundation to all that makes up a photograph. We all work with the same five qualities of light: direction, shape, quality, quantity, and color. However, beyond the definition and the technique, I feel that light is my *religion.* I feel to be successful and fully dedicated to this craft, one must be obsessed with all of the lighting details, or the project will fail to reach its mark. Done right, the lighting shapes the interpretation of the story and gives purpose by the detailed control of production design, wardrobe, hair, makeup, and space.

The three *Untitled* photographs presented are works by Gregory Crewdson. For reference purposes only, descriptive names were designated to

Figure 7-46

Richard Sands, left, and Gregory Crewdson on location. Courtesy of Richard Sands.

each image. *The Letter* and *Forest Clearing* are from Gregory's body of work entitled *Beneath The Roses*. The *Gwyneth from Dream House* image is from Gregory Crewdson's *Twilight* series.

Untitled, Winter, 2007 (*The Letter*)

The lighting of this entire image is balanced with intensities, coloration, and a detailed gradation. The image can be viewed as a yielding of a supernatural off-balance inspection of sadness or maybe a special order of never-ending/never-fulfilled hope.

This piece could not have succeeded without the detailed execution and relentless craftsmanship of an incredibly experienced stage crew. This remains one of my favorite images created for Gregory.

Table 7-2

The Letter

Instrument Schedule
Richard Sands, Director of Photography
Lighting instruments for *The Letter*

1. 36° Source4 Ellipsoidal with 3/8 color temperature blue (CTB) on a two-riser baby stand. Hampshire Frost diffusion in the gel holder. This light touches the upstage left window wall, giving a hint of detail to the sheer that is in frame. Medium-soft barrel focus.
2. Arri Baby 1K with full + 1/4 CTB on a two-riser stand. Projecting through a two × three-foot frame of Opal Frost diffusion. The light rakes the downstage left window treatment with blue highlights.
3. Mole Richardson 650-W Tweenie on a two-riser stand outside the upstage left window

Figure 7-47

Untitled, Winter, 2007 (*The Letter*). Courtesy of Gregory Crewdson and Luhring Augustine, New York.

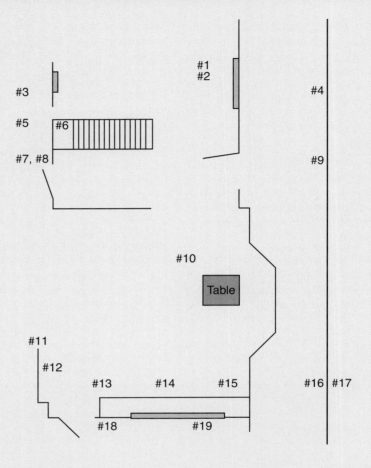

Figure 7-48

The lighting diagram for *The Letter*. Courtesy of Richard Sands.

#3

#1
#2

#4

#5 #6

#7, #8

#9

#10

Table

#11

#12

#13   #14   #15   #16 #17

#18   #19

with 1/4 CTB gel. This is the light that supplies color contrast and balance, along with the stairway, to the camera right half of the frame.

4. Eight-foot 5600K T12 Kino Flo tube without the fixture, taped and stapled to underneath the eave of the porch overhang with ND.30 and 3/4 CTB gel. This supplies fill level to the detail of the camera right foreground house exterior and is controlled with two-inch black paper tape.

5. Arri 1.2K PAR (parabolic) HMI with a medium lens on a Lowboy Combo stand with 5/8 CTB gel. This luminaire is focused upward into a four × four-foot hard frame of Roscoflex SS, giving the stairway treads/handrail definition.

6. Arri 650-W Tweenie on a two-riser stand on the top stairway landing with 1/2 CTB. Projecting through a two × three-foot frame

of Opal Frost diffusion. Back/top light for the furniture in the camera right room.

7. Six-foot 5600 K T12 Kino Flo tube positioned vertically via 40-inch C stand and Mafer clamp and gelled with 1/4 CTS. Works in conjunction with unit 8 by pushing light through the door behind the stairway. Gives definition and color balance to the door.

8. Six-foot 5600 K T12 Kino Flo tube positioned vertically via 40-inch C stand and Mafer clamp and gelled with 1/4 CTS. Works in conjunction with unit 7 by pushing light through the door behind the stairway. Gives definition and color balance to the door.

9. Six-foot 5600 K T12 Kino Flo tube without the fixture, taped and stapled to underneath the eave of the porch overhang with ND.30 and 3/4 CTB gel. This supplies fill level to the detail of the camera center foreground

house exterior and is controlled with two-inch black paper tape.

10. Two-foot 2 Bank 5600 K T12 Kino Flo fixture vertically positioned on a 20-inch C stand with 1/8 CTS gel. This adds shape as a hairlight and brings focus to the woman sitting.

11. Sixty-watt Reveal type A bulb screwed into an out-of-frame practical fixture on a dimmer. Adds shape and detail to the upstage kitchen counter.

12. Four- × four-foot Bank 5600 K Kino Flo fixture rigged directly overhead and in line with the upstage right kitchen counter with 1/8 CTS gel. This luminaire, along with units 13 and 14, is motivated by out-of-frame kitchen overhead lights and splashes the countertops with a neutral colored effect. Brings focus to frame left through color offset and intensity.

13. Four- × four-foot Bank 5600 K Kino Flo fixture rigged directly overhead and in line with the midstage right kitchen counter with 1/8 CTS gel. This luminaire, along with units 12 and 14, is motivated by out-of-frame kitchen overhead lights and splashes the countertops with a neutral colored effect. Brings focus to frame left through color offset and intensity.

14. Four- × four-foot Bank 5600 K Kino Flo fixture rigged directly overhead and in line with the upstage right kitchen counter with 1/8 CTS gel. This luminaire, along with units 12 and 13, is motivated by out-of-frame kitchen overhead lights and splashes the countertops with a neutral colored effect. Brings focus to frame left through color offset and intensity.

15. Mole Richardson Mighty on a two-riser stand, gelled with 3/4 CTB. This unit is tucked out of frame and bounces onto a three- × three-foot silver-sided bead board mounted of the stage right interior kitchen wall. This bounce light is softened through a four- × four-foot frame of Lee 251 and side lights the woman sitting with a low, soft, yet directional key.

16. Two-foot 5600 K T12 Kino Flo tube without the fixture, taped and stapled to underneath the eave of the porch overhang with ND.60 and 3/4 CTB gel. This supplies fill level to the detail of the camera left foreground house exterior and is controlled with two-inch black paper tape.

17. Arri 6K HMI PAR with a stippled lens on a Turtle stand, gelled with 1/4 CTB. This unit is focused upward into a 36-inch convex mirror, which is on a high roller stand about 16 feet above the stage floor. The convex mirror, in effect, miniaturizes the physical size of the 6 K source output; thus, a much harder shadow is produced. The harder light is then broken up by several leafless tree branches rigged on high roller stands. These shadows can be seen on the face of the house as a "spidery" moonlight effect.

18. Arri Baby 1 K high up on a three-riser stand outside the upstage right kitchen "back door," with 1/4 CTB and projecting through a four- × four-foot frame of Lee 250 diffusion. This adds shape to the kitchen door and maintains the warm color palette.

19. Arri 6K HMI PAR with a medium lens, a medium Chimera with 1/2 grid, and a 40° fabric grid on a four-riser crank-up stand, gelled with 1/4 CTS. This luminaire is positioned high, shooting through the kitchen window, supplying a soft, directional light maintaining a slightly warm feel as a cross key on the woman sitting. Subject separation and intensity are its purpose.

Untitled, Summer, 2006 (Forest Clearing)

The beauty of this image's light, upon first glance, may seem quite natural. In reality, a great deal of effort went into its creation. Gregory worked with landscape artist Bill Markham, until seconds before "time to shoot" (i.e., "we're losing ambient light too fast!"). As our shoot time grew shorter, I would find myself anxiously looking into the 8 × 10 ground glass to check the framing for our various lighting rigs and to see whether Gregory had any "surprises" that I should be aware of. Right before shoot time, as is typical, Gregory had crafted a beautifully poetic landscape that was exactly what was needed to tell this particular story. Photographs that were shot the week before near the same riverbank required suspending eight × eight-foot reflective frames of bounce material from helium-filled weather balloons for the correct lighting effect. In this set, the trees above the "hero area" were a bit too close for the balloon treatment. In lieu of puncturing our last balloons, we turned to one of the crew's resident troubleshooters. "Greensman/snowmaker/tree surgeon" Bill Markham tossed a thin black line (*trick line*) high into the precise branches that, in turn, were used to hoist the top soft bounce into the exact position needed.

Figure 7-49

Untitled, Summer, 2006 (*Forest Clearing*). Courtesy of Gregory Crewdson and Luhring Augustine, New York.

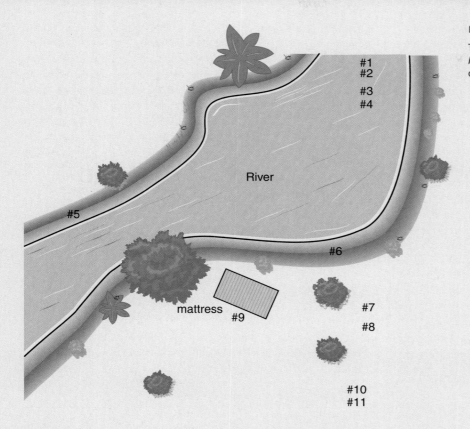

Figure 7-50

The lighting diagram for *Forest Clearing.* Courtesy of Richard Sands.

River

#1
#2
#3
#4

#5

#6

mattress #9

#7
#8

#10
#11

Table 7-3

Forest Clearing

Instrument Schedule
Richard Sands, DP
Lighting instruments for *Forest Clearing*.

1. Arri 6K HMI PAR in a 40-foot aerial boom lift has a medium/wide lens and is gelled with 1/2 CTB. This luminaire is raking the background and backlighting our generated atmospheric haze across the river.

2. Arri 4K HMI PAR in a 40-foot aerial boom lift has a medium lens and is gelled with 1/2 CTB. This luminaire is raking the background and backlighting our generated atmospheric haze across the river in concert with 1.

3. Arri 6K HMI PAR in a 60-foot aerial boom lift has a medium/wide lens and is gelled with 1/2 CTB. This luminaire is raking the background and backlighting our generated atmospheric haze across the river.

4. Arri 4K HMI PAR in a 60-foot aerial boom lift has a medium lens and is gelled with 1/2 CTB. This luminaire is raking the background and backlighting our generated atmospheric haze across the river in concert with 3.

5. Arri 6K HMI PAR in a 100-foot aerial boom lift has a medium/wide lens and is gelled with 1/2 CTB. This lift was difficult to position. It is across the river in a moderately graded backyard that was very muddy from a downpour. The purpose of the lift is to position the luminaire over a group of tall trees that line the riverbank. The light from this unit added a few highlights to the leaves on the group of trees.

6. Arri 4K HMI PAR, medium/wide lens, on a Low-boy Combo stand gelled with 1/4 CTB and projecting through a

four × four-foot frame of Lee 216 diffusion. This 4K is in-frame but hidden behind a tree and the thick brush. It backlights the man sitting and the woman lying down. This light falling on them is motivated by the bright sky. There are several flags set to contain light from unwanted areas.

7. Arri 1.2K HMI PAR, medium lens, on Low-boy Combo stand gelled with 1/4 CTB projecting through a two × three-foot frame of Lee 251 diffusion and broken up with a branch cutter rigged from a C stand. This unit sidelights the camera right midground tree from a low angle, which keeps the light off the ground, giving the set more depth.

8. Arri 1.2K HMI PAR, medium lens, on Low-boy Combo stand gelled with 1/4 CTB projecting through a two × three-foot frame of Lee 251 diffusion and broken up with a branch cutter rigged from a C stand. This unit sidelights the camera right downstage tree from a low angle, which keeps the light off the ground, giving the set more depth through contrast.

9. This is not a lighting unit but an eight × eight-foot PVC frame of silver lame with the silver side down. In the center of the silver side is safety-pinned a hard silver show card. This frame is suspended approximately 35 feet, just out of frame, by four lengths of black 3/16-inch trick line thrown high over tree branches, with each line tied to a corner of the frame and to a point on the ground. Some trick lines are, necessarily, in the shot.

With units 10 and 11 focused on the silver lame from underneath, the light bounces back down onto the subject and falls off fairly rapidly, giving focus to the center of the set. The hard silver show card takes the same light and gives even greater focus to the mattress area and also touches the man sitting before falling off significantly.

10 and 11. Each an Arri 6K HMI PAR, medium lenses, on Turtle stands, gelled with 1/4 CTB and focused upward to the center of the suspended eight × eight-foot frame.

Untitled, 2002 (Gwyneth from Dream House)

This is an image where I felt that the set should be lit with impunity. The lighting was to be without distraction or judgment, more presentational yet giving in to the comfort of shame.

Figure 7-51

Untitled, 2002 (*Gwyneth from Dream House*). Courtesy of Gregory Crewdson and Luhring Augustine, New York.

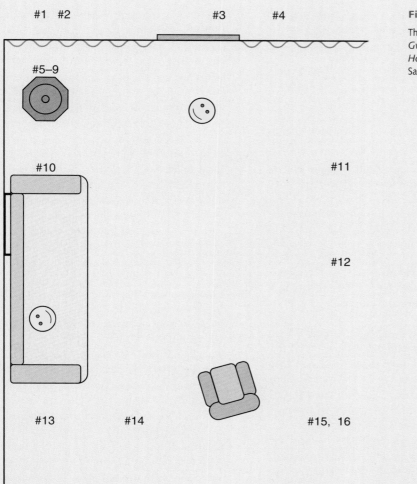

#1 #2   #3   #4

#5–9

#10   #11

                                       #12

#13   #14   #15, 16

Figure 7-52

The lighting diagram for *Gwyneth from Dream House*. Courtesy of Richard Sands.

Table 7-4
Gwyneth from Dream House

Instrument Schedule
Richard Sands, DP
Lighting instruments for *Gwyneth from Dream House*.

1. LTM4K HMI Fresnel with 1/2 CTB on Low Combo stand. No diffusion. This unit is backlighting the upstage left thick drapery.
2. LTM 4K HMI Fresnel with 1/2 CTB on Low Combo stand. No diffusion. This unit is backlighting the upstage left thick drapery.
3. LTM 4K HMI Fresnel with 1/2 CTB on Combo stand shooting through a four × four-foot frame of Lee 216 diffusion. This unit is separating *Gwenyth from the Background*.
4. LTM 6K HMI Fresnel with 1/2 CTB on Low Combo stand. No diffusion. This unit is backlighting the downstage left thick drapery. The focus is toward upstage to give more strength as a drapery highlight

when seen in the mirror. This unit is flagged off of the sliding glass door as to not contaminate the mirror wall.

5–9. These are all small units rigged behind the practical lamp via a slit cut through the shade on the Upstage side. Two short C stand arms both connected to a Mafer clamped onto the lamp post hold all five luminaires, allowing for complete articulation.

Note: The practical is lamped with a PH212 and is gelled with Full CTB. The camera side of the shade is gelled with ND.90. The force of the PH212 is intended to add a *practical motivated* glow on the wall.

5. Two hundred-watt LTM Pepper with a wide snoot pointing straight up supplies a *practical motivated* circle of light on the ceiling. It is scrimmed to taste and is gelled with 1/2 CTB.
6. Two hundred-watt LTM Pepper with a narrow snoot focused on the flowers with falloff on the chair. Gelled with 1/2 CTB.
7. One hundred-fifty-watt Great American Stick-Up light gelled with 1/2 CTB focused upward to augment the natural glow from the PH212. This unit is further controlled with black wrap, fine-tuning its unwanted spill.
8. One hundred-fifty-watt Great American Stick-Up light gelled with 1/2 CTB focused downward to augment the natural glow from the PH212. This unit hits the arm of the couch and the lamp table and is further controlled with black wrap, fine-tuning its unwanted spill.
9. Two hundred-watt LTM Pepper with barn doors and 1/2 CTB. This unit merges with the falloff of 8 and continues to light the rest of the couch, supplying a cross key for the woman on the couch. The barn door takes all of the light off of the wall, eliminating contamination from the window pattern on the wall.

10. This Mole-Richardson Baby 1K Fresnel is on a low floor stand, gelled with 1/2 CTB, and is hidden by the couch. The unit is spotted up as a *practical motivated* backlight for the woman standing. The full spot at this distance allows for significant falloff from the waist down. The unit hits nothing else, and its intensity is adjusted primarily for the woman's reflection in the mirror.
11. Mole-Richardson Baby 5K with Full CTB. This luminaire supplies the couch wall with a window pattern and giving the woman sitting a bluish frontal light. The pattern is achieved by projecting the baby 5K through a black silk fabric pattern hanging from a C stand arm. The lens is taken out of the 5K for a harder shadow. All spill is flagged off of the set.
12. Mole-Richardson IK PAR light with 1/4 CTB on a low baby stand. This unit is bouncing into a white card taped to the ceiling for minimal front fill.
13. Mole-Richardson Mighty with 1/4 CTB bouncing into an overhead four × four-foot bead board clamped onto a C stand. The bead board is almost directly above the downstage right foreground chair yielding a top/back light that leaves the camera side of the chair dark.
14. Mole-Richardson Mighty with 1/4 CTB bouncing into an overhead three × three-foot silver-sided bead board. The light from this rig gives the standing woman a back cross key that transitions the *practical motivated* edge light. The quality from this cross key is realized on the camera side of her face only because the image in the mirror merely picks up shapeless quantity.

15 and 16. These are two Source4 575-W 50° ellipsoidal spotlights adding vertical shape and separation to the background in the mirror.

CHAPTER EIGHT

PORTRAIT

Figure 8-1   A portrait can be made with simple lighting and little or no background. Shown here is a very elaborate set with complex lighting created for the purpose of making a narrative portrait of a fictional character. A product of the light painting trend of the late 1980s and early 1990s, the Aaron Jones Turbofilter used a unique design to create various degrees of selective diffusion in an image. *Lonnie Swept the Playroom and Swallowed Up All He Found*, a 1994 image by Daniel Overturf, was lit with five light sources and seven heads. The Turbofilter consists of a large circular disc rotating at 2000 rpm that is positioned in front of the camera lens. The 12-inch Plexiglas disc is divided into thirds, including a clear wedge, another slightly diffused wedge, and finally a wedge that is substantially diffused. Three separate flash units are wired into a central control unit that triggers each connected flash or set of flash units separately, providing each area's flash illumination with a different look. For this image, the clear channel had two flash units and three heads, the slightly diffused channel had two units and three heads, and the diffused channel used one source and a single head. The silhouetted figure at top left is a child who is lying on a rear projection screen. No post-exposure image manipulation was used.

The portrait may be the most popular type of photograph in the world. Because definitions of a portrait usually contain terms such as "a likeness of a person" or "a photograph of a person," the idea of how to complete a portrait is quite open to interpretation.

How many portraits are made each year? Research indicates that an exact figure is impossible to confirm. However, the 2002 U.S. Census Bureau's Economic Census states that 63,880 people were in paid positions at 14,545 photographic portrait studios in the United States alone. Portrait studios maintain their clientele with specific styles and approaches that are often based in well-established lighting arrangements.

Amateur and professional photographers create portraits using a variety of light sources. Certainly, the portraits created at any professional portrait studio are lit, if not entirely, then partially, by artificial light. Editorial photographers and photojournalists also use artificial light to create location portraits for various assignments and projects.

The greatest or, at least, better known names in photography will often choose an approach that ranges from the simple to the most intricate lighting schemes for their photographs of the greatest or, at least, most popular celebrities of our day. Many of the most respected photographers in the world are in that position because they are known for a particular lighting treatment that transforms their celebrity portrait subjects. Although the authors are not in total agreement with the following sentiment, photographer/writer Bill Jay did have a point when he wrote in 1998 that "Famous people are best to photograph because you borrow their fame in order to increase your own."

Photographs of people for personal and professional purposes continue to be a highly popular subject for photographers. Depending on one's definition of a portrait, there will always be a place in the photographic discipline for portraits of family members and friends, of coworkers, for use in advertising, school portraits, and elsewhere. Photography often defies absolute rules or tendencies, but one could wager that there will always be photographic operations whose primary activity and source of income will be portraiture.

Photography has a well understood capability to preserve the facts or create a fantasy that someone desires for their portrait.

Others may prefer to engage a photographer to create a portrait of someone close to them. Portrait "sessions" are even given as gifts. A portrait of someone during a particularly crucial transition in their life, such as graduation, marriage, or while in the military, can become a priceless family heirloom.

What are the objects created from these portrait sittings? Hard copies or prints have traditionally been the primary goal, but the Internet and electronic communications have provided another avenue for the portrait photographer. Often, a photographer will offer portrait packages, and, along with prints of various sizes, there might also be a Web-friendly file option, which can be used to send the image anywhere via the customer's computer. That electronic file might also be sold with an unlimited reproduction option, which can be considered an acknowledgment of home printing popularity.

One adage remains the same throughout all forms of portraiture. The subject, or subjects, will be the key element in the image. Additional visual components may be included that are intended to support or further inform us about the subject. The photographer will weigh a variety of factors to determine the best possible approach for the portrait's composition. Carefully considered lighting is a primary method with which to assign appropriate status to the subject and the background in a portrait.

If the portrait is one of the most popular forms of photography then, consequently, there have been numerous forms of instruction on how to create the portrait. A would-be portrait photographer can go to school or learn while interning at an established studio. Countless guides, instructional DVDs, and workshops also add to the industry of learning how to make a successful portrait.

As previously mentioned, repetition is a key element to the portrait studio. A certain lighting approach may become a tradition or trademark for the photographer. Those specific studio styles are passed down or sometimes even sold as part of the studio's property to the next owner. A portrait style, in certain cases, has initiated long-standing studio franchises. Successful portrait photographers will regularly pass along their particular lighting approaches to student photographers at workshops that explain their specific techniques.

What follows is a discussion of basic lighting techniques that can be used in the creation of a portrait. An overview of this length cannot replace complete guides or extended coursework that cover the portrait and all related photographic elements. The beginning portrait maker should understand, though, that guidelines about portraiture are similar to other formalized, proven techniques. Starting with established techniques should form a basis for experimentation that will lead to a personal approach to the portrait.

Three-Source Portrait Lighting

Many portraits are made with only natural or ambient lighting. Many others are made with a combination of both natural and artificial light. However, for those portrait photographers who choose to control the light for their subjects, there will usually be the combination of three basic elements or sources: main, fill, and **background**. The three components will typically be present in every portrait, although there will be instances where the photographer will choose fewer sources or different forms of the basic three (figs. 8-2 through 8-6). Examining the core role of each source is only the beginning to understanding the potential for an artificially lit portrait. Whichever lighting variation a photographer chooses, within the framework of the basic three sources or an alternative, remains the critical aesthetic measure available to the portrait photographer.

The main light, also called the **key light**, is the essential light source in any lighting arrangement. The name of this light signifies the importance of the position and intensity of the source. Normally the brightest

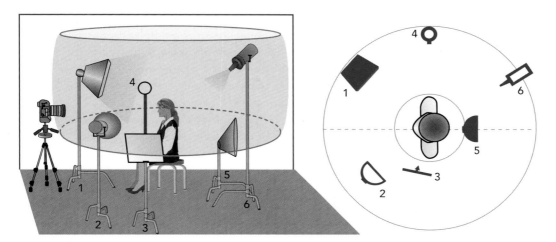

Figure 8-2

The circular pattern indicates the traditional approach to lighting placement for portraiture. The subject is placed into the center of a virtual circle that indicates lighting arrangements that are infinitely adjustable.

Source 1: The key or main light's placement may be located along an arc from one side to the other or placed center/on-axis exactly over or around the lens. This example is a soft box placed to the subject's right side.

Sources 2 & 3: Fill options can be created from a variety of sources. The diagram shows two basic types. Source 2 is a light head with a reflector and source 3 is a fill card. Both options will supplement the key light, but the effectiveness of a fill card is dependent on the key light's intensity and the card angle. Typically only one of the two would be used.

Source 4: One possible placement for a kicker, rim light or other supplementary sources that are placed in support of the front and rear lights.

Source 5: The background light is pointed toward whatever surface is located behind the subject to provide spatial separation.

Source 6: The hair light can be created with a basic reflector fitted with a snoot or a grid that can be shifted around the arc behind the subject.

Photographing on location, working with multiple subjects and other factors may render further adjustment necessary when lighting the portrait. However, many contemporary lighting schemes remain consistent with these well-known placements.

light, the main light should illuminate the subject but not be further evidenced in the background. To accomplish this exclusive treatment, the subject will need to be positioned away from the background to eliminate the main light's shadows. Keeping the subject as far away from the background as practically possible will prevent unwanted shadows caused by the main light.

The type of light chosen for the main light will define the subject as no other source included in the making of the portrait. The main light will indicate the mood or tone that the photographer has chosen for the portrait. Harsh sources will create surface dimension that will emphasize the human character and texture of a face. Conversely, a soft light source will provide a softer and more gentle illumination. Both

Figure 8-3

The key or main light on portrait subject Sarah is created from a 60-inch umbrella and single flash head.

Figure 8-4

An additional flash head and a small soft box create the fill source. The function of the fill source in this illustration is to somewhat open the shadows on the left side of the face. Alone, this light source is very faint. Many photographers will use a fill card or reflector panel instead of a light head.

effects will be altered, as has been established in previous chapters, by the distance to the subject and the angle of the light source. The soft source will wrap around the face and subject only as long as the source is close to and larger than the subject.

For one light to be the main light, there must exist some manner of secondary support for the main or key light. The fill source can be a second light head or another type of additional light source that fills in shadow areas that are caused by the main light. A window, a strong ambient or available light source from the correct direction, a large reflector card, or the previously mentioned additional light head can function as the fill source. Tradition holds that the fill light be adjusted to a level nearly half or less as intense as the main light. The greater the difference between the two sources, the greater the contrast in the final image. There are many formulae for lighting but to create a fill source that dominates the main light would essentially reverse their roles. The supporting fill source is often the least noticed gesture in the making of a portrait. Although the main light creates the character in the portrait, the fill light can subtly reveal a bit of detail where the main light might have caused a dark void.

Put in basic composition terms and to build on a visual topic introduced in Chapter 5, the background light exists to establish the *ground* while the subject is the *figure*. Done by lighting a surface or object that is usually not in focus, the background light is critical to creating an environment for the subject. Why should so much consideration be dedicated to an out-of-focus background area that is of minor concern when compared with the subject? The background light affirms the prominence of the subject in a portrait. The space that is created between the subject and the background puts important compositional emphasis on the subject. The subject is altered and put into the intended context as the photographer dials in the tonality or pattern of the background.

The background light can serve a variety of visual purposes. The background surface and the chosen lighting for that area will often be part of the signature look for a photographer. Depending on the subject and the purpose of the portrait, the main light might be consistently placed, whereas background lighting applications can change. The photographer who may want to deviate from a familiar tradition or style will sometimes look to background variations as points of departure.

Single-Source Light Positions

Three sources may be considered traditional when making a portrait, but many photographers will use but one light for the portrait. The following section will explore the placement variations of a single light. Once understood, the difference in the placement of a single light will aid the photographer in planning for the location of the main light in a multiple-source portrait setup. However, the single-light experience will also show the beginning photographer that certain light placement options should be used with caution because their characteristics may be extreme. Once a photographer discovers a number of starting points, the experimentation in lighting for a subject during a session will often come in fine adjustments. Broad changes in placement are not unthinkable, but usually, such alterations indicate a complete revision from the photographer's previsualized lighting plan.

Single-Source Light: On-Axis

When keeping the light **on-axis**, the photographer has chosen the light that is most similar to the built-in flash found on a snapshot camera. The result of placing the light on the same axis as the lens will provide the flattest light of all. Shadows are diminished, texture is obscured, and the face is lit evenly. A ring light encircles the camera lens and provides the most extreme example of on-axis lighting (fig. 8-7). The effect commonly known as *red eye*, when the iris in the eye does not close, is most pronounced in a ring light image made in low light. Small circles will be reflected in each eye. Depending on the goals of the

Figure 8-5

The background lighting, in most cases, should be solely planned for that purpose and not mix with the main light on the subject. If the background surface is too close, reflected light will bounce into the back of the subject. By ensuring the mutual exclusivity of the main light and the background, the edge between the subject and the background will retain a specific clarity.

Figure 8-6

The background, main, and fill lights are combined to complete a lighting arrangement. Different ratios among all three sources can be applied to create a variety of different contrast levels and effects without moving any of the lights.

Figure 8-7

A ring light is the most literal form of an on-axis light source. Surrounding the lens, the ring light creates unique catchlights in the eyes and specific shadows that edge a subject when placed closely to a background surface. Used by many fashion and editorial photographers, the ring light is often used for close-up photography, too.

Figure 8-8

Placing the flash head to the side of and at the same level as the subject's head creates side lighting.

Figure 8-9

Only the background is lit to create a silhouette.

portrait, these characteristics may or may not be desirable.

Single-Source Light: Side Lighting

Just as dawn and dusk provide the most shadows and dimension in natural light, **side lighting** with artificial light will create variations in depth and texture in a portrait. Side lighting can be performed from any side angle (fig. 8-8). Many photographers will bring the main light to nearly 45° from the center of the face.

Single-Source Light: Backlighting

Backlighting will often be the starting point for a tabletop or still life image to emphasize an object's shape and dimension. When a light is placed at any location behind a portrait subject, the source is considered a backlight. In portraiture, the term backlighting can bring to mind a silhouette (fig. 8-9). However, if a portrait that is exclusively a silhouette is the goal, the light is directed away from the subject. An intentional silhouette is usually the result of lighting the furthermost background surface, with little or no light being reflected onto the silhouetted subject. If a photographer directs the backlight toward the subject, this will create effects beyond a simple silhouette. Two versions of lights that originate from the background that are

meant to add light to the subject are called hair light and rim light. The two lights are shown in figures 8-14 and 8-15, respectively. Note that backlighting is an entirely different lighting treatment apart from the background light. Backlighting is directed *at* the subject and background lighting affects the supporting area beyond the subject.

Portrait Lighting with Multiple Sources, from Multiple Directions

The starting points described so far allow for infinite adjustments to refine the portrait. Lights can be rotated to change the emphasis of each source and to change the overall appearance of the subject. Because of the limitless possibilities, an experienced photographer will return to the aforementioned starting points to begin each new portrait. The following discussion will primarily review the general adjustment parameters available to the photographer.

Adjusting the Height of the Main Light

The subject and the type of light used will inform how high and how far to one side the main light is placed. The main light is often placed off-axis, right or left, and slightly higher than level with the subject.

Too low or level, and the light will cause an odd nose shadow on one cheek. Move the light too high, and the eyes will often be lost into detail-less shadows.

Another consideration when adjusting the height of the main light, or any light in the portrait, can be the possibility of eyeglasses on a subject. The light's reflection can be eliminated, in certain cases, by elevating the source. If using a flash unit's model light or tungsten lighting, it is easy to see whether this remedy has been successful. If the eyeglasses have lenses that are quite round or large, the size of the light source may also need to be considered. A large rectangular soft box, placed above, rotated so that the long dimensions are horizontal, may be the best option to remove the reflection. Some photographers employ a horizontal strip or narrow box for this purpose. Conversely, the reflection of a round umbrella can prove difficult to remove because of its shape and size, especially with certain large-diameter models.

Adjusting the Fill Light Location
As described previously, a photographer will usually use another light head or a fill card

Figure 8-10
A main light without a reflector card.

Figure 8-11
A main light with a white reflector card for fill.

Figure 8-12
A main light with a gold reflector card for fill.

Figure 8-13
A main light with a mirror for fill.

that reflects light to provide a fill source. The second source is employed to open the shadows that are too deep and lacking information. The main light is placed slightly "up" and to one side or the other, whereas the fill can be located in a variety of angles. Some photographers will place the fill light on-axis with the lens as a counterpoint to the angled main light. Others will use a head with a soft source that may be similar to, but less intense than, the main light.

Another option for providing a fill source is a card placed close to the subject and opposite from the main light. Reflector cards will vary in size, sometimes being nearly twice the size of the subject. Large reflectors are generally referred to as panels. Moving a reflector card or panel closer or further from the subject will control the amount of fill and the contrast of the portrait lighting. Two other reflector card/fill surface attributes to consider are reflectance and color. A soft white surface will provide less fill intensity than a bright silver surface. Mirrors will provide yet another fill character. When photographing in color, the use of a gold or a gold/white-striped surface will warm the subject's skin tone (figs. 8-10 through 8-13).

Accent Lights: Hair Light, Rim Light, and Kickers

There are many methods that have been used to describe the additional lights used in portraiture. For our discussion, we will group the three most traditional lights under the heading of **accent lights**.

Accent lights are positioned at different angles from the rear and to the side. The **hair light**, used to light a top portion of the subject's head, provides an accent and lit edge on the top of the subject (fig. 8-14). A **kicker** source, sometimes used from the rear at one side, provides an accent from considerably lower than the hair light. **Rim lighting** can be best described as similar to a hair light but larger in application and located directly behind the subject. The rim light provides definition to the entire rear edge of the subject. How best to apply these sources, which to exclude or include,

and their intensity represent questions that are answered only by attending to the individual needs of the subject.

The hair light is the most common of accent lights. The hair light is another method to provide separation between the subject and the background. A specifically aimed source, the hair light is usually placed above, behind, and to one side of the subject. Selecting the position or side for the hair light is often determined by which side of the subject needs greater spatial separation from the background.

The color and texture of the hair will determine the exact placement of the light. The decision to photograph a dark-haired subject on a dark background generally mandates the use of a hair light for separation. Various hairstyles or types will react differently to the hair light. Light-colored, frizzy hair requires less intensity than a darker, thicker head of hair. Again, the placement is specific, so a variable power head best accomplishes the adjustment. Simply moving the light to increase or diminish intensity could easily divert the hair light from the scope of the original spot and change the lighting gesture entirely.

The hair light is intended to produce a slight touch of light on the rear of the head. If the hair light is misdirected into a part of the face such as the nose or onto a large portion of the ear, the intended subtle effect will become a far too obvious and usually inappropriate highlight. If the hair light misses or barely touches the subject, the effect will be unnoticed and wasted. The electronic flash hair light, as with many of the specifically aimed lights that serve to augment the main light, benefit from the use of a model light to guide precise placement. The hair light is often fitted with a grid or a snoot, although some photographers will use a combination of the two. The narrow beam created from these sources will necessitate a fairly stationary subject. If the subject moves even slightly, the main light will probably still light the subject while the hair light might miss the subject altogether.

Often the largest of the accent lights, rim lighting defines the back edges of the entire subject by pointing the light source at the back of the subject (fig. 8-15). The light source is pointed nearly at the camera, with the subject in between, and produces a fully lit back edge.

A kicker light provides a touch of light on the side of the subject (fig. 8-16). A kicker source is typically a small, bright spot source that defines the side of the subject.

Modifying the Light Source for Portraiture

The large range of light modifiers is described in Chapter 7. The use of modifiers in portraiture, though, merits specific discussion. Photographers will use a range of modifiers on their main lights, from soft to hard, to obtain the intended portrait. Modifiers of varying sizes can also be used for fill lights and other purposes.

Soft Sources for Portraiture: Umbrella and Soft Box

The umbrella and soft box are modifiers used by photographers who have chosen soft lighting for their subjects. A soft source is the choice for many portraits, but there is usually a preference between the two. Portrait photographers may also use a hybrid of the two soft lighting types. Photographers who prefer umbrellas can choose to use the light reflected from within the umbrella or use the transparent type that allows the light to pass through and diffuse. Known also as shoot-through umbrellas, this type of light is a combination of the umbrella shape and the diffused light quality of the soft box. A round-shaped soft box combines the essential shape of the umbrella with the lighting quality and control of a soft box.

Usually referred to as **catchlights**, these small reflections in the eyes are the most telling method to discern the photographer's choice of a light source's modifier. In fact, photographers and their subjects may discuss catchlights as a determining character in a planned portrait. To that end,

Figure 8-14

The hair light is a minimal yet critical gesture that separates the hair from the background. This is particularly crucial when photographing a dark-haired subject against a dark background.

Figure 8-15

The rim light creates a bright backlight that edges the subject entirely.

Figure 8-16

A flash head with a snoot creates a kicker or small, spot accent light.

Figure 8-17

A flash head outfitted with an umbrella creates rounded catchlights. Some photographers prefer the umbrella's catchlights because they are round, following the natural shape of the eye.

Figure 8-18

A flash head with a soft box produces catchlights with harder, squarer edges.

Figure 8-19

A three- × four-foot soft box positioned two feet away. The light is soft and wraps around the face.

Figure 8-20

A three × four-foot soft box positioned twelve feet away, with the flash power increased for an equivalent exposure. Positioning the light this far away causes stronger shadows and contrast.

and with the availability of possible digital manipulation, catchlights can be altered and adjusted to taste after the portrait is made. The umbrella, available in many sizes and surfaces, provides catchlights that are rounded (fig. 8-17). The soft box creates reflections with square-edged shapes because the soft box is typically either square or rectangular shaped (fig. 8-18).

A general guideline to understanding a soft source is simple and helpful. The longest dimension of a soft box or the diameter of an umbrella is also the maximum distance between the subject and the source to maintain a soft affect. For example, when a three × four-foot soft box is placed twelve feet away from the subject, the soft box becomes a large directional source. The soft box becomes a directional because the proximity has exceeded the longest dimension (figs. 8-19 and 8-20).

Figure 8-21

The view from above a portrait set. Note that the single flash head attached to the pipe grid above the set creates the background light. Also shown is a large reflector panel that, once positioned, will function as a fill card. Keeping the main light on a boom allows the photographer to precisely position the light while keeping the studio free of obstacles on the floor.

Figure 8-22

A bridal photograph is one category that has long been photographed with high-key lighting. A white dress on a white background has been seen in wedding portfolios for generations. Virtually shadowless lighting in an infinity space is an example of a high-key portrait that can also be employed when the traditional white attire is not selected for a wedding. This photograph was begun with two large soft boxes at the front and two flash heads in the rear with open 20-inch reflectors. A third, medium-sized soft box was added at the front, placed at floor level, and pointed up at the subjects to complete the overall even illumination.

Hard Sources for Portraiture: Grid, Fresnel, and Projector

Using a grid inserted into a reflector for the main light, for example, will function as a hard main light source. The hard light source shows detail in the face that promotes what is often thought of as character and which some may consider unflattering. Many portrait subjects might not prefer this type of examination, but photographers will employ this unforgiving light source to create a portrait that hides very little.

High-Key Portraiture

High-key lighting has a long-standing tradition in portraiture. The bridal portrait, the high school portrait, and others have long employed the technique of using bright tonality and very few shadows. The bright background must be lit separately, and the light on the subject is also bright and without shadows. Light-colored clothing and a white background is the norm, but the high-key lighting approach can be applied to any subject with equally stark results (fig. 8-22).

Figure 8-23

A 20° grid spot for the main light serves to make a somewhat harshly lit low-key portrait. Inverting the methods used in creating the high-key image makes a low-key portrait. Placing areas in deep shadow helps to makes prominent the features that are revealed through selective lighting. The flash head was positioned above the subject because of his eyeglasses. Fine-tuning the flash head position with a model light is important to the balance between illuminating the eyes and avoiding glare in the eyeglass lenses.

Low-Key Portraiture

Many versions of low-key lighting may be used for a range of portraits. Compared to the uniform consistency of high-key lighting, the dark tones of a low-key photograph can be varied to allow strategic highlights. The direction of the lights can be adjusted to the portions of the face and/or other parts of the figure to be included in the portrait. By concealing selected elements in deep shadow, the parts lit with specific sources are effectively floating pools of detail in a dark abyss. Depending on the degree of concealment desired, the photographer can choose to use small accent lights to add slight, often backlit edges of detail that will help convey the subject's three dimensions.

The low-key portrait is a favorite among those new to studio lighting, for good reason. The direct light requires little balancing with other sources because there is often only a single light source. The small, discreetly lit pocket or pockets of light provide an instant dramatic affect on the subject. After the technique of low-key lighting is mastered, the infinite black background has aesthetic limits (fig. 8-23). Other than moving the subject around the dark frame, the low-key approach provides very few challenges to the photographer who is attempting to evidence a greater understanding of the more subtle possibilities of tonality and color in lighting. However, the low-key portrait remains a consistently popular lighting technique, perhaps because of its inverse relationship to the equally common high-key approach.

Two Lights and Alternating Tonality

A very effective portrait can be made against a blank wall with only two light sources and an optional fill card (fig. 8-24). As simple as the arrangement may be, there is a key ingredient that may be the most difficult to obtain, especially when on location. Critical to this portrait lighting technique will be the space between the subject and the background surface. There must be enough room

Figure 8-24

The foreground light, coming from the left side of the image, creates light that falls off to darker tones on the subject's left cheek. The background light, coming from the right side of the image, provides light that goes from brighter to darker in the opposite direction. This alternating tonality, when sandwiched upon each other, forms a simple and effective portrait.

provided to isolate both light sources and their intended targets. If the space is ample, the lighting for this portrait can be placed effectively in minimal time (fig. 8-25).

The two lights are pointed into the set in two different directions. One source is on the subject, and the other is pointed at the background. After the subject light has been adjusted, and it is understood where the subject will be located in the frame, the second or background light can be positioned.

The background light is aimed across the surface so that the light begins to fall off, and the surface gradually becomes darker. The transitional division between the brighter area, closest to the light source, and the dark or furthest area, is kept discreetly behind the subject.

The subject is lit with a source that is complimentary to the subject's face. This can be accomplished with any type of

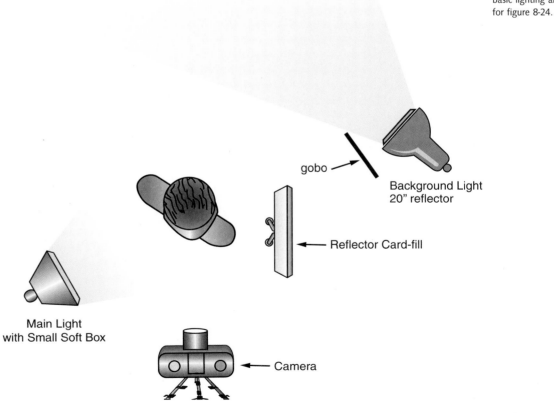

Background surface

Figure 8-25

The diagram describes the basic lighting arrangement for figure 8-24.

gobo

Background Light
20" reflector

Reflector Card-fill

Main Light
with Small Soft Box

Camera

modifier, from a more typical soft source such as an umbrella to a harsh grid spot. The source selected to light the subject cannot, however, cast a shadow or affect the background surface whatsoever.

In figure 8-24, the subject's body is turned to the main light, placed on his right. The main light is a flash head with a small soft box. The background light is pointed across the studio wall from the subject's left. The background light is a flash head with a 20-inch reflector. A 36-inch gobo is placed at one edge of the reflector to help create the transition between the light and dark background.

As one reads the photograph, scanning laterally, the tones alternate. The results read left to right as follows: dark wall, light side of the face, darker side of the face, and finally lighter wall. The lighter side of the face is set off against a background of dark wall, and the darker side of the face is in front of a lighter wall tone. The combination of tones and layered information creates depth in the space and dimension in the subject.

In this example, a reflector panel was placed on the subject's left side to maintain a modicum of detail on the left side of the face. If this approach is attempted while on location, the fill may come from a window or a bright wall just out of camera range.

Location Portraiture

To summarize the challenges of making portraits on location would be nearly impossible. Most photographers have dozens of anecdotes that detail one extreme set of circumstances after another. No two situations will have identical conditions. However, that is precisely why many portraits are made on location. Because the photographer may have new challenges in each situation, the possibility for a fresh image also exists. The studio has the security of absolute control and repeatability. The location photographer can rely on a fresh set

Figure 8-26

Deckhands on The Orleanian, by Daniel Overturf. Three barge workers were photographed in the middle of the night using a single 400-W battery-powered flash source. The camera was handheld, and the shutter speed was 1/4 s. This combination of daylight film, a relatively slow shutter speed, and daylight-balanced flash separated the subjects from the tungsten-lit surrounding boat deck. As described in the preceding chapter, the shutter speed allows the ambient light to register, and the flash intensity determined the aperture.

of circumstances to accent each situation's potential.

Some photographers attempt to recreate the control on location that they enjoy in their studios. Most assistants employed by studio photographers who only occasionally go on location will describe their packing procedure quite simply. The answer to whether or not certain gear should be packed is usually met positively. Better to have more than may be needed than to assume something may not be necessary. As many photographers will agree, chancing the latter will usually lead to a time-consuming trip back to the studio or to a store. Even with the constraints of air travel and within practical reason, packing or shipping ahead more equipment than what may be apparent at the point of initial planning is wisest. Many professional photographers who travel regularly will opt for yet another efficient method. They may engage a rental studio and/or a rental equipment service to facilitate an out-of-town project. The photographer may or may not even bring their own camera or even their regular assistant, depending on the rental services available.

On the other hand, for a variety of possible reasons, some photographers will take only minimal equipment and travel without an assistant to a location. Depending on the situation, the more "minimalist" photographer will make due with what little has been brought and/or creatively engineer what can be found on location. If a single lighting source has been transported, reflector surfaces can be fashioned to provide fill. Converting a wide range of transparent materials can create *diffusion* modifiers.

Flags or gobos can be made from a variety of materials or even clothing. The spartan photographer is often the most inventive when on location.

The photographer who is making a portrait in color often makes use of the spatial and visual separation that can be obtained from using ambient light as a background. Using a daylight-balanced flash and daylight-balanced capture media will provide a neutral rendition of a subject's skin tones. Meanwhile, in certain locations, the background may provide the warmth of tungsten ambient lights, the odd coloration of contemporary industrial vapor lights, the toxic green of certain fluorescent fixtures, or even the familiar tonality of a deeply colorful sunset.

Location portraiture is usually best described through examples and their related anecdotes. Figure 8-26 provides one example, and there are others included in this text. Every situation has different requirements, and every photographer will have an individual solution to the challenges.

Summary

The previously described portrait techniques and approaches can serve to form the basis of a lighting plan for a given portrait. However, superior portraiture demands more than knowing basic lighting technique. Learning how to translate the key elements of a sitter's personality into a photograph will require an interpersonal appreciation and understanding of the subject. Camera controls and lighting will only serve to underscore that interpretation in a successful portrait.

Keith Cotton

Keith Cotton, from Cobden, Illinois, has a studio that specializes in all forms of the portrait. Demand for Cotton's particular portrait approach has led to clients from Chicago to Colorado. He was enlisted by a relief organization to make photographs in New York after September 11. Cotton also works with a number of commercial clients, from casinos to healthcare to vineyards (www.keithcotton.com).

Title: *Arnold Newman, Cobden, Illinois, 2004*

In 2004, I met the environmental portrait photographer, Arnold Newman. At that time, my work had been informed and influenced by Newman more than any other photographer. After we had this session, that influence would never be diminished.

I was able to arrange for a portrait session, through a series of unusual circumstances, in my small, southern Illinois studio. Knowing there was one degree of separation between me and many influential world leaders, artists, musicians, and writers over the past five decades was quite exhilarating.

I wasn't sure how many rolls of film and how much time Mr. Newman would kindly allow me, so I had the technical details and general concept of composition planned beforehand. His personality and comfort level in front of the camera was the key to a perfectly efficient and productive 30-minute session. His genuine expression and connection with the process truly provided the moment I believe all portrait photographers seek with the subject. In this case, the "subject" happened to be the *reason* I gravitated toward people photography in the first place. As I concluded the shoot, I only hoped that I had held up my end of the encounter. I feel that the resulting image does indeed reflect my continued respect for the late Mr. Newman.

Figure 8-27

Arnold Newman, Cobden, Illinois, 2004. Courtesy of Keith Cotton.

My concept for the portrait started with a respectful nod to great portraits created by Mr. Newman. Although most photographers will recognize the influence, I did hope to specifically reference the trademark compositions of Newman's Henry Miller (1976), Igor Stravinsky (1946), and Pablo Picasso (1954).

Film:	Ilford FP4 @ ISO 50
Camera:	Hasselblad 500C/M, 120-mm macro with 1.0 Proxar
Exposure:	f11 @ 125th
Presentation note:	Both frames were scanned and combined as a diptych

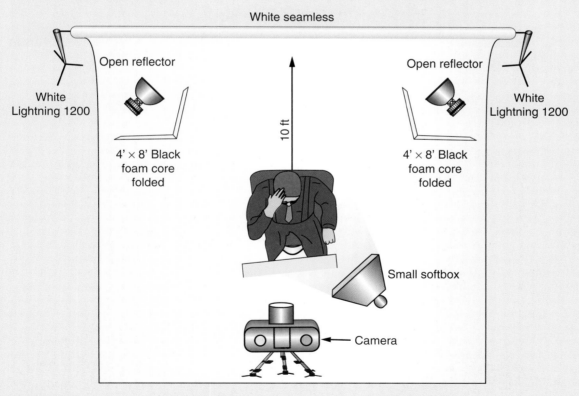

Figure 8-28

Lighting diagram for *Arnold Newman, Cobden, Illinois, 2004.*

Figure 8-29

Keith Cotton (left, with his son, Jeremy, driving on the eve of Jeremy's 16th birthday). Courtesy of Keith Cotton.

Pramoonchai Nopsuwanvong

Pramoonchai Nopsuwanvong, born in Buriram and now living in Bangkok, Thailand, is a freelance documentary and fashion/editorial photographer. Known to his friends as "Mod", he received his education in Thailand and the United States, worked as a commercial photography studio assistant in Chicago, and then returned to Thailand to pursue his career. His latest photographic project is a documentary examination of Thai folk culture festivals for the Thai Khadi Research Institute at Thammasat University in Bangkok (www.modder-photography.com).

Title: Amy, Chicago, 2003

Amy was lit with a single flash head, outfitted with a 60-inch umbrella that was powered by a 2400-W power pack. Although I was using 4x5 film, I decided to use the 8×10 camera to employ the longer bellows and a 300-mm lens for this close-up image. I was an assistant at the time when I made this photograph. Consequently, my

Figure 8-30

Amy, Chicago, 2003. Courtesy of Pramoonchai Nopsuwanvong.

Figure 8-31

Lighting diagram for *Amy, Chicago, 2003.*

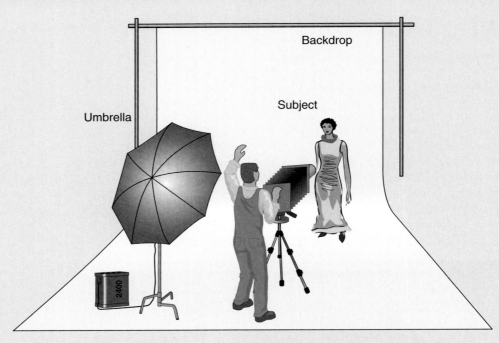

film budget was at the 4×5 "level," rather than the 8×10.

The airy, brown background was rendered soft and creamy because of the wider aperture. Amy wore clothing that was similar in color to the background tone. I placed her close to the background to create a specific shadow. I angled the single head to create enough shadow to present separation between Amy and the background.

My goal with the resulting smoothness of the background was to envelope Amy's face. Her makeup was designed to blend with the color scheme as well.

Film: Polaroid Type 59
Camera: Cambo 8×10 camera, fitted with a
             4×5 reducing back
Lens: 300-mm Rodenstock Apo-Symmar lens

Figure 8-32

Pramoonchai Nopsuwanvong. Courtesy of Pramoonchai Nopsuwanvong.

III GRIP GLOSSARY HANDBOOK

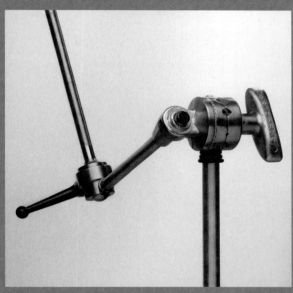

A Matthews Broken Arm is attached to a C stand. The Broken Arm is a unique member of the Matthews Gobo and Hollywood family of extension arms.

A Grip Glossary

Introduction

Years ago, immediately after graduation with a photography degree, one of author Overturf's former students went to work in Chicago. Pramoonchai Nopsuwanvong, a native of Thailand, found English challenging enough without the jargon associated with grip equipment and the common nicknames used for the gear. Now a professional photographer in his home country, Nopsuwanvong recalls receiving a photocopied *Grip Glossary* at Helix Camera and Video. He would consult the guide for understanding the myriad equipment names that he encountered during his first months in the field.

Mr. Clay Bannister, Manager of Helix Camera Rental and Repair, compiled the *Glossary* for educational reasons. In 2007, the authors contacted Mr. Bannister and sought permission to publish *A Grip Glossary* in this text. He was a tad surprised at our request, but he quickly agreed to share this resource nonetheless. We learned that countless new assistants, sales professionals, and photographers still benefit from the *Grip Glossary*.

Mr. Bannister explains:

"Professor Overturf, I have no objection to your use of the Glossary in a textbook."

"The Glossary was originally compiled in the mid 1980s when I worked in Los Angeles. Its purpose was to educate still photographers about the incredible range of grip equipment available in the Los Angeles area."

"A Bogen sales representative asked for and received my permission to distribute copies of the Glossary to the Bogen sales force. The Glossary became a way of educating the Bogen people about selling the Manfrotto/Bogen Avenger grip equipment line. Until your e-mail, I had no idea my memo's distribution went beyond my employees and Bogen."

"I haven't actively updated the Glossary in many years. The initial compilation and distribution of the glossary from Photographic Rental Service in Los Angeles seemed to coincide with the introduction of a rash of quirky, semi-useful pieces of grip equipment. The new grip all came with overly cute names, i.e. 'pigeon plate,' 'poultry bracket,' and 'quaker clamp.' I decided to wait until the furor subsided. It didn't."

"Hope this helps."

Clay Bannister, Manager
Helix Camera Rental and Repair

CHAPTER NINE

BANNISTER'S GUIDE

Name:	The name we would call it if we had to order it from a manufacturer or another grip house.
a.k.a.:	Also known as—Current jargon may include different manufacturer's names for essentially the same product.
i.k.a.:	Incorrectly known as—Current terms that are ambiguous or stem from misconceptions about the use of the equipment.
Prompt:	Questions one can ask a client to quickly determine what equipment is needed.
Definition:	A short definition of the term as used in still photography.
Use:	Special uses of the equipment not covered by the main definition. This glossary will limit itself to grip equipment wherever possible. Lighting equipment to follow next semester, but first a few general definitions to establish some size relationships.

BABY:

a.k.a.:	407 (Mole-Richardson model #), baby keg, 1K Fresnel (freh'nel), baby spot, keg, keg light.
i.k.a.:	1K…1000 of anything, Klieg… a theatrical type spot.
Prompt:	Does it have a lens?
Definition:	A lensed spotlight with a 6″ Fresnel type condenser lens. Baby spotlights were originally lamped at 500-750 Watts. The 1K designation wasn't possible until seven or eight years ago, when the EGT lamp was developed. The spotlight is "keg" shape and weighs 8-10 pounds or more with its cable coiled up and hung from the yoke.
Use:	The term *"baby"* applies to any piece of grip or support equipment strong enough (M.P. light enough) to keep an 8-10-pound spotlight from falling on its face. The standard baby stand mount (male) or receiver (OK-OK) is 5/8 inches. For years, American manufacturers hung onto a system of stand mounts that progressed in 1/8 inches and 1/4-inch increments from 3/8 to one inch. An attempt at standardization with metric photographic sizing resulted in the 5/8-inch (16-mm) mount. Americans still insist on a stand mount twice as long as the European mount, I have no idea why.

JUNIOR:

a.k.a.:	412 (Mole-Richardson model #), junior keg, 2K spot.
Prompt:	Does it have a lens? How big?
Definition:	A lensed spotlight with a 10-inch Fresnel-type condenser lens.
	The junior usually lamps at 1500–2000 W at 3200 K. A 10-inch Fresnel spotlight usually weighs 22–30 pounds.
Use:	The term *junior* applies to grip or support equipment in the 25-pound range. Because of the weight factor, there is far less variety of grip equipment available in the junior size. The relative wattages of baby and junior spotlights mean that baby spots tend to be used in close on stand mounts. Junior spots can achieve the same light levels at greater distances and are frequently hung above a set.
	NOTE: Never store a junior stand with the lockdown screw tightened all the way in. It is hard to support a 25-pound light fixture at arm's length and loosen a lockdown screw at the same time!
	There are senior stands, but these have the basic 1-1/8-inch junior mount with more bracing for the heavier senior (50+ pounds), tener (100+ pounds), or the brute (200+ pounds). The development of quartz-halogen technology has been followed by an increase in the permissible wattages used in various sized spotlights. The normal associations of wattage and lens size have broken down to produce such variations as baby-baby, baby-junior, baby tener, and would you believe "tweenie," but the baby and junior designations still apply because of the reduced weight.

BABY PLATE:

a.k.a.:	Floor plate, floor mount, baby nail-on, and wall plate.
i.k.a.:	Floor stand. All stands sit on the floor. What they do on their own time is their business.
Prompt:	How tall?
Definition:	A flat steel plate with a baby stand mount welded to it. The plate has holes drilled in it so that it can be nailed to wood floors or set walls. Baby plates are available in 3″, 6″, and 12-inch-long mounts. A 12-inch-long right angle mount is available, and Lowell has a short right angle version called a tape-up bracket.
Use:	Still photographers use baby plates to mount lights low on the floor or on a table. A 3/8 × 16-inch machine bolt stuck through a piece of plywood can serve as a Balcar baby plate.

BUTTERFLY:

a.k.a.:	None
i.k.a.:	None yet.
Prompt:	What size: 4 × 4, 4 × 5, 5 × 5, 5 × 6, 6 × 6 feet (depending on what we stock)?
Definition:	A lightweight collapsible frame (sometimes tubular) designed to support a variety of light-control materials. A butterfly's only restriction is that it be supported by one stand. A lightweight material such as silk or china

silk can be supported at the end of a 40-inch extension arm. Heavier materials should be clamped directly into the 4-1/2″ clamp head at the top of a combo roller stand.

Use:	Used to control light quality hitting a camera frame area approximately half its size, i.e., 3 × 3 feet.

CLIPBOARD:

a.k.a.:	None
i.k.a.:	None
Prompt:	Clipboards should be suggested when clients complain of "leaky" barn doors and burning black cards.
Definition:	A clipboard is usually a rectangular piece of wood with a large ACCO-type paper clamp on one end. Clipboards come in three sizes (all too small to hold paper). Their main use is as front or rear extensions to barn doors to sharpen the "cut" of the barn door edge. They are also useful as blinders to prevent stray light from escaping past accessory holders and rear barn door edges.
Use:	Four-leaf barn doors are most frequently used to adjacent leaves at a time, i.e., to block light from one wall and the ceiling in a room set. Clipboards can be used to cover or blind the intersecting space between barn door edges.

CHINA SILK:

a.k.a.:	Crowder hanger
i.k.a.:	None
Prompt:	None
Definition:	A crowder in an L-shaped piece of sheet metal with a baby mount welded to the long part of the "L". A crowder may be nailed to a 2x4-inch or it may have a locking knob to allow temporary attachment to a board.
Use:	Crowders are used to crowd several light units onto a temporary support, such as a 2 × 4-inch or a 2 × 6-inch. The board itself may be held between two roller stands.

CUCALORIS:

a.k.a.:	Cookie or Cuke
i.k.a.:	One really has to see the waving arms of someone who wants a cucaloris but doesn't know what to call it to understand i.k.a.
Definition:	A panel of indistinct shapes and patterns placed between a hard light source and plain background to break the light pattern into interesting shadows. Many different types are in use. The wooden cookie is opaque with open areas. Lowell makes a clear plastic sheet with black blobs painted onto it. A cello cookie may be wire or cloth mesh with open areas. The cello cookie is used for more subtle patterns.
Use:	Like the barn doors or snoots, the closer the cookie is to the light source, the less distinct the pattern.

CUTTER:

a.k.a.:	None
i.k.a.:	Long cutter, long flag
Prompt:	What are you doing with it?
Definition:	A cutter is an opaque light-blocking device like a flag. Its dimensions are normally on a ratio of 1:3. Cutters are used closer to the subject than flags to produce a harder edge. Although a flag is normally used to block light from reaching a subject, a cutter is used to define the edge of a light.
Use:	For some strange reason, large square flags are also known as cutters, possibly because 48 inches square are rarely feathered in a light pattern.

COLOR CODING:

Purpose:	To allow identification of light-control materials by color. When large numbers and different varieties of light controls are stored together, coding permits quick separation of types. Coding is done by painting the metal support handles or by sewing colored borders on the frames. Some manufactures have different coding for fabric and wire screen light-control materials. Fabric coding is as follows:

Silk-gold
Single net-white
Double net-red
Triple net-royal blue
Lavender-light blue (dilly-dilly)

DICHROIC (See FILTER)

DIPSTICK:

a.k.a.:	Pattern holder
i.k.a.:	None
Prompt:	None
Definition:	A dipstick or pattern holder is a paddle-shaped piece of metal with a heat-insulating handle on one end and a 2.-1/2 inch circular hole in the other. The dipstick is designed to fit into the projection gate of a 6-inch ellipsoidal (read Profoto Zoom) spotlight and hold patterns. The patterns themselves are available in hundreds of designs and cut out of stainless steel. Most dipsticks allow rotation of the pattern so that the projected images can be positioned.

DOT:

a.k.a.:	Dots larger than 8 inches in diameter are sometimes known as targets.
i.k.a.:	Little round flags
Prompt:	How big is your light?
Definition:	A dot is a small circular light-control device generally used to alter or modify a problem within a light pattern. Dots come in the same variety

of materials as flags and nets. Dots have long 1/4 inch diameter handles and can be gripped in gobo heads, grip heads, or flex arms.

Use: The small size of dots and targets make them ideal for use in small-product photography where small accent lights are commonly used.

EGG CRATE:

a.k.a.: None
i.k.a.: None
Prompt: None
Definition: For still photographic purposes, an egg crate is essentially a large grid spot make of black anodized metal and is used to control flare in large aperture soft light sources such as soft lights, sky pans, cone lights, etc. The openings in an egg crate are square, deep (1-1/2–3 inches), and usually large enough to accommodate a hen's egg.

FINGER:

a.k.a.: I shudder to think!
i.k.a.: None
Prompt: You mean a little tiny cutter?
Definition: A finger is the rectangular equivalent of a dot. Fingers are sized either 2 × 12 or 4 × 14 inches.

FLAG:

a.k.a.: Gobo, block, solid.
i.k.a.: Black scrim
Prompt: None.
Definition: Flags are opaque light-control devices used to keep light from reaching the camera, the photographer, or the subject. Flags can be used to *feather* the edge of a light beam. Flags are 50% longer than they are wide, i.e., 12 × 18, 18 × 24, and 24 × 36 inches. Flags are equipped with a 3/8-inch steel handle and are held in a gobo or grip heads.

Use: The purpose of the basic black flag is to block light from hitting the subject. Still photographers, because of their work habits and subject matter, tend to use flags to protect their camera and themselves from flare. When camera flare becomes a problem, a special small flag called a French flag does a better job. Because the black cloth material normally used on flag is not opaque enough to properly shield a camera lens, the flag on a French flag is generally heavy black plastic. The French flag is not for use with lights. The plastic blocking material melts quickly when exposed to hot or flash lighting. French flags are sold or rented complete with blocking panel and ball-and-socket arm. A more versatile version of the French flag is the flex flag system.

FLEX ARM:

a.k.a.: French arm, articulating arm
i.k.a.: Goose neck
Prompt: What do you want to hold up with it?

Definition: A longer, heavy-duty version of the French arm, the flex arm has lockable ball-and-socket joints and ends in a 2-inch spring clamp or snap-in super clamp mount. The heavier arm is used to support flex flags, flex silks, and flex scrims. Because of its length (36 inches), the flex arm is designed to be too light to support cameras and should never be recommended for that purpose. The 1/4-inch female receiver can be slotted to take a French flag or show card.

DICHROIC FILTER:

a.k.a.:   Dich (Dike)
i.k.a.:   None
Prompt: Requests for color correction filters are usually preceded by the question, "How do you correct tungsten to daylight?" The first prompt is, "Tungsten what to daylight what?" When it is established that a client wants to convert tungsten light to daylight film, the next piece of necessary information is whether the filter medium should be glass or gel. If the client's choice is glass, one needs to know whether the customer wants blue glass or dichroic glass. Mole-Richardson still makes and sells a blue glass color correction filter called a Molocolor filter.

Definition: A glass daylight conversion filter used to convert the 3200 K color temperature of quartz-halogen lighting to "daylight." Dichs are a long-lasting type of filtration made by depositing a thin film of metal on Pyrex glass in a vacuum. The metallic film is so thin that it reflects certain wavelengths of light while transmitting others. This creates a dichroic (two-color) effect, usually gold on one side and blue on the other. Dichs also have their disadvantages. Fingerprints cause the dichroic coating to boil away, which changes the filter's effect. Light hitting the filter at an acute angle will not be affected and create an orange fringe around the corrected light pattern. This is solved by using diched lights in banks to weigh overlapping patterns or by resorting to expensive curved glass dichroics that keep the light angle close to perpendicular to the glass filter surface.

Use: Dichroic filters are designed only for use as fill for ambient sunlight. They do not fully correct tungsten illumination to daylight, falling short by about 500–800 K. The use of banked lights can be useful in filling daylight because the filter has an exposure factor of 1.5 f-stops. The light quality of this multiple highlight bank is not normally suitable for still photography.

FURNITURE CLAMP:

a.k.a.:   Bar Clamp, space clamp
i.k.a.:   None
Prompt: Furniture clamps can span relatively large distanced (36 inches), but the clamping pads are small (less than one square inch). One needs to know the approximate weight of the light fixture and the object clamped to it.

Definition: This is a common garden-variety carpenter's clamp with an adapter allowing baby-sized lighting gear to be attached to the end of the bar. The baby mount on the end of the Lowell space clamp can be attached anywhere on the bar. Clamps are available in 6-, 12-, 18-, 24-, and 36-inch lengths. Furniture clamps have one fixed jaw and one sliding jaw, which are locked by sliding the jaw up to the clamping surface and screwing it tight.

GAG:

a.k.a.:   Double grip head, double knuckle.

i.k.a.:   Swivel, gag mount

Prompt: It is easier to haul one out and show it to a client than it is to describe one. Visually, a gag is reminiscent of the round wooden plugs used to gag prisoners way back when.

Definition: A gag is two sets of grip head-clamping discs locked by a common spin handle. Gags are used in special frame construction and light mounts. A gag mount is generally a piece of slotted metal with a light mount or special clamp mounted to it. The slotted metal piece is inserted between the clamping discs of the gag.

DOUBLE GAG:

a.k.a.:   Lollipop

i.k.a.:   None

Definition: Two sets of grip head clamping discs independently locked to either side of a common bas. The base is a 2-inch-round disc with a 6-inch long shaft welded to it. The shaft allows double gags to be mounted in double gags as infinitum.

Use: Double gags are used in the construction of special supports and bracing for set rigging.

GOBO:

a.k.a.:   Block, flag, solid

i.k.a.:   Scrim, black screen

Prompt: How big?

Definition   The definition of the word *gobo* is probably lost forever, but most people believe the term started as *go-between*. A gobo (or flag or block) is used between a light source and a subject to block the light path and shade the subject.

GRIP HEAD:

a.k.a.:   Knuckle

i.k.a.:   Swivel, grip clamp

Prompt: Do you want a head for a C stand?

Definition: The 2-1/2-inch grip head mounts on any baby-sized stand mount including C (century) stands and grips other accessories with two 2-1/2-inch clamping discs. Grip head discs are slotted to accept 5/8-, 1/2-, 3/8-, and 1/4-inch-diameter accessories. The paddle-shaped fixed mount has an open-ended hollow mounting receiver with an off-center lockdown screw to lock on either short or long 5/8-inch stand mounts. The open end also facilitates sliding the grip head along the 40-inch shaft of a gobo arm.

Use: The grip head has two locking knobs, a small stand lockdown knob like those used to lock stand risers, and a large spin handle used to tighten the clamping discs. When using a grip head to clamp a light-control device projecting into the set, it is common practice to keep small handles to the operator's left and the large handles to the right. This places any weight clamped to the head in a clockwise orientation, which is self-tightening.

4-1/2-INCH GRIP HEAD:

a.k.a.:	Clamp head
i.k.a.:	None
Definition:	The 4-1/2-inch: grip head is designed with a male junior mount on the lower end, and a female junior receiver on the upper end. The 4-1/2–inch clamping discs in the middle are locked with a large spin or butterfly (two-winged) handle. The 4-1/2-inch clamp head is intended for heavy-duty clamping of overhead frames, or for wooden 2 × 4-inch to 2 × 6-inch constructions.

GOBO ARM:

a.k.a.:	Extension arm, knuckle arm, single arm, C arm
i.k.a.:	None
Prompt:	None
Definition:	The 40-inch gobo arm or its 20-inch "mini" cousin have grip-type heads on one end and are used to place extended gobos, scrims, silks, and other devices into the set. The gobo head differs from the grip head in that it should not be mounted directly on a stand.
Use:	Photographers have been known to clamp the gobo head to a stand top and use the extension arm as a boom. This is not a good application in that it places a light unit at maximum extension from the stand with no possibility of counterweighting the opposite end of the arm. It also forced light adjustments to be made in wide arcs, a risky business when no counterweights are available.

GRID CLAMP:

a.k.a.:	None
i.k.a.:	Knuckle
Prompt:	None
Definition:	A grid clamp is a hinged two-piece clamp designed to clamp to pipe or tubing and lock with a thumb nut or standard nut. Grid clamps are intended to be almost permanent and are strong enough to be fitted with either baby or juniors mounts.
Use:	Several manufacturers have attempted to make side arms for light stands using this type of clamp. It is almost impossible to move or adjust this clamp with a light unit positioned on the mount unless, of course, one has three hands.

GAFFER GRIP:

a.k.a.:	Skyhook, Molegator grip
i.k.a.:	Gator grip
Prompt:	Does it have teeth or pads on the jaws?

Definition: A heavy-duty cast metal spring clamp, sometimes with adjustable jaws and one or two baby-sized light mounts attached to it. The gripping jaws are lined with rubber pads. The clamping pressure of a gaffer grip is better on flat surfaces than round tubes and never quite strong enough to hold the weight of a baby spotlight. Gaffer grips are very useful for holding flash units in a variety of positions.

GATOR GRIP:

a.k.a.: Grip a light.
i.k.a.: Gaffer grip
Prompt: Does it have teeth?
Definition: Originally developed to hold light-weight 10- or 12-inch reflector pans, gator grips are made from stamped sheet metal and do not exert enough clamping pressure to hold any current heavy-duty lighting fixtures.

GRIFFOLYN:

a.k.a.: Griff, T55
i.k.a.: Tarp
Prompt: Griffolyn is an excellent material to suggest when a large white bounce panel or a large black reflection seems to be required.
Definition: Griffolyn is a tough vinyl-type material rain protection. Normal construction is two layers bonded to a net/ripstop material, making griffolyn very durable. The two-layer construction makes possible combinations of white/white, black/black, white/black, and clear. Griffolyn is available in the same standard sizes as other light-control materials. Bulk griffolyn may be purchased and sealed together with "fab" tape, which makes a permanent molecular bond between two sheets of griffolyn.

GRIP, LOWEL:

a.k.a.: Grip, crossbar grip head
i.k.a.: None
Prompt: A standard grip head is made of cast metal, the Lowell grip is made of heavy stamped metal. Ask the client to describe the grip head.
Definition; A clamping device designed by Ross Lowell to mount large irregularly shaped objects on baby-sized stands. The device consists of a female stand mount bolted to a movable, stamped metal clamp capable of fastening to a 2 × 4-inch, 2-inch pipe, chairs, doors, crossbars, etc. Its main disadvantage is the distance between clamping bars and locking screw make the Lowell grip perfect for dimpling tripod columns and aluminum stand risers.
Use: The Lowell grip is especially useful for clamping crossbars to light stands. The locking, movable clamp permits one person to raise a background to working height without assistance.

HI-ROLLER (See ROLLER STAND)

HI-HI-ROLLER (See ROLLER STAND)

HI-BOY (See ROLLER STAND)

TALL-BOY (See ROLLER STAND)

INKY:

a.k.a.:	Midget, Minimole, Tiny mac, Tenny, Inky-dinky, Mini-spot
i.k.a.:	None
Prompt:	None
Definition:	Any of a class of lensed spotlights with Fresnel-type condensers, a wattage rating of 300 W or less, and a lens diameter of 4 inches or less. These spotlights are excellent for small product photography or as accents in product photography. The large range of accessories available and small beam patterns produced mean the inky spot can be used close to a subject without overpowering large, nondirectional key sources.
Use:	Inkys are among the only quartz-halogen light sources that can benefit from gel conversions to daylight. The 1-1/2 f-stop loss allows close working distances in conjunction with electronic flash. The absence of an inky-type light source for electronic flash makes the quartz-halogen spotlight do double duty.

INTERLINK:

a.k.a.:	None
i.k.a.:	None
Prompt:	None
Definition:	The Lowell interlink consists of a 5/8-inch female double receiver with locking screws and two double-male 5/8-inch stand mounts. The double-female receiver is keyed with a V groove to accept all male stand mounts from 3/8–5/8 inches. The three pieces may be locked together to form right angle mounts, frame corners, multiple head mounts, etc.
Use:	Interlinks frequently rent with the Lowell grip as a clamping device to secure lighting and camera units in awkward or remote locations.

LAVENDER:

a.k.a.:	Lavender scrim
i.k.a.:	Doris Day diffusion
Prompt:	None
Definition:	Lavenders are pink bobbinet stretched on a tree-sided spring steel frame. The fourth side is fine wire so that the lavender can be blended into the light pattern. Lavenders provide light diffusion with slight warming. Color code is light blue.
Use:	Lavenders have been used in front of a camera lens to diffuse and warm an image at the same time.

MEAT AXE:

a.k.a.:	Some versions of this are called bear traps.
i.k.a.:	None

Prompt:	None
Definition:	A long gobo arm attached to a C clamp or pipe clamp by an adjustable pivot similar to a boom swivel clamp. The C clamp is attached to a grid, catwalk, ceiling beam, or overhead surface. The pivot adjusts vertically and horizontally and can be locked. The gobo arm has a handle to allow precise handling of nets or flags held by the gobo head.

NET:

a.k.a.:	Scrim, bobbinet
i.k.a.:	None
Prompt:	Single, double, or triple
Definition:	One or more layers of (usually) black bobbinet fastened to a spring steel frame with one open side. Nets are supported by century stands (C stands) between the light source and subject to cut or feather the light pattern. Nets are also called scrims, but the term scrim has too many correct uses to be convenient. Nets are color coded to make identification or multilayered assemblies easier. White for single layers, red for double, royal blue for triples.
Use:	Some people object to color coding the frame edge on the grounds that the colored edge can affect the color balance of the netted light source. This can be avoided by using a net of sufficient size. The colored borders help prevent inadvertently placing the net from in the light beam. When a net reached 48 inches square, the support frame is made solid for rigidity's sake

OFFSET ARM:

a.k.a.:	Side arm
i.k.a.:	None
Prompt:	Where do you want to mount the light?
Definition:	An offset arm extends to the side or offsets the light mount to which it is attached. Offset arms cannot be attached to the lower portions of light stands. Offset arms are available in baby or junior mounts and in fixed and extendable lengths.

OPEN FACED:

a.k.a.:	None
i.k.a.:	None
Prompt:	None
Definition:	Any lighting unit without a Fresnel- or condenser-type lens on the front. Although the tern "open-faced" applies to any non-lensed light source, it is usually used to distinguish between focusing light units such as the Mole-Richardson® Mickey Moles, Lowell® DP lights, or Ianiro® Ianebeams from lensed spotlights.

OVERHEAD:

a.k.a.:	None
i.k.a.:	None
Prompt:	None

Definition:	A tubular frame supporting two to four sides of a large piece of fabric diffusion, netting, light blocking, or reflective material. Overheads range in size from 9 × 12 feet to 30 × 40 feet with the largest sizes, and the rectangular shapes using a two- sided frame and guy ropes for support. The square 12 × 12 foot and 20 × 20 foot overheads have four- sided tubular frames supported by two and four medium hi or hi-hi roller stands. Some deluxe versions of the 20 × 20-foot frame use a guy wire support systems requiring only two stands for support.
Use:	*Caution:* A 20 × 20-foot overhead is, in fact, a large sail. A sudden gust of wind can lift a poorly anchored overhead, a 30-pound hi-hi roller stand, two 35-pound sandbags, and the assistant responsible 10 or 15 feet in the air and set them down hard!

PIPE CLAMP:

a.k.a.:	C hanger, C clamp, C clamp with hanger
i.k.a.:	None
Prompt:	It is necessary to distinguish between pipe clamps and ordinary C clamps. Find out specifically if pipes or battens.
Definition:	Pipe clamps are specially shaped cast metal C clamps, designed to hang light units from horizontal pipes. Pipe clamps hook over the pipe top and lock with a screw. Their function is for semipermanent installation of lighting with only minor changes in light spacing necessary. Pipe clamp design is specialized, but many adapters are available to attach baby, junior, heavy senior, and multiple lighting units to pipes, battens, and catwalks.
Use:	Pipe clamps are usually left attached to their lighting units for quick placement and removal from pipes. Their use requires a wrench to loosen the lockdown screw. These clamps are not recommended for temporary light positioning.

POLITO BRACKET:

a.k.a.:	None
i.k.a.:	None
Prompt:	Do you need something to hold foam core in a grip head?
Definition:	The Polito bracket is designed to hold an expendable reflector (Matthboard) to a C stand. The bracket is approximately 48 inches long and has a one-inch-wide clamp at either end to hold the reflector board. A gag plate in the middle of the bracket and a 5/8-inch pin on the end allow holding and rotating the board/end allow holding and rotating the board/bracket at a variety of heights and positions. On soft ground, the bracket end pin can be used as a ground spike.
Use:	The Polito bracket can hold a variety of materials, including foam core and Styrofoam insulation.

ROCKY MOUNTAIN LEG:

a.k.a.:	Mountain leg, sliding leg
i.k.a.:	None
Prompt:	Is the stand going to sit on level ground?

Definition:	Several manufacturers make a variation of their standard light stand with one or more variable extension legs. This variable leg allows placing the light stand in positions where the floor or terrain is not level, hence the "rocky mountain" label. Lowell grand stands, Matthews beefy baby and sliding leg C stands, Mole-Richardson lightweight location, and Moleflector stands are all available with a rocky mountain leg. All Matthews combo-type stands are available with a R.M. leg, although this option is not listed in their catalog. It is a good idea to keep one or two rocky mountain leg stands in any location lighting kit.

ROLLER STAND, E.G., MEDIUM HI-ROLLER (14 FEET), HI-HI ROLLER (20 FEET), SKY HI ROLLER (25 FEET)

a.k.a.:	Hi-boys, sky-hi boys, tall boys, and overhead roller stand
i.k.a.:	None
Prompt:	The support legs of roller stands are almost parallel to the ground and end in casters. The low profile makes the stand easy to sand bag and depend on a comparatively wide base for stability. Ask about the need for sand bags to establish which type of stand is best suited to the assignment.
Definition:	A series of heavy-duty, wide-based roller stands intended for use in supporting butterflies and larger overheads. Sizes range from 14–25 feet. Roller stand tops end in 4 1/2.-inch clamp heads and junior 1 1/8-inch receivers. The size and height of roller stands is necessary to raise overheads high enough to pivot from vertical to horizontal or any position in between. The relatively low center of gravity of the base legs is designed to allow the easy positioning of sand bags. Tripod-style legs tend to get into the picture area under a 12-foot overhead. Overhead stands are designed for outdoor use.

SCRIM:

a.k.a.:	Screens
i.k.a.:	Wire diffusion, nets
Prompt:	The word scrim covers too many uses to be an effective term. Most requests for scrim material involve a need to modify light intensity. The key may be where the scrim needs to be used. Nets cut down light intensity away from the light source. Screens work at or on the light source.
Definition:	For Helix purposes, a scrim is a piece of metal-framed wire screen used to cut light output over all or part of a light pattern. Scrims are sometimes called screens, which they are, or wire diffusion, *which they are not!* In fact, wire scrims are used specifically to cut light without diffusing it. Most scrims are available in full or half coverage and in single or double strengths. Single scrims cut light output almost one f-stop. Double scrims are made from closer screening than single scrims. Wire screening used in front of open-faced lights should be made of stainless steel. The stainless wire will not discolor in the intense heat generated by open-faced fixtures.

Color-coding is:

Green, full single	Red, full double
Green/silver, half single	Red/silver, half double

SPRING CLAMP:

a.k.a.:   A clamp, grip clamp, pinch clamp, "Pony Clamp"

i.k.a.:   Skin clamp. Ouch! Who thought up this one?

Prompt: Spring claps are used for everything. They are like gaffer's tape, bubble gum, baling wire, etc. What one needs to know is what is being clamped to what. Spring clamps normally clamp soft goods, e.g. paper, cardboard, foam core, etc. to hardware.

Definition: The common spring clamp is manufactured by any number of hardware companies and is supposed to be used for light gluing jobs. The clamp is metal, shaped like an A, and spring loaded. The current "clamp of choice" is manufactured by Adjustable and comes with vinyl-covered handles and clamp tips to protect the clamped material. The adjustable design permits opening a 3-inch clamp with one hand without stretching fingers to the limit. The clamps are available in 1, 2, 3 and 4″ inches. This dimension reflects the clamp's maximum opening size.

Use: The spring clamp is the photographic equivalent of the "bobby pin," but one can't pick locks with it, I think.

SUPER CLAMP:

a.k.a.:   A variation of the super clamp by Matthews is called a Mafer clamp.

i.k.a.:   None

Prompt: The super clamp should be suggested to anyone who needs to attach anything to anything else, and accompanies their inquiry with frantic hand gestures. They obviously haven't seen a super clamp.

Definition: The super clamp was originally manufactured and I think designed by Manfrotto. The clamp has one fixed and one spring loaded moveable jaw tightened by a large locking handle and is shaped to clamp to anything vaguely round and less than 2-1/2 inches in diameter. Both jaws are padded, the fixed jaw is V-shaped, and the moveable jaw is flat. The back of the fixed jaw is truly amazing. It has been provided with a centered female 1/4-inch × 20 threaded hole. Surrounding this are four holes oriented at 90°, two of which are threaded for 10 × 32 machine screws, and placed opposite one another. This allows super clamps to be attached to walls, boards, and even each other. In addition, the super clamp is provided with a removable standard European length 5/8-inch mounting spud. The spud is held in place by both a lockdown screw and a quick release button.. The socket for the 5/8-inch spud is hex shaped and 5/8-inch or 16-mm measured acrss the socket flats. This allows the clamp to be mounted on 5/8-inch stand tops or the ends of gobo arms. The hex shape and lockdown knob allow 10-mm hex head machine bolts (or the American equivalent) to be secured in the socket. In addition, Manfrotto sells a large array of attachments designed socket mounting, including crossbar holders, vertical and horizontal glass shelf holders, threaded European and American tripod adaptors, tripod heads, articulated camera and gobo arms, extension arms, joining studs, ad infinitum.

Use: The super clamp has only two limitations. Theoretically, there should be a limit to the weight a super clamp will support. I have seen heavy

8 × 10 view cameras supported by a super clamp, but i do not recommend it! Second, the 60° hexagonal orientation of the spud socket means that most of the Manfrotto-designed accessories will only mount at 0° or 60° to the V-shaped clamping face of the super clamp.

SILK:

a.k.a.:	Artificial silk
i.k.a.:	Silk scrim. The two are contradictory in purpose.
Prompt:	Is what you want white? Is it a diffuser?
Definition:	Silk is a white, nylon-blend, diffusion material used to soften and diffuse the pattern of any light source placed behind it. Silks may range in size from 3-inch dots to 30- × 40-foot overheads. The term silk is used to describe a diffusion density of approximately one f-stop. The nylon fabric tends to diffuse light in a way different from Mylar-, acetate-, or spun-type materials. Specular sources tend to radiate axially (star) as light passes through the woven fabric. The density of the fabric lets the sun or lensed spotlights retain some of their directional character. This results in a "hazy-bright" diffusion light "look." In an attempt to provide photographers with some intensity control, grip equipment manufacturers now offer silks in addition to other "weights" for diffusion control, there are two other types of silk diffusion material: "china silk" and "taffeta". China silk is thinner than artificial silk and is used to open shadows without dramatically altering the foreground-background lighting character. Taffeta is a heavier material than silk and will be discussed under its own heading.

SIDE ARM:

a.k.a.:	Low arm
i.k.a.:	Offset arm
Prompt:	Do you want to mount the light off the top of the stand or off the side?
Definition:	A side arm is used to place a lighting fixture to the side of a light stand or other support. Different from an offset arm, a side arm may be used to place a light fixture lower on a light stand than the stand's minimum extension. Side arms are available in junior and baby sizes and in fixed or adjustable lengths. Many side arms have both upper and lower pin mounts. The lower pin mount can be used to place lights very close to the floor or to accept grip heads and gobo arms, permitting light-control devices to be added to those designed to mount directly on the light fixture.

SOLID:

a.k.a.:	Gobo, duvetyne, block, flag
i.k.a.:	None
Prompt:	None
Definition:	A solid is a large piece of opaque fabric attached to a butterfly or over-head frame. Solids are usually made of duvetyne or griffolyn material with grommets or rope ties attached to the edges. Stretched across the

four-sided frame of a butterfly or overhead, the solid forms a very large gobo or light block. Solids range in size from 4 × 4 to 30 × 60 feet and larger. When one or more of a solid's dimensions exceed the 20-foot side of the largest closed overhead frame, the solid is sometimes referred to as a black. Solids should be stored folded and dried in cloth bags to prevent mildew and footprints.

Use: The duvetyne material used in solids has a shiny side and a dull side. Still photographers use the dull side as a nonreflective background for in-camera montage and photography of highly reflective subjects.

SOUND BLANKETS:

a.k.a.: Furniture pad, mover's pad
i.k.a.: None
Prompt: None
Definition: The sound blanket is indeed a mover's blanket or furniture pad. The term sound blanket probably originated when touring musicians found that the same furniture pads used for protecting and transporting musical instruments worked acoustical wonders when draped over isolation walls in recording studios, although sound blankets are generally used in still photography for padding and the occasional temporary dressing room. Motion picture rental house people delight in correcting any still photographer silly enough to ask for furniture pads instead of sound blankets.

STAIR BLOCK:

a.k.a.: Step wedge
i.k.a.: None
Prompt: None
Definition: Stair blocks are small wooden-stepped blocks used to elevate tables and chairs or to gently tilt a piece of furniture toward the camera. Stair blocks are made from ices of 2 × 4 inch wood nailed together. The height difference between the three steps is approximately 1-1/2-inch. The lands (flat area) of each step are usually large enough to accommodate a cup block used to prevent a stand or chair leg from slipping off the stair block. Because cup blocks have a hole drilled in their center for storage purposes, they can be nailed or screwed to the stair block in long-term situations. Stair blocks are normally sold and rented in sets of four.

STIRRUP:

a.k.a.: None
i.k.a.: None
Prompt: The stirrup is one of a series of special light-mounting adapters that can be bolted to the end of telescoping hangers. A stirrup looks like a stirrup or spade handle. The stirrup and telescoping hanger come into use as a quick way to extend a single light fixture down into a set. The hundreds of light fixtures normally found hanging overhead in a sound stage are attached to battens in groups so that several may be raised, lowered, and aimed together. These fixtures are equipped with a pivoting C clamp instead of a

light stand mount. When a single light fixture must be positioned higher or lower than the others in a group, the hanger/stirrup combination allows a gaffer to remove a fixture from a batten and reposition it without converting the light mount from the C clamp to the stand mount. The pivoting capability of the C clamp is not lost, and the light fixture may be returned to its normal position when necessary.

SPIDER/OCTOPUS:

a.k.a.:	None
i.k.a.:	None
Prompt:	Say what?
Definition:	These two terms may be among the most misused in the photographic industry and are applied unilaterally to describe any electrical, fluid, or support junction with more than two connection arms or receptacles. The only vague distinction between the two terms seems to be that the arms of any item described as an octopus are... usually... flexible, and the arms of a spider are rigid or jointed.

TAFFETA:

a.k.a.:	Double silk
i.k.a.:	None
Prompt:	None
Definition:	Taffeta is a form of white light diffusion material that should be heavier than artificial silk and have twice the diffusion density. In reality, the many suppliers of diffusion material for silks, butterflies, and overheads are at least standardized at this weight of material. I have seen taffeta material that appears to just a heavier, more closely woven version of artificial silk. I have also seen taffeta that looks like normal taffeta and diffuses light much differently than heavy artificial silk. Woven fabric has threads running at right angles to one another. The thread directions are called "warp" and "woof" (another glossary entirely), but the threads in the fabric tend to make light sources "star" depending on the light source size and its distance from the fabric. The looser (read taffeta) weaves star more easily than the tighter weaves. Anyone trying to maintain basic light quality while increasing diffusion would do well to visually inspect the taffeta cloth before accepting it as a "double silk."

T-BONE:

a.k.a.:	Floor spider, boat anchor
i.k.a.:	None
Prompt:	None
Definition:	A T-bone is basically a "senior-"sized floor plate or nail on with some significant differences. T-bones are heavily constructed or cast to support large HMI fixtures or arc lights. The T shape allows this mount to be nailed at the edge of a catwalk, parallel, or tower. T-bones always come with heavy safety chain, just in case one misses the junior size receiver when mounting the light fixture.

TURTLE:

a.k.a.: None

i.k.a.: None

Prompt: None

Definition: A turtle is essentially the three-legged base of a C stand, usually with the same staggered leg height and spring-loaded base features of a regular C stand. Because turtles are low to the ground and can be nested and sandbagged like C stands, they are used to support heavy lights and ground-level gobo arm configurations. The light mount on a turtle is a 1-1/8-inch female receiver.

VANNER:

a.k.a.: Alternating current (AC) inverter

i.k.a.: Motor generator

Prompt: You want a 2000-W battery-operated flash?

Definition: The vanner is a piece of electrical equipment that converts battery power direct current into 120-V full wave AC. Smaller models can be connected to the 12-V D.C. sources. The most popular rental size is a 12-V D.C. unit with a rated output of 2200 W at 120 V AC, and a surge capacity of 3600 W. By dividing the surge capacity of 3600 W by the AC line voltage of 120 V, one gets a current output of 30 amps. Dividing the circuit breaker rating of electronic flash power supply into the vanner amp rating tells approximately how many flash power supplies can be operated from a vanner.* Flash units designed for fast recycling, e.g. Speedotron black line, should be given lots of amps to work with. Rapid flashing builds up heat quickly, which can tend to overload the surge capacity of the vanner. A vanner of the size noted above is capable of powering studio flash units (2000 W) from the battery of a running automobile. The vanner unit weighs between 50 and 55 pounds.
Caution: Be careful about comparing this kind of inverter with the inverters found in some rental recreational vehicle. Some of these inverters may not put out a full-wave alternating current and will seriously damage an electronic flash unit.

---

*If the answer to this division problem is 1.5, it means you can run one power supply with power to spare. It does not mean you can run two power supplies if you run one at half power. Electronic flash units usually draw the same current at all power settings. Lower power settings just draw current for less time.

GLOSSARY

AC (alternating current). Standard electrical power found in studios and locations, accessed from a standard electrical outlet.

Accent lights. Hair lights, rim lights, and kickers.

Accessory shoe. A shoe on a camera that provides for accessories to be attached, but that does not have any flash contact.

Actinic. Refers to actinicism, measuring the light that causes chemicals to combine and decompose.

Actinograph. A device patented by Hurter and Driffield to measure the actinic intensity of sunlight for exposure calculations. Variations of the actinograph include early forms of light meters that could measure light intensity.

Angle of Incidence. The direction light travels from the light source toward an object.

Apparent color temperature (ACT). Color temperature assigned to pulsing light that cannot be measured by continuous light waves.

Arm. Extension poles that attach to light stands or other rigid bases.

Autopole. A telescoping apparatus that can be firmly positioned between ceiling and floor.

Backlighting. Light placed behind the subject which is directed toward the rear of the subject.

Background light. Light illuminating the background of a set or portrait.

Background reflector. A purpose-built attachment or hand-crafted tool created by employing a standard reflector with a small flag or other handmade alteration to create the taper.

Barn doors. A modifier with two or four adjustable metal blades used to flag the light at the source.

Boom. An arm or extension mounted to the top of a light stand that can extend a light head into a set or over the top of a subject.

Bright-field lighting. Lighting for glass that produces dark edges and a bright background.

Brightness. The intensity of the light.

Broad lighting. A portrait technique in which the subject's face is illuminated across the side of the face and wrapping around the head.

Butterfly lighting. Light placed high and at the camera position to create a small shadow under the nose and beneath the chin.

Cadmium sulfide (CdS). Material used in specific light meters to determine light intensity.

Catchlights. Small reflections in the eyes that are the most telling method to discern the photographer's choice of light source modifier.

Ceiling systems. Ceiling-mounted rail system designed to hold light heads, keeping the studio floor clear.

Cell. A section of the power pack that provides power to the flash head, operating independently from the other cells.

Channel. See *Cell*.

Charge-coupled device (CCD). Image sensor found in some digital cameras; see also *Complimentary metal oxide semiconductor (CMOS)*.

Cinefoil. Moldable, flameproof, metal sheeting that comes in a roll.

Clipping points. Exposure extremes in digital capture.

Color. Light waves reflecting off an object perceived by the human eye and divided into hue names such a blue, green, red and others.

Color meter. A meter that measures the color temperature in Kelvin degrees and, in some models, also Mired values.

Color temperature. Term applied to the color of light waves, measured in degrees Kelvin, that assigns a numerical value. For instance, nominal tungsten illumination is rated at 3200 K and photographic daylight is generally rated at 5500 K.

Color Temperature Blue (CTB). A group of blue filters that are available in various densities from 1/8 to 2x.

Color Temperature Orange (CTO). A group of orange filters that are available in various densities from 1/8 to 2x.

Combination meter. A light meter that is equipped with a spot, flash, incident, and incident metering system into one single meter.

Complimentary metal oxide semiconductor (CMOS). Image sensor found in some digital cameras; see also *Charge-coupled device (CCD)*.

Continuous lighting. Light, such as quartz and incandescent, that is turned on and remains on until it is turned off.

Contrast. Quality of light that indicates dissimilar tonality or colors.

Cord mode. The mode in which a light meter will read flash lighting when connected to the flash source with a PC cord.

Cordless mode. A method of making a flash measurement without connecting a PC cord to the meter.

Correlated color temperature (CCT). Color temperature assigned to pulsing light that cannot be measured by continuous light waves.

Cucaloris. A sheet of material with irregular shapes cut out that creates irregular shadows when light shines through onto a surface, subject, or both.

Cutter. A large, rectangular flag.

Dark-field lighting. Lighting for glass that produces a bright edge and a dark background.

DC (direct current). Unidirectional electrical charge, found in a battery or generator, used to produce electrical power.

Diffraction. Light waves bending as they pass through the lens.

Diffused light. Scattered light resulting in even illumination and soft shadows.

Diffused reflections. Reflected light rays that are scattered and changed by object surfaces.

Diffusion panel. Device for diffusing a hard light source to make even, soft illumination.

Direct reflections. A mirror of the light source that produces it or any light source within the family of angles.

Discontinuous spectrum. Pulsing light that spikes at certain wavelengths.

Dot. A round flag.

Double polarizing. Using a polarizing filter on the camera lens and the light source to effectively remove glare, despite where the camera may be placed.

Dynamic range data. Maintaining a certain dynamic range or lighting contrast in the capture that is suitable for an intended method of reproduction.

18% Gray. Refers to the popular standard that holds that a gray card reflects 18% of the light that is falling on it.

EXIF. Also referred to as Exif, the acronym refers to Exchangeable Image File Format. Developed in Japan and common to most digital cameras, EXIF is the standard for storing interchange information in image files. For instance, JPEG format capture on most digital cameras will also provide metadata that will be located in the image's EXIF.

Exposure value (EV) scales. A numerical system dispensing a wide range of aperture/shutter speed relationships derived from a meter reading.

Extinction meters. Antique light meter measuring reflective light.

Falloff. The effect of illumination decreasing as a light source is moved farther from the subject. May also reference the edge of an intended illumination effect where the intensity diminishes.

Family of angles. The angle at which the light source is recorded by the camera.

Fill light. (1) The light that fills in the shadow or adds additional illumination to the darker part of the setup. (2) An additional light source or second head that fills the shadows caused by the main light.

Finger. Narrow, rectangular flag.

Flash. A rapid burst of light.

Flash duration. The measurable fraction of a second that the flash fires.

Flashmeter. Meter used to measure flash or electronic strobe intensity.

Fresnel. A specific lens designed to be placed in front of a light source to control and focus the shape of the light.

Front lighting. Light that comes from the direction of the camera.

Gaffer tape/gaffer's tape. A standard adhesive tape used for securing cords and attaching virtually anything to any surface without leaving residue.

Gel filters. A thin plastic material that slides into a holder on the front of the light source used as a color conversion or correction type.

Glare. Polarized direct reflections.

Gobo. A black board or a thick card used for blocking errant light from the lens or other elements of the photo set, also known as a flag.

Grid or grid spots. A modifier with a honeycomb pattern that is inserted into the front edge of the strobe head reflector used to control the size of the beam of light.

Grip. An assistant on a film set or the collected lighting gear on a film set. It is also a generic name for lighting gear.

H&D curve. Named after Ferdinand Hurter and Vero Driffield, the H&D curve is a chart reflecting film density variations that can be used for film density and development comparisons.

Hair light. Common accent light that is used to light a top rear portion of the subject's head to provide an accenting, lit edge on the top of the subject.

Halogen. Refers to the gas contained within the bulb that helps to protect the tungsten filament in a quartz-halogen light source.

Hard light. Light produced from the sun or a strobe light source resulting in bright areas and dark, distinct shadows. The light source creating a hard shadow.

Hard shadow. Dark with clearly defined edges.

High contrast. Very bright highlights and dark shadows with few midtone areas.

Highlight alert. A signal that automatically signals any overexposed areas in the digital image.

Histogram. A graphic representation of the image that indicates the range of darkness to light. Can be found on cameras or in computer applications.

HMI. Hydrargyrum medium-arc iodide, employing a mercury-halide gas to discharge an arc between electrodes to create a continuous light source related at approximately 5600 K or close to daylight.

Hot lights. Common term for tungsten light sources such as quartz and incandescent.

Hot shoe. The term for the accessory shoe that has a syncing contact used to set off a flash unit

Incandescent light source. Light usually found in household applications, such as a basic light bulb

Incident light meter. A device that reads the light falling on the subject.

Intensity. The level of light brightness.

Inverse Square Law. Light intensity changes proportionally to the inverse of the square of distance.

Kelvin degrees. A numerical method to express the color temperature of light.

Kelvin Scale. The scale created by William Thomson, later titled Baron or Lord Kelvin, to identify the different colors of light by comparing them with a black body heated to different temperatures Celsius. Zero Kelvin equals −273.15 Celsius or absolute zero.

Key light. The main light source.

Kicker. Provides a touch of light on the side of the subject.

Latitude. The amount of acceptable latitude of over- or underexposure tolerated by the material or sensor.

Law of Reflection. The angle at which the light reflects off an object. It is exactly the opposite of the angle at which the light strikes the object.

Light stand. Stands originally designed to hold light heads but that can be used for a variety of utilitarian purposes in photography. Light stands come in a wide range of materials, designs, and sizes.

Lighting ratio. The difference between the brightest area and shadow areas of any scene caused by the difference in intensity between the key light and the fill source.

Low contrast. Even lighting but few bright highlights or dark shadows.

Mafer Clamp. A tool used to attach many tubular grip elements to stands and to each other.

Main light. The light that provides the primary and brightest illumination on the subject, also called the key light.

Metadata. Information data stored with a digitally captured image that can include date, time, location, file type, camera or scanner, assigned name and other related details about an image. See also EXIF.

Metering modes. Meters can read light in different modes: ambient, reflected, flash, or variations of all three.

Metering probe. A kind of sensor inserted into the rear of a view camera and positioned to the desired area for a meter reading near the film plane.

Model light. The continuous quartz or tungsten light built into most studio and some portable flash units. Also known as model lamps.

Modeling lights. A low-wattage tungsten light source housed within a strobe light head.

Modifier. An attachment to the light head that will change the quality of the raw light emitted from the light source.

Monolight. A strobe light source where the power is contained within the lighting unit.

Multiple mode. Building exposure intensity through multiple firings of a single flash that is recorded or designated by the meter.

Omnidirectional. Light head modifiers that are primarily intended to be soft, overhead area lights.

On-axis. Light placed on the same axis as the lens, producing flat lighting.

Optical spot. Also called a projector head, it contains a lens that allows the light to be precisely focused and zoomed to alter the beam size.

Penumbra. The transition between bright areas and shadow areas.

Perspective distortion. When an object appears as much larger than it is relative to the rest of the scene and when the spatial distance appears shorter between foreground and background objects.

Photoelectric cells. Device that responds to light, used to set off multiple flash units without hard wiring, also called a slave or photo-eye.

Piping. Lighting a glass object from the bottom through a small hole at the base of the glass.

Polarization material. A filter designed to reduce obvious glare from surfaces such as glass, acrylic material, and liquids.

Polarized light. Lightwaves traveling in only one direction or on a single plane.

Polarizer. A filter that organizes light's naturally erratic pattern, which is designed to reduce unwanted glare from highly polished surfaces.

Power invertors. Used mostly in a vehicle to recharge a battery while driving or powering equipment on location; available in different sizes.

Power pack. A single power source that controls light output for multiple strobe lighting heads.

Preproduction. Refers to planning out the photography session in advance. This may involve arranging for models, light sources, lighting diagrams, and additional details.

Prontor-Compur (PC) cord. The most common sync cord.

Putty knife. A grip term that refers to the familiar flat-surfaced tool with a solid handle and a 5/8-inch mounting pin attached to it to create a temporary mount

Quartz. The glass that is used to enclose the bulb in a quartz-halogen light source.

Quartz halogen. A bulb that contains an inert gas that helps to protect the tungsten filament.

Radio trigger system. A transmitter/receiver cordlessly synchronizes a camera and flash unit. The triggering system does not rely on sensing an original flash like a photo-eye, thus enabling radio units to read each other around corners and through other physical obstacles.

Raking. Placing the light to the right or the left of the object, causing the light to shine directly across the texture of the subject, creating shadow and depth.

Recycle. When the flash's power supply is recharged and ready to give its next burst of light.

Recycle rate. The amount of time that a flash requires to recharge for the next burst of light.

Reflectance. The amount of light reflected off the object surface.

Reflector. The most basic and efficient modifier for a flash head or continuous light source.

Rembrandt lighting. Denoted by the inverted triangle of light over one eye that travels down the cheek to a point even with the base of the nose.

Rim lighting. Defines the back edges of the entire subject by pointing the light source at the back of the subject.

Scene contrast. The comparison of reflective surfaces of many objects within a scene.

Scrims. A flat, mesh-covered device placed between a light and the subject to form a neutral color method of reducing light intensity.

Selenium type meter. A type of meter that produces readings directly related to the sun's energy and requires no batteries

Shot. Lead shot is used in *shot bags* that are used to provide more weight at the base of a stand or panel for support.

Side lighting. Placing the light on the side of an object that creates a visible shadow.

Silicon. The key element found in some light meters.

Slaves. Common term for the electronic photo-eye unit built into the strobe light that receives a signal to fire the flash head automatically when the main flash fires.

Snoot. A conical tube light modifier that is placed on the end of a reflector used to pinpoint light to a small portion of the image.

Soft box. A light modifier that is an enclosed box with a diffusion panel on the front.

Soft light. The illumination from a diffused light source producing soft shadow.

Specular highlights. The bright, small highlights within a larger one or a small reflection from a small bright light.

Specular reflections. Direct reflections.

Spider boxes. Specialized boxes with multiple outlets that are connected to dedicated circuits in the studio's electrical system designed for flash systems or any equipment that requires heavy amperage levels.

Spot meter. A light-metering device that is used to measure small areas of reflective surfaces.

Strobe. An electronic flash that fires an intense burst of light.

Subject contrast. The difference between the most reflective surface and the least reflective surface within a subject.

Sunshine recorder, or heliograph. Invented by T.B. Jordan, ca. 1839, to measure light intensity.

Synchronization. The term that notes a camera's minimum shutter speed that can be used with a flash; refers to the connection between a camera and a flash.

Syncing. Designates the different methods to connect a flash with a camera so that the flash will fire in conjunction with the camera's shutter.

Tabletop coves. Nearly seamless enclosures for specialized lighting applications.

Tabletop reflector card. Typically a homemade white, silver, or gold card used to reflect light into the tabletop setup.

Tabletop sets. Small setups that literally sit on a table.

Temporary mounts. A device created to securely hold lights, flags, and other devices while on location.

Tents. Enclosures designed for even illumination on objects.

Tethered. Term commonly used to describe digital cameras when attached to a computer.

Three-quarter lighting. Requires the light to be placed somewhere between the camera position directly across from the subject and side-light position.

Tungsten. General term to describe quartz halogen or a standard incandescent bulb for continuous lighting with a temperature of approximately 3200 or 3400 K.

Tungsten lighting. Using continuous light sources to make a photograph.

Umbrella. A light modifier that attaches to the light head in different configurations, depending on the material. The light head can be pointed away from the subject and into an umbrella that emits soft light. The light head can be pointed at the subject but through a translucent umbrella for a different type of diffused light.

White balance. Adjustments made by digital still or video cameras to compensate for differing light sources and color temperatures.

Y cords. PC cords that are manufactured to connect three devices: light meter, flash unit and camera.

BIBLIOGRAPHY

Adams, Ansel, Artificial Light Photography. Hastings-on-Hudson, New York: Morgan and Morgan, 1968.

Albers, Joseph, The Interaction of Color. New Haven, Connecticut: Yale University Press, 1963.

Broecker, W.L., Morgan, D.O., and Vestal, D. (Eds.), Leica Manual: The Complete Book of 35mm Photography (15th Edition). Hastings-on-Hudson, New York: Morgan & Morgan, 1973.

Compton, J., Current, I., Stroebel, L. and Zakia, R., Photographic Materials and Processes. Boston: Focal Press, 1986.

Eastman Kodak Company, Kodak Professional Photoguide (Sixth edition). Rochester, New York: Author, 2001.

Hirsch, Robert, Exploring Color Photography (Fourth Edition). London: Laurence King Publishing, 2005.

Horenstein, Henry, Color Photography. Boston: Little, Brown and Company, 1995.

Hunter, F., Biver, S., and Fuqua, P., Light Science & Magic (Third Edition). Burlington, Massachusetts: Focal Press, 2007.

Kolb, Gary, Photographing in the Studio. Madison, Wisconsin: Brown and Benchmark, 1993.

Lowell, Ross, Matters of Light and Depth. New York: Lowel-Light Manufacturing, 1992.

McKenzie, Joy, Exploring Basic Black and White Photography. Clifton Park, New Jersey: Thomson Delmar Learning, 2004.

Miller, Katie, Photography for the 21st Century. Clifton Park, New Jersey: Thomson Delmar Learning, 2007.

Mees, C. E. Kenneth and James, T.H. (Eds.), The Theory of the Photographic Process (Third Edition). New York: The Macmillan Company, 1966.

Mitchell, Earl N., Photographic Science. New York: John Wiley and Sons, 1984.

Nurnberg, Walter, Lighting for Portraiture: Technique and Application. London: The Focal Press, 1948.

Tood, Hollis and Zakia, Richard, Photographic Sensitometry. Dobbs Ferry, New York: Morgan and Morgan, 1968.

Wall, E.J., The Dictionary of Photography. London: Hazell, Watzon & Viney, 1912.

INDEX